Remembrance

of

Love and War

Carol Astbury

Copyright

 Published by Carol Astbury with the assistance of Dragonfly Publishing, February 2022

© All rights reserved.

No part of this book may be used or reproduced by any means, graphic, electronic, or mechanical, including photocopying, recording, taping or by any information storage retrieval system without the written permission of the copyright owner except in the case of brief quotations embodied in critical articles and reviews.

This book is copyright. Apart from any fair dealing for private study, research, criticism or review, as permitted under the Copyright Act, no part may be reproduced by any process without written permission from the author.

The author acknowledges the trademark status and trademark owners of various products referenced in this work which may have been used without permission. The publication/use of these trademarks is not authorised, associated with, or sponsored by the trademark owners or Dragonfly Publishing.

 A catalogue record for this work is available from the National Library of Australia

ISBN(sc): 978-0-6453505-3-1

Dedication

To my beloved mother and grandmother, the storytellers, who faithfully passed down our family history.

To my grandfather, on whose story this book is based. He was a quiet man, but his silence spoke volumes.

Cherished for the memory of his bravery, wisdom, and ageless love.

Special Thanks

To my good friends from Katharine Susannah Prichard Writers' Centre, thank you for your honest critique, helpful suggestions, and encouragement along the way.

Contents

Part One - REBOUND

CHAPTER ONE	1
CHAPTER TWO	17
CHAPTER THREE	31
CHAPTER FOUR	43
CHAPTER FIVE	51

Part Two - WAR YEARS 1914-1918

CHAPTER SIX	71
CHAPTER SEVEN	82
CHAPTER EIGHT	100
CHAPTER NINE	105
CHAPTER TEN	117
CHAPTER ELEVEN	128
CHAPTER TWELVE	139
CHAPTER THIRTEEN	157
CHAPTER FOURTEEN	167
CHAPTER FIFTEEN	185
CHAPTER SIXTEEN	200
CHAPTER SEVENTEEN	209
CHAPTER EIGHTEEN	226

Part Three - AFTERMATH

CHAPTER NINETEEN	233
CHAPTER TWENTY	252
CHAPTER TWENTY-ONE	274
CHAPTER TWENTY-TWO	297
CHAPTER TWENTY-THREE	326
CHAPTER TWENTY-FOUR	330
CHAPTER TWENTY-FIVE	351
CHAPTER TWENTY-SIX	375
EPILOGUE	387

About the Author

Part One

REBOUND

CHAPTER ONE

February 1919

Shadows played in the moonlit garden, full in the grip of winter. A light from the kitchen window spread arcs of yellow across the untrod snow. No pathways between the garden beds were visible, only a blanket of white with trees rising out of it; each bough adorned with thick pillows.

High in a leafless oak, a blackbird's yellow-rimmed eyes surveyed the scene below. His flutelike call interrupted the stillness of the small hours. Food scraps, thrown from the window, seduced the watcher. With a flick of the blackbird's wing, the branches stirred, sending powdery snowflakes, soft as icing sugar, drifting to the ground.

'Is the snow piled high above you, my love, wherever you lie?'

Grace opened her desk draw and ran her fingers over two books lying there. The first, *A Collection of Poems, by Emily Bronte.* She picked up the second book, a pocket journal, its leather cover, gnarled and wrinkled. She held it to her chest for a moment before opening it and reading these words, written in fine cursive script:

> *I expect to pass through this world but once.*
>
> *If, therefore, there be any kindness I can show,*
>
> *Or any good thing I can do for my fellow human beings,*
>
> *Let me do it now.*
>
> *Let me not defer nor neglect it,*
>
> *For I will not pass this way again. (S. Grellett 1835)*

The soft light of dawn, silver-edged with rose, spread across the sky. Grace shivered; the fire had faded in the hearth. She poked at the coals, took a page of yesterday's newspaper, and held it across the cavity. Soon the chimney pulled the draught up, and the coals ignited. As the fire blazed, hot coals shaped themselves into a thousand memories of the past. She sat in silence as shadows crept noiselessly about the room. A familiar vision returned ... she watched from the window as Freddie walked beneath the oaks. He stopped, turned, blew a kiss, and was gone. 'Why didn't I follow him? Why did I let him walk away? I could have grabbed my hat and coat, ran out the door and shouted: Freddie, wait for me.'

~

Grace woke to the sound of trolleys rattling down the hallway and the muffled exchange of greetings. There was a knock on the office door.

'Good morning, Sister, I've brought you some tea,' said a young maid, placing a tray on the desk. 'I'll fetch your clean collar and cuffs, back in a jiffy.'

'Thank you, Doris,' she replied as the young woman left. Grace removed her shawl and shivered as she entered the bathroom. She quickly performed her ablutions and pulled on her corset, adjusting the laced slits down the sides, confident that she had chosen wisely, as this corset was unboned, made specifically to curve around her rather than press into her abdomen. Looking in the mirror at the profile of her body, she felt satisfied that no one would guess her secret. She pulled on her grey serge dress and black woollen stockings.

Doris returned with the freshly starched items. 'Finished your tea? Good, I'll take the tray.'

Grace clipped on her collar and cuffs, adjusted her white

linen cap, draped her cape over her shoulders, and with a final glance at the fire still glowing in the hearth, she headed to the wards. As she arrived, the night nurse was handing over to the day staff. 'Good morning, ladies.'

The nurses responded warmly.

'Quiet night, Nurse Parkes?'

'Reasonably so, Sister, apart from Mr Six, who decided he wanted to dance in the wee hours and Mr Nine, who had an unsettled night and wet his bed.'

'Alright, we'll deal with that; you head off now and get some rest.'

~

The patient, alias Mr Nine, was emerging from a nightmare. Moisture gathered along the rim of his eyelids and spilled down his cheeks. He caught the salty tears on his tongue. He knew, without opening his eyes, that pastel morning light permeated the room. He held that lightness in his mind to keep the darkness at bay.

~

'Good morning, are you awake?' Grace asked.

Mr Nine did not respond.

'We're going to change your sheets. Won't you sit up?'

He did not move.

'Here, let's help you.' Gentle hands raised him from the pillow. 'That's it, swing your legs over the side of the bed. Good lad. Nurse, help me get him into the chair, please. We're taking you for a bath now.' With a swish, the wet sheets were removed.

He was led to the washroom, where a nurse tenderly undressed him. His unbuttoned pyjamas fell to the floor, he stepped out of them and into the warm bath water.

Grace held his arm and guided him to sit. She squeezed the soapy sponge over his shoulders as she examined his skin, pockmarked from lice-bites, puckered with ragged lines from neck to buttock. He bent his head, and she washed behind his ears; lifted his chin to swab his face and neck. *So thin,* she thought, as the water slipped past the sharp bones of his cheek and jaw. She bathed his arms and torso, separated his knees, and smoothed the sponge around his groin, down his thighs and finally to his feet. 'There, we are all done. Nurse, please dry Mr Nine and find him some clean pyjamas.'

'Come along, Mr Nine, it's nearly time for breakfast,' said the nurse.

With all the patients bathed and breakfasted, Grace completed her rounds, ensuring all the men were comfortable. 'Staff, I'm going to my office now.' On the way, she called into the kitchen where she found Doris up to her elbows in soapy suds.

'Mornin' Sister Phillips, can I get you something?' Cook called from behind the long table, where she was busy chopping vegetables. 'We still got some warm porridge.'

'Lovely, thank you, Cook.'

'I'll get Doris to bring it in, soon as she's finished those pots.'

'Don't worry, I can take it myself.'

Cook ladled the porridge into a bowl and placed it on a tray with milk and sugar. 'We'll bring in morning tea when the Doc arrives.'

Porridge consumed; Grace began the daily treadmill of tasks. Her duties included the administration of prescribed medicines, meticulously recording patients' observations.

She opened the box of patient files and began her work. 'Ah, Mr Nine, our unknown man of endless silence.' She sat back in her chair and read his file notes.

~

Knock, knock. 'Good morning, Sister.' Doctor Kirke entered, followed by Doris, carrying a tea tray.

'Lovely, thank you,' he said, removing his gloves and rubbing his hands.

'I've been reviewing Mr Nine's medical notes.'

'Mr Nine?'

'Yes, we call the patients' who are without names, Mr *bed-number*. It seems friendlier.'

'Yes, good.'

'His journey to Broadleigh was a long one. He was found by Danish Red Cross in a POW camp in Hochfenitz, near the Drehmen salt mine in November. Condition described as *severe malnutrition, Typhus, and lice infestation*. He was cleaned up and transported to Rouen Field Hospital, where it appears they kept him for several weeks. At this point, the record says he was repeatedly interrogated but failed to provide his name, rank or regimental number.'

'In Heaven's name,' exclaimed the doctor.

Grace continued. 'He was then transferred to HMHS Grantilly Castle hospital ship, arrived Southampton Casualty Unit where he was again interrogated. Oh my. His condition there was reported as *multiple scarring from shrapnel, whipping, bayonet wound to left scapula.* Then hospital train to Weston, admitted to Broadleigh Repat on 22nd January.'

'May I see?'

Grace handed the folder to Kirke. 'He has had unsettled

nights since his arrival five days' ago.'

'Mr Nine most likely has a case of general neurasthenia, in other words, exhaustion of the nervous system due to physical or nervous strain. We will have to keep a close eye on him. Anything else before we begin the rounds? Then let's proceed. Shall we start with Mr Nine?'

They were greeted in the ward by the staff nurse.

'Staff, we'll see Mr Nine first.'

'Yes, Sister, He was agitated when I last checked, half an hour ago. I closed the screen to avoid any disturbances.'

~

An eagle is hanging like a sepia shadow in the bright white sky. I lie on cold earth. My prostrate body throbs with the drumming retreat of horses' hooves. My blood seeps into the fissures and cracks of the churned brown earth. My fingers grasp for a hold on the sticky soil. I'm struggling to lift myself out of the cloying mud. Then I hear the unremitting cry of the eagle until, as it departs, its massive wings draw the breath from my lungs and silence descends upon me.

~

Grace pulled the screen aside and found the patient shaking uncontrollably, curled in a foetal position on the bed. His eyes had rolled back into his head. Saliva dribbled from the corner of his mouth. She touched his thin arm and felt the muscles hard as stone, skin hot, his pulse racing. 'Quick, Nurse, fetch cool water and sponges.'

She and the doctor tried to turn him without success, so she pushed up his pyjama shirt and applied the cool sponge to his back and neck.

'Alright, you're safe now, you're here with friends,' she

spoke softly as she applied the cooling water until his heart rate slowed and the heat left his skin.

Kirke examined the patient. 'Hmm, considering the intensity of this seizure, along with pupillary reactions and his state of consciousness, I can confirm he is suffering from a form of neurasthenia. I'm prescribing phenobarbital,' he said, 'that should keep him well sedated for now and it contains an anti-convulsant just in case there are any more episodes. I'll find him a bed at the Neurological Clinic, but that may not be for a day or two, so you'll have to keep an eye on him until he can be moved.' Kirke added some notes to the record sheet. 'God only knows what he's been through.'

Grace had seen firsthand the horrific injuries of men brought to the field hospital. She knew she would remember forever the faces shredded by shrapnel, sucking chest wounds, limbs torn apart, gangrene, the dirt and stench. She shivered at the memory. She checked her patient's vital signs. His skin still felt hot, and his breathing laboured. She helped him take the medication and sip water to wash down the pills.

He groaned and his muscles tightened.

'There now,' she said, wiping his brow with a cool flannel. 'The medicine will help.' She held his hand gently in hers. *What happened to you? Who are you? I wonder if you have family somewhere who are wondering where you are? Perhaps they think you were killed or still believe in the hope that you are alive.* Grace thought about all the letters she had written from field hospitals to families, either warning their son was about to die or recording their final moments. She had always hoped that, in some way, she had illuminated that time of darkness as much as possible for a soldier in his last moments. Merely the awareness that a nurse was by his bedside to give him sips of water, brush his hair and, all the time with pen and paper, record everything he said before eventually writing to his family.

Kirke checked his pocket watch. 'Shall we continue, Sister?'

'Yes, of course. Keep an eye on him, please Staff, call if you need me.'

They finished the rounds and Grace escorted the doctor to the front door.

'And you, Sister. I hear you are leaving us soon?'

'Yes, at the end of March.' Grace blushed. She hoped her girdle concealed the bulge of her belly.

'Well, you'll be sorely missed,' said the doctor reaching for his bag. 'Righto, I'll be off. I'll be in touch about the bed at the clinic.'

Grace returned to the ward to check on Mr Nine. *Good, the phenobarbital is working.* Now that his facial muscles were relaxed, she studied his face. *There is something familiar about you. Have we met I wonder?* Tucking the sheets in tightly around him, she whispered, 'Rest now.'

~

> *I feel the darkness rising. How can I shut it out and find the light that glimmers from another place so deep it seems beyond reach? What is this ... a memory tugging at the corner of my mind? It's so quiet. There's a window, but I can't see through it ... is it rain that is blurring the view? I'm moving closer and now I see a grey sky tinged with pink and endless green that seems unnatural, too fresh, too pure. I'm through the window, lying on fragrant grass. There are trees murmuring and leaves dancing in the breeze, revealing the bluest sky and white clouds and sparkling pinholes of sunlight.*

I can rest here for a while.
Dizzy ... I'm spinning round and round, I hold my arms out wide, faster and faster. There's someone here. Who? She's calling to me. I can hear her ...
"You'll make yourself sick if you keep doing that. Look at you; you're all red in the face. Come and sit for a while and calm yourself. Here, I have a picture book."
I'm a child standing by her side. Mother? She is wearing a dress the colour of cornflowers; she smells like roses. She draws me close.

~

In the early hours before dawn, Nurse Parkes took a candle and walked quietly down the ward. She reflected on the difficult conditions of working in the dimmed light. Ten beds on the right-hand side, ten beds on the left. Some patients silent, some snoring, some crying, muffled by pillows. *How they contrast with the man experiencing violent nightmares*, she thought. She hesitated for a few minutes beside Mr Nine's bed and watched him grip the blanket in his fists. His clasp was spasmodic. He thrashed his head from side to side. Spittle sprayed from his mouth and a guttural groan grew steadily louder.

Parkes hurried to the emergency bell and pulled on the rope. She fetched a cold flannel and returned to the man's side. 'Alright, calm down,' she whispered, wiping his brow.

Minutes later, Grace arrived.

'Sister, I checked him at nine o'clock and again at midnight and he seemed to be sleeping soundly. On my third round, I found him like this.'

'He needs medication. Nurse, please take my keys and find the phenobarbital in the medicine cupboard. Bring two tablets and some water.'

'Yes, Sister.'

~

> *Rough hands are forcing me to my knees. Shrieking incomprehensible commands. Please don't hurt me. It's so dark, someone is screaming. Is it me? They are beating me and kicking. Please stop.*
>
> *They've gone. I must get up. No, I can't stand. So much pain ... hard to breathe ...*
>
> *They're coming back.*

~

The noise of breaking glass was like the shock of memory returning. He opened his eyes.

'Sorry, Sister,' said the nurse, mopping up the spilt water. 'I'll fetch some more, here are the pills.'

'Relax,' said Grace, holding the man's shaking hand. 'Can you tell me what frightened you? Was it a bad dream? Did you remember something?'

He held her hand tightly.

'Here, sit up, take these pills, a sip of water.'

Gradually his grip weakened, and his eyes closed.

She remained by his side until his breathing returned to normal and she slipped her hand from his.

'That should make him comfortable for a few hours. I'll call Doctor Kirke later. Hopefully, there will be a bed for him at the clinic and he can begin treatment soon.' Grace checked her watch. 'Well done, Nurse, only a few hours to go. I'll be in my office if you need me.'

~

> *I see a child, straddled on a stile and she's calling me.*

'Wait for me.'

I try to help her. 'Put your other foot over.'

'Where?'

'Here, where my hand is.'

'I can't see. I'll fall.'

'No, you won't, c'mon. There you go, now turn round, sit down and slide. I'll catch you.'

We're in an orchard. Her short legs are struggling against knee high weeds. The air is still, it's quiet except for the sound of bees amongst the blossoms.

'I don't like it. Can we go back now?'

'Don't be scared.'

We're running, her blue sunbonnet, falls back and her auburn hair gleams in the sunshine as it streams behind her.

~

In the early afternoon, Doctor Kirke arrived to see Grace. 'Good news, we have a spot in the clinic for Mr Nine. I'll arrange for an ambulance to collect him in the morning.'

'That is good news.'

'Yes ... and how about you, my dear? You're looking pale and those dark circles beneath your eyes indicate you may not be getting enough rest. You must take care of yourself, especially now.'

'What do you mean?'

'Come now, I'm a doctor. I presume this is Frederick's infant you are carrying?'

Grace had not anticipated Kirke's forthright questions. 'Yes, you're right.' She blushed.

'Do you have family support?'

'Well, I haven't told anyone yet but I'm sure my family will be supportive.'

'Let me take your temperature. Pop this under your tongue.' He checked her pulse. 'Are you eating well?'

She nodded.

'I want to help you. Please don't feel you are alone. I was fond of Frederick, and I know he would have cared for you. Have you considered speaking to his mother?'

'Lady Morton? I would rather not speak to her about this. She was angry with Freddie. She could not accept his decision to become a conscientious objector. She said he brought shame on his family name, denying their history of past regimental honours. If only she knew how brave and dedicated he was to saving lives.'

'I understand and I sympathise with your predicament. You must understand that Frederick was her only child. He was groomed to become his father's successor, who was a member of the Lords Temporal in the Parliament. Her Ladyship was a devout Catholic, did you know? Well, I'm not sure Frederick held quite the same beliefs or ambitions. I recall speaking with him about his decision to become a conscientious objector ... it was not a decision he made easily. He was greatly disturbed by the fate of a man called Everett, a schoolteacher, who was jailed for two years for his refusal to fight in 1914. Frederick quoted the man as saying, "I am prepared to do work of national importance which does not include military service, so long as I do not thereby release some other man to do what I am not prepared to do myself." The rest you know, he volunteered for the Medical Corps at the outbreak of war.'

Remembrance of Love and War

'When I think back, he spoke little of himself or his life before the war.'

'Anyway, my dear, I am here for you if you need me. I will monitor your pregnancy while you remain here. If there is anything I can do for you when you prepare to return home, please let me know.'

Grace thanked the doctor for his kindness; however, she was pleased to see him out as she felt desperate for some time to herself. She ran a warm bath, removed her clothes and the cloying corset, immersed herself in warmth and leaned back to allow her head to rest on the rim. As she relaxed, she felt the infant kick and slip inside. She cradled her swollen belly and allowed the tears to flow.

~

Later that day, Grace responded to a knock on her office door.

'There's someone here to see you, Sister.' The nurse held the door open to allow the visitor to enter.

'Percy.' Grace embraced her brother. 'Let me look at you.' She held him at arms' length and looked him up and down, her eyes met his as she examined the contours of his face, the deep lines, and cruel purple scars.

'Be honest, I look like a broken gargoyle. Nothing like your little brother who went off to war.' Percy lowered his eyes.

'The surgeon has done a remarkable job. Is it painful still? Are you taking medication? Come and sit down, tell me all about it.'

'They were exceedingly kind at Sidcup. We were in a world of our own. The doctor referred to us patients as "my boys' and "my brave lot". We supported one another. I made a few good friends. I used to think about what Ma said when we were little: "When you smile, your personality shines through your face. Keep smiling." It just seemed inappropriate when I thought about the men who had to learn how to talk again, how to breathe again ... you know, you can't just smile at someone when you no longer have a mouth to smile with. We all had the same fears, mostly of how people will react once we return home.'

'Percy, dear. The scars will fade in time.'

'I know,' he said.

'You are so thin. Didn't they feed you at Sidcup?'

'They fed me alright, but I was busy chasing the nurses. They took some catching, I'll tell you.'

Grace laughed and hugged Percy again. She felt a lightness she hadn't felt for weeks.

'It's so good to see you. The last few months ...'

'I know, love.' He reached across and held Grace's hand.

'So, what are your plans now?'

Percy sighed. 'Well, firstly I have to go to Battalion HQ in Birmingham. It seems I slipped through the cracks, so I have to be officially discharged.' He shifted awkwardly on his seat. 'Then I've got to deliver some things. There's a letter for my pal's mum, which I promised I'd take if ... well I promised. And, I have this watch, it was Edmund Farrington's. D'you remember him?'

'Dr Farrington's son? Yes, I do remember him.'

'He was a good man. It all seems like a lifetime ago. Do you remember my friend Tom? We were at school together and Edmund was the head boy. He used to walk Tom home when we were in junior school. It's bad enough that Edmund died but I still can't believe Tom's gone.'

'I know what you mean. This war has taken so much from

us. From so many people.'

'God, I'm sorry, love. That was so stupid of me. I should've thought about Freddie.'

'It's alright. Really ... It's just that I can't forget the longing for him and endless nights praying that the next day I might receive some news of his return. Finally, the realisation that he would never be coming home. And here, in this house, his house, surrounded by his things ... I'm sorry.'

'Don't say sorry, Grace. Freddie was a wonderful man. It's a tragedy that he went back and yet, you know, he could never have stayed here while he knew there was still a need for him at the front. I thank God he got you home safely. For that, we will always be grateful. Cherish his memory. What a bloody mess this is. You know, in battle, we lost men, friends, so suddenly. The danger of the moment meant we didn't have time to think, let alone grieve. But now it's over, we do have time to think and remember. How we articulate that grief to our family and the community at home, I don't know.'

'Now this dreadful war has ended, there generally appears to be a sense of relief, but I fear the blood sacrifices of our men and women will bring a never-ending sadness to the families who lost a loved one. As dearly as I loved Freddie, his death has not affected me nearly as much as the memory of all those men slaughtered during the war. I don't think we'll ever forget something like that. The most important thing we can do now is to learn to appreciate better the joy of being alive.

'I agree, the first test for me will be to take Edmund's watch to his family. That won't be easy.'

'No, dear, but you will manage.' Grace checked her watch, 'I have to go to the wards now. Are you hungry? Come with me and I'll ask Cook to find you something. Will you stay for a few days before you go to Birmingham? I'll get a bed organised for you. Will you mind if the bed is set up here in my office, it's nice and warm? It would be lovely to have your company for a little while.'

'Yes, love. I can stay until Wednesday, that's when I have to get to HQ.'

~

The following morning, Grace supervised the transport of Mr Nine into the care of the ambulance officers. She walked beside the trolley, escorting him along the corridor.

Percy stood near her office door, his head bowed, his left hand covering the scarred side of his face, his right hand resting on his walking stick.

Poor darling, she thought. *While he was at Sidcup, he was protected from direct contact with the public but now he must learn to deal with people responding to his disfigurement and it won't be easy.*

As the trolley slowed near the front door, the patient tried to sit up. He began to thrash around on the stretcher. The ambulance officers reached out to prevent him from falling.

Percy stepped closer to help. He stared at the man's face. 'Oh my God,' he exclaimed. 'Tom Bellamy? We thought you were dead.'

CHAPTER TWO

'Good morning,' Doctor Kirke said, shaking Percy's hand and pulling out a chair for him to sit. 'Sister Phillips tells me you think you know the identity of the patient.'

'Yes, I believe I do, although his features have changed, his eyes have not. We were boyhood friends. I feel sure it his him.'

'The patient has suffered severe trauma and malnutrition, so it's not surprising his features have changed. My diagnosis is that he is suffering from a mental paralysis. In other words, his brain is attempting to shut out horrific memories as a form of self-protection. I believe he has experienced glimpses of those past events, resulting in seizures. Thus, we must give his mind and body a chance to heal so he can regain sufficient strength to cope with a full return of memory.'

'What can I do to help?'

'For the moment, we will be keeping him sedated, at least until he regains some strength. How you can help would be to spend time talking to the patient. I caution you to only speak of gentle things, we don't want to stimulate any harmful memories, particularly in this critical period of healing. The Red Cross record indicates he was found in a forced labour camp, where we believe he was near death.'

'I understand.'

'There are procedures that must be followed. However, if we can nurture a slow return of his memory and confirm his identity, we can then inform the authorities and in turn, of course, his family will be contacted and told of his situation.

One fears to think of the grief of loss they must have had to deal with.'

'Yes, indeed. When can I start?'

'No time like the present. The patient's level of consciousness will be lessened by the medication; however, this is simply to decrease his level of anxiety. Although he will appear to be asleep, I am quite confident he will hear you. If you're ready, I will take you along to the patient.'

Percy followed the doctor down the corridor to a small cubicle.

Kirke pulled back a screen and spoke softly. 'Here is a chair for you. Will you be comfortable?'

'Yes, thank you.'

'Then I'll leave you to talk to your friend.'

Percy looked at the face of the man beside him. He felt a lump grow in his throat. *Old friend, you have endured so many injuries and gone through so much,* he thought. He swallowed hard, took the man's hand in his and began. 'Hello, old chum, it's Percy here. Where to begin? When we first met? Our first year at Lord Scudamore School. My Uncle George paid my school fees, otherwise, I would never have met you. My pa just being the station master and yours being chief inspector and all. So, thank you, Uncle ...' Percy drew a deep breath.

'So, the end of our first day of class and our teacher, Mr Cornwall, what a funny old thing he was, calls out, "Class dismissed. Exit in an orderly fashion if you please." We had to walk in pairs down the long tree-lined laneway; you and I were placed together. It was autumn and the conkers were starting to fall. *Oddly-onker, my first conker.* I found one for each of us and told you to take it home and drill a hole through the middle of it, get a piece of string and push it through, tie a knot in the end so the string won't fall out ... bring it tomorrow and we'll have a game. That was the beginning and who would have guessed we would become Conker Kings of Scudamore.'

Percy paused to think for a few minutes and wondered if Tom had indeed heard him speaking. 'That's it, old chum, you sleep on. You're safe here.' He remembered what the doctor had said about keeping the conversation simple. *Righto, better not mention how Edmund Farrington walked you home then, even if you don't know that he was killed in France.*

Percy continued. 'I remember the first time I came to visit you at your home. I'd never seen such a big house. I rang the bell and that old housekeeper of yours opened the door and looked down her nose at me. So, I quickly whipped off my cap and asked if you were home. "He is. Who wants to see him?" she said. I told her I was your friend from school, and she said: "Come in then. 'Ere wipe your feet carefully if you don't mind." So, I did and then I followed her down the hall, past all the portraits of your ancestors, their black eyes following me. I'll never forget how my boots squeaked on the polished boards. Her skirt swayed like a great ship in full sail, and I followed in her wake to the back door. "Thomas, you have a visitor," she called, and you hollered: "Percy, how splendid." I wondered why you were on your knees and that's when I saw her ... your sister, Alice. I'll never forget ... she had a long white stick in one hand, a lace cloak around her shoulders and a paper crown adorning her gleaming red hair. I thought she was ... magical. Until she started shouting: "Tom! You're supposed to be *Bottom*!" and stamping her foot, she threw off the crown and gossamer cape, folded her arms and sliced the air with her wand. I'll tell you now, I was so shocked ... I didn't know what to think.'

Percy reflected on the naivety of their childhood years. *The things we most often joked about were often the things that embarrassed us, just like this unexpected experience. I suppose we held a secret hope that the blush on our cheeks was merely a sign that the sun had warmed our faces.*

'Hello,' said a nurse, pulling aside the screen. 'Would you like a break? You've been there for a while now.'

'Yes,' Percy replied. 'I'm getting a bit stiff sitting here.'

'Come with me. I'll show you to the conservatory. You can stretch your legs and I'll see if I can rustle up some lunch and a cup of tea for you.'

He followed her down the corridor and she pushed open a glass door.

'Oh, goodness,' exclaimed Percy as he stepped into the conservatory. He marvelled at the warmth of the room, constructed of glass, wrought iron frame on three sides and a glazed pitched roof. The floor consisted of old flagstones, yellowed and indented with footsteps over time. A variety of soft green ferns and aspidistra protruded from their colourful pots. Two majestic palms edged the walls, interspersed with a variety of citrus trees. Baskets of purple and white heliotropes, suspended from ceiling beams, were set against a backdrop of sweet-shop-coloured orchids and a vast array of herbs. He breathed in the heady scents as he walked the length and breadth of the room.

'Here is your tea and a sandwich,' said the nurse placing a tray on the edge of the potting table. 'What do you think?'

'It's wonderful,' replied Percy.

'Yes, all our patients love this place. Will you find your own way back to the ward? Enjoy your lunch.'

'Tom, I've just been to visit the conservatory. It's bursting with colourful plants. You know, it reminds me of your back garden and that big old orchard across the lane. We had some adventures in there. I remember the first time we went into the orchard ... it was cold and muddy, must have been late autumn. Suddenly you said: "Bob down, quick." A shadowy shape darted from tree to tree. Off we ran, keeping low. We came across an old timber structure with a rusted metal roof and scrambled beneath it. One of the posts had almost rotted away, which caused the corner to tilt downwards. We crouched in the shadows, peering through a crack in the timbers. A sudden thump on the roof frightened the life out of me. Strands of dirty grey cobwebs fell on our heads and a smelly, sticky substance dripped through the cracks. Another thump. We bolted out from the shelter as mouldy apples hurtled past and exploded on a nearby tree trunk, splashing the two of us. I caught at least two direct hits as we ran away. I was in for it when I got home, and you got a serve from your housekeeper, I'll bet.'

Funny thing was, thought Percy. *That red-headed rascal who scared us in the orchard turned out to be Ron.* A vision of Ron came to him as a young gung-ho chap, always cheerful and laughing, a friend to all. *So again, I shouldn't speak of Ron to you, Tom. You didn't know him as well as I did. He turned out to be a great friend. We went to war together. He saved my life.*

Percy sat quietly for a while reminiscing, but then childhood memories came flooding back. He spoke of them practising cricket with the lamppost as the wicket, playing leapfrog and the time he missed his jump and little Billy Worshoppe got a clout on the head. He talked of the endless races across the common, collecting tadpoles, of adventures and misadventures ... of laughter and innocence.

'Percy, it's three o'clock,' said Kirke. 'You were having a

little doze, I see.'

'Oh heck, I didn't realise ...'

'No, no, that's fine. Nurse tells me you have been entertaining our guest with wonderful stories.'

'I'm not sure he's heard me.'

'Oh, I think he has. Nurse?'

'He's resting peacefully, Doctor. Temperature normal. Pulse steady.'

'Come along, let's get you back to Broadleigh. Your lift is here.'

'Should I come back tomorrow?'

'Yes, indeed.'

~

'Hello love, how did it go?' asked Grace, kicking off her shoes and stretching her toes.

'I don't really know. When I first saw him on the stretcher, I was sure it was Tom, but today, I talked about our friendship, memories of school and people we knew and yet absolutely no reaction. Not a twitch of his eyelids, nothing.'

'Hmm, that doesn't surprise me. Doctor Kirke did explain that the patient was heavily sedated. Don't give up heart.'

'No, I won't, of course. I wish ... I don't know, some sign.'

'It won't happen straight away. Will you go again tomorrow?'

'Yes, the driver is picking me up at ten o'clock. Then on Wednesday, I must go to Birmingham, and I should go to Hereford, although I might put that off for a while.'

'You're welcome to stay here for as long as you wish. You know I love having you around. As long as you're comfortable on that hospital bed.'

'It's fine,' Percy laughed, bouncing on the mattress. 'I'm starving. Can we go and find something to eat?'

~

The following morning Percy arrived at the clinic and was greeted by the nurse he had met the day before.

'Good morning,' she said. 'I couldn't help but overhear some of your stories.'

Percy laughed and followed the nurse to the patient's bedside. 'Hello, old friend, it's Percy. I've been thinking about some of our adventures and the games we played. Saturday mornings on the Castle Green ... you were always *Sir Lancelot the Brave,* and I was *Sir Robin the-not-quite-so-brave* companion. Somehow or other, we always conquered the *Black Knight* and his dastardly companions. Especially when Gerald Barker and his motley friends from Upper IVB were our opponents.'

The screen opened. 'Ah, those dreadful Upper IV's.'

'Good morning, Doctor. Still no response.'

'That is to be expected. I believe our patient has damage to the areas of his brain responsible for consciousness, self-awareness and personality. Owing to the extreme conditions he has experienced, his brain virtually shut down as a form of self-protection and an instinctual impulse for survival. The medication we have administered has placed him in a state of consciousness like a deep sleep. We are carefully monitoring his condition because the last thing we want is for him to descend into a more troubled state. His awakening must be a slow process to protect his neurological condition.'

'I understand.'

'Keep up the good work, you are doing very well.' Kirke patted his shoulder before leaving.

Percy leaned closer to the patient's bed and examined his face. *So many similarities and yet ... perhaps due to injury, your face ... hmm. How long is it since I last saw you?* He thought of his own injuries and how his features had changed so dramatically. *I remember at Sidcup, the first time they let me look into a mirror and I was met with a stranger in the reflection. It's still me inside.*

~

'Ah, yes, one of our best times. The last day of term, I was waiting for you at the school gate. "What? No school uniform. You'll catch it," you said. I told you that school days were over for me, Uncle George had got me a job at the Cartwright's Cider Mill. You responded: "Oh, that's rotten luck. It's the match today, Upper Fifth versus Lower Sixth." Typical reaction from you. I could tell you were anxious to get to the match, so I said: "How about coming with me to Cartwright's stables? Uncle George says I could earn a penny or two polishing the brasses. We could do it together."

'A couple of days later, we met at the stables. Old Bob Clune, the drayman, let us in. I'll never forget the smell ... fresh straw, dust, horse and dung. I thought I was going to be sick, but you breathed it in. I'll have a go at Old Bob's broad Hereford accent. "Righto, lads, not afraid o' these beauties are ye?" Afraid? We were dwarfed by those powerful creatures and watched in awe as he walked easily amongst them, scratching their cheeks and huge shoulder muscles. "Here we have Daisy, she's the matriarch." Daisy nuzzled him affectionately. "An' this 'ere's Petal, she's Daisy's sister. There's Rosie, she's the youngest and this 'un's Puddin'", he slapped the rump of round-bellied Puddin' and she retorted with a snort. "C'mon ladies, let's get you fed and watered, then we'll get ye all tacked up ready for your outing. Oh, and that's

Punch, he's a fine old gentleman, aren't ye boy?" He reached up to rub the white muzzle. Punch bowed his massive head to rest on Old Bob's shoulder, his deep, dark eyes level with ours. The beast shifted his weight from one hoof to another, making a loud clopping sound on the flagstones. Old Bob rubbed the muscled neck, "You've done your bit, no work for you anymore, old man. Ron, pump some water, will 'e?" Well, that's how we discovered that Ron, the red-headed scoundrel who terrorised us in the orchard, was Old Bob's boy.'

In deep thought, he paused for a moment's reflection; *darn, I shouldn't have mentioned Ron, although ... I think in the context it is alright.*

'How can I forget our bicycle ride to Llancillow. Now that was a real adventure.'

He reached forward and held the patient's hand. 'If that is you in there, Tom; if you're in some dark, fearful place, just know that there are people here who love you.' He sat back and gathered his thoughts.

'I'm afraid the brass-polishing incident landed you in a bit of trouble with your father, so you weren't allowed any more adventures for the rest of the school holiday. I was working at Cartwright's by now and you were about to start the Lower Sixth. I found out that old carthorse had been put out to graze at Llancillow Hall. I called round to your house to let you know and suggested we could go and visit him.'

'We planned a bike hike for the following Saturday; you wanted to take your new Raleigh for a spin while I borrowed my Uncle George's bicycle. That was the first time you came to my house. You were early. I was eating my breakfast; you came into the kitchen. My ma asked if you would like a piece of toast and you said: "No thank you." Then our Gracie piped up: "That's funny, a boy saying 'no' to food." She was teasing, of course. She held the long toasting fork aloft. You went quiet. You told me later: "Her cheeks, reddened from the fire, glowed like spring roses, her blue eyes sparkled like sapphires." Hahaha, talk about gush. Anyway, off we went.'

'We pedalled hard and made good progress on those dusty roads. Finally, we arrived at Llancillow, pushed our bicycles through the gate, closed it behind us walked up the potholed driveway. We turned a bend and caught our first glimpse of the house. I'll never forget it ... a towering grey building, with a castellated roof, like something out of a Grimm's fairy tale. To be honest, it took my breath away. You called: "Hello." Dogs barked. A tall, wiry man and two sheepdogs appeared through the front door. "Be still," he commanded. The dogs sat, their tongues lolling and tails wagging. I can tell you now, I was ready to bolt. Instead, we both stood there like we were frozen to the spot and removed our caps.'

Percy leaned back in his chair and smiled at the memory before continuing.

'Major Crabbe was a formidable looking chap. Ice-blue eyes beneath vast grey eyebrows, then he said: "Are you lost?" Well, I was speechless, but you said: "No sir, my name is Thomas Bellamy. This is my friend, Percy Phillips. We wondered if we might visit old Punch, the dray horse, recently retired from Cartwright's Cider Factory."

'I thought he'd tell us to be off, but instead, he said to follow him. Off we went, around the side of the house, through a gate, past the stables. I nearly jumped out of my skin when I heard this horse kick the stable door and snort at us, shaking its head and spraying spit. Crabbe rubbed the horse's muzzle and said: "Manners, Phoebe, we have visitors." Then to my horror, you touched the horse's neck, tracing your finger along old scars. "What happened to her?" you asked. Crabbe explained that she was an old cavalry horse, he reached into his pocket and pulled out a carrot. She curled her lips, exposing long, cracked teeth, took the carrot, and retreated inside her stall. I breathed again for the first time in what seemed like ten minutes. "Take a few of those with you." Crabbe pointed to a sack of misshapen carrots, and we shoved a handful in our pockets. "Stay," he instructed the dogs and we followed him through another gate. Crabbe whistled and two black ponies, followed by the old dray, trotted up to him. "Hold your palm out flat, like this," he said as he offered a carrot to Punch. The horse lowered his enormous head and gently scooped up the carrot. I couldn't do it ... all that slobber and big teeth but you got the hang of it straight away.'

Percy paused, he needed to stand for a while, his wounded leg was hurting, sitting too long was no good for it. *How we've changed,* he thought. *Are you my old friend? I feel it rather than recognise you. God knows what you would think if you saw me now. Gammy leg ... and my face ... reinvented ...*

'It turned out Crabbe had lots of horses. The two little ponies he had rescued from the pits, four old carriage hacks and a chestnut mare, all of whom were destined for the glue factory.

'I'm sure Crabbe noticed how easily you moved amongst the horses, gently yet confidently offering carrots on your open palm, because he asked: "Do either of you ride?" and then you said: "No, sir, but we would love to learn." "Speak for yourself," I said, and Crabbe replied: "Well, there's work here if you're up for it, cleaning the stalls, and of course, exercising the horses. I could use the help and in return, I'll teach you to ride." I knew at that point you were hooked.

'I was glad he invited us back to the house. I was hungry and saddle-sore from the ride up. We settled down to a tremendous tea of sardines on toast and crumpets with jam before collecting our bicycles and riding home.'

Percy sat back in his chair. 'Was that a life-changing adventure? It was for you, I believe, but not so much for me. You had two more years at school and would spend every Saturday at Llancillow. While I was a working lad now, with a proper job at the cider mill and a weekly wage. When we did bump into each other, I wanted to talk about whopping great machines, huge wheels, giant presses, plumes of steam and boiling pumice. Whereas your interests became Crabbe's stories about the Boer War, his floor to ceiling bookshelves filled with antiquated leather-bound tomes, his brigade of tiny tin soldiers on horseback, with sabres raised against an unseen foe ... and most of all ... the thrill of riding the chestnut mare.'

When Percy leaned forward, he saw moisture had formed on the patient's eyes. He watched as a single tear slipped across his cheek. 'Well blow me down,' he whispered and then called, 'Nurse!'

~

Back in Grace's apartment, Percy poked at the coals while he waited for her to finish her rounds. He was tired yet anxious. He walked around the office, straightened the cover on his bed, plumped up the cushions on the sofa, picked up a book and flicked through the pages.

'You're back early,' said Grace.

'Yes, I ran out of stories.'

'Really? That surprises me.'

'Hmm.'

'Is everything alright?'

'Yes, well, sort of. You see, I had no idea that I would get so

... emotional.'

'Come and sit by me. Tell me what happened.'

'I won't lie, I'm in a bit of a hole right now ... I really had no idea that remembering childhood events would bring such sadness.'

'Oh, Percy, dear. You have put yourself in a vulnerable position. By trying to help the man you believe is Tom, spending time at his side, telling stories of your shared childhood ... of course, this will bring up emotions and sadness. I fear those halcyon days we knew as children are gone; I doubt we'll ever experience such an age of innocence again.'

'You're right, of course. Something odd happened this afternoon.'

'Tell me.'

'I'd just finished a story about our visit to Llancillow. Um, then, I suppose I became maudlin, talking about how that had changed our friendship. When I looked at his face, I thought I saw moisture on his eyelids, so I bent closer and saw a tear run down his cheek. I called the nurse.'

'That's a very good sign. What did the nurse say?'

'She was going to talk to Doctor Kirke. He was out and my driver turned up, so I came back here. The driver said he would pick me up early, it's Wednesday tomorrow and I have to go to Birmingham, but I'll call into the clinic first and then the driver is going to give me a lift to the railway station.'

'Very good. Will you still go on to Hereford after that?'

'No, I think I'll come back here first. There's no rush for me to get to Hereford.'

~

The following morning Percy arrived at the clinic and was escorted to Doctor Kirke's office.

'Good morning, Percy. Nurse Giles told me about the tear incident, a good sign, hence, we have commenced a reduction in the patient's dose of medication in the hope of bringing him gently to consciousness. I believe you are going to be away for a while.'

'No, I've decided to change my plans. I do have to go to Birmingham today, but I will return as soon as I can; it shouldn't take more than a day or two.'

'That's excellent news. Your continued visits to the patient will be appreciated.'

'I'll pop and see him now if that's alright.'

Percy sat by the patient's bed. 'Good morning. I can't stay long today, I'm off to Birmingham on the train. I was thinking of going to Hereford after that, there are some things I need to do but I've decided to come back here first.' *How inane, think of something cheerful,* he thought. 'I'm looking forward to getting back home but it can wait for a while.' *Groan.* 'It's Wednesday today. Market Day in Hereford. I used to love all those animal smells and the auctioneers shouting out the bids. D'you remember how we used to try to avoid riding through the puddles in case we accidentally sprayed water and dung at innocent passers-by? We didn't always manage to avoid them, did we?' He chuckled at the memory.

He leaned closer and held the patient's hand. 'I have to get along now. Don't worry, old chum. I'll be back to see you soon.'

The patient responded with a light squeeze of his hand.

CHAPTER THREE

On Friday morning, Grace received a telephone call.

'Kirke here, Sister. Would you come along to the clinic this afternoon, please? I want to consult with you about the patient, Mr Nine.'

'Yes, of course, Doctor.'

'Good, I'll send the driver for you at three o'clock.'

On her arrival, a nurse escorted Grace to the doctor's office.

'Thank you for coming, my dear, take a seat. I wanted to talk to you about your brother's visit. I believe he has had quite a remarkable effect. During the last visit, Percy announced that our patient had squeezed his hand.'

'Oh, that's good, isn't it?'

'Yes, indeed. The sleep enhancing medication has been discontinued, there have been no more seizures and the patient is awake. We have conducted several neurological tests, and he has been able to respond verbally, albeit monosyllabic. Here is the report.'

Grace read from the chart:

> Palpitations—fear of suffocation, of constriction of the throat.
>
> Exhaustion still evident and pain in the chest.
>
> Headaches, nervousness.
>
> Patient fears sudden loud noises and the dark.
>
> Suffers much from head and ear pain.

Exhibits a marked defect of recent and remote memory. His mental condition is non-assertive. He is docile.

'We are making headway, although I would like to keep him in the clinic, as you know, we are desperately short of beds. I believe in his periods of semi-wakefulness, he visualises beatings and whippings, feels terror of confinement, which may be the source of his nightmares. I recommend he return to Broadleigh early next week. Do you have any smaller rooms available, as I don't want him back in the general ward?'

'Yes, we still have two officers in one of the small rooms upstairs; there is another room, I will have to get staff onto preparing it as it has been used for storage.'

'Does it have a window?'

'Yes, it has a view over the garden.'

'Excellent. So, we have a plan. All being well, the patient will be transferred on Monday. When will your brother be back?'

'I believe he's returning this evening.'

'Good. As soon as we can get the patient's identity confirmed, the sooner we can put the wheels in motion and get him back to his family. Having said that, I feel it would be most beneficial if we can have the patient comfortably accommodated in his own room before Percy visits him again.'

'Of course, Doctor, I'll get onto that straight away.'

'And Grace ... are you keeping well? Getting some rest?'

'I am, thank you. It has cheered me no end having Percy around for a while.'

'Very good. We'll see you on Monday.'

~

When Grace arrived back at Broadleigh, Percy was waiting in the office. 'Hello, love, good trip?'

'Not the best experience,' he said, rubbing his temples. 'I suppose I should have expected it ... people staring, I mean. I hid behind a newspaper once I was on the train but the people on the platform and in the street looked at me with disgust. One woman pulled her child away and it started crying.'

'Oh, that's awful.'

'Yes, well, that's how it's going to be from now on. Best get used to it.'

Grace felt great sadness for Percy. *He was such a good-looking young man with a cheerful disposition. I only pray his character will sustain him.*

Percy stretched. 'I ache from top to toe. Bloody uncomfortable train ride and then standing around at HQ for hours ... what a shambles.'

'Oh dear.'

'They gave me this *demobilisation account*. It says: Balance due to soldier on the date of arrival at the dispersal station; two pounds and eighteen shillings. Twenty-eight days' leave at eight and tuppence equals eleven pounds, eight shillings and eight pence. Twenty-eight days' ration allowance at two and a penny equals two pounds, eleven shillings and four pence. Allowance for plain clothes ... two pounds, twelve and sixpence. The total is nineteen pounds, eighteen shillings and four pence. So that's it, not a lot to show for nearly four years' service. Oh, and I got a greatcoat and a voucher, Army Form Z50 for the return of the greatcoat to a railway station within twelve months, in exchange for one pound.'

They looked at each other and laughed at the irony.

'Any news from the clinic?'

'I've just come back from a meeting with Doctor Kirke. Good news, Mr Nine is conscious and, all being well, he is being transferred back to Broadleigh on Monday.'

'Oh my, that's wonderful news. I didn't expect that so soon. I must go and see him.'

'No, Percy, not yet. Doctor Kirke wants him accommodated in one of the small upstairs rooms and suggested we get him settled before you visit. I've got to organise the room to be cleaned and furnished, so it will be a busy weekend.'

'Alright, that's good. I can help. Right now, I need something to eat followed by a hot bath.'

'It's good to have you back,' Grace said, hugging her brother.

~

The next morning, Grace instructed two orderlies to clear out the spare room. She supervised the removal of boxes. *This is Freddie's stuff,* she thought. *Where on earth can I put it?* There was one room upstairs that, for some reason, had remained locked. Her thoughts were interrupted by Percy's arrival.

'Made it,' he said, leaning on his stick to get his breath back. 'Crikey, that was a heck of a climb.'

Grace addressed the orderlies. 'I think, for now, if you just stack these boxes at the end of the corridor, out of the way, so we can get in and clean the room. Please take care, there may be breakable items.'

Doris arrived at the top of the stairs, carrying cleaning rags and a mop and bucket.

'What can I do to help?' Percy asked.

'I'm not sure, dear, help with the boxes perhaps?'

Soon the room was empty, and Doris began cleaning while

the two orderlies went to fetch a bed.

Grace stepped inside. 'Oh, it's bigger than I thought,' she said.

Percy followed. 'It's light and airy and has a pleasant view of the gardens.' He opened the French window and stepped out onto the balcony. 'Brrr ... a bit chilly out there,' he said, closing it. 'I've got an idea.'

'Do tell.'

'Why don't I move up here as well? You'll easily fit two beds in here,' he said, looking around ... 'room for a nice armchair or two. I can keep an eye on him, and it would save me walking up and down those stairs, not to mention give you back your privacy.'

'Yes, I think that would work. I'll check with Doctor Kirke.'

''Scuse me, I'd like to do the floor now, please,' said Doris.

'C'mon, we're in the way. I'll go ahead and make that call. Please be careful coming down the stairs.'

By the time Percy reached the ground floor, Grace had spoken to the doctor. 'Yes, he said that is a fine idea.'

'Good, but I'm not planning on climbing up there again too soon. I'll move up on Monday morning if that's alright. Now it must be time for morning tea ... that's a thought, how about meals?'

'Don't worry, the two officers in the other upstairs room have their meals brought up. You won't go hungry. And before you ask, yes, there's a bathroom up there too.'

~

On Monday morning, the two orderlies took Percy's bed out of Grace's office to the upstairs room. Doris followed with clean linen for the beds.

'Percy, don't go up until the patient gets here. Would you like to have these things?' Grace opened the desk drawer and pulled out a small chess set, pack of playing cards, notebook, and pencils. 'Have you got a book to read? You're welcome to take one from the bookshelves.'

'Thank you, I'll pop them in my case. A book ... let me see ... um, they look a bit highbrow for me. What's this? "Tarzan of the Apes," that sounds more like my cup of tea.'

~

Later that afternoon, Kirke arrived. 'Well, here we are then. Percy, this is where your help is going to be truly valued. It is not unusual for a patient, in the initial stages of regaining memory, to behave in this way. Much of what he has learned in his lifetime is still present in his brain, however, severed connections block access to this information and he may not recall how to perform many activities. He must relearn not just how to dress himself but perhaps even how to move from a prone to a sitting position. Now here's how you can help, and for that matter, all nursing and domestic staff should be advised of these procedures.'

'I'll see to it, Doctor,' said Grace.

'Always name yourself when you enter his room or in your case, Percy, when you approach his bed. Tell him that it is morning, afternoon, or evening to help him orient to time. Warn him when you are going to touch him. Continue to talk to him about pleasant, shared experiences. Show him pictures of familiar places. You may tell him that he has been unwell and is recovering in hospital. Assure him that he is safe from harm now. Don't ask him to recall anything as it may frustrate him. Avoid saying, "do you remember ...?" And importantly, don't take any of his hurtful words or actions personally. This can be a challenge when a patient is in this condition, he truly does not know what he's doing, and he should not be held responsible for his deeds.'

'I understand.'

'Percy, I would like you to keep a journal, beginning today, make a note of any significant changes or reactions. You will spend more time with your friend than anyone else. We will rely on you to inform us of any of these changes. Please pay special attention to anything that occurs that may help us to prove his identity. Only address him as Mr Nine, or friend, don't use the name you believe belongs to him. As soon as we know for sure, we can start the procedure of confirming that with the authorities and putting his family out of the misery they must have been suffering.'

Grace pulled a book off the shelf. 'Take this with you, Percy. It's a picture book of some of the historic buildings in Hereford; I'm sure it has Lord Scudamore's in it. Freddie bought it for me. It might help.'

'I'll be off now. Call if you need me; otherwise, I will see you on Thursday for the usual rounds.'

After saying goodbye to the doctor, Grace went with Percy up the handsome oak staircase that led under an ornate glass dome to the upper floor. She carried his suitcase and the picture book.

Percy tapped lightly on the door before entering. 'Good afternoon, old chum. It's me, Percy. I've brought Grace to see you too.'

'Hello,' said Grace.

The patient pulled the sheet up to his chin.

'She's the nurse,' Percy explained. 'Well, we're going to be roommates. This must be my bed,' he said, taking the suitcase. 'I'm alright, you can go now,' he whispered, kissing her on the cheek.

Grace listened outside for a few minutes and heard Percy saying: "This is a nice room, isn't it? We have a lovely view of the garden. We're in hospital, you know. You weren't well and they've brought you here to get better ..." *Good on you, Percy.*

As Grace walked back to the staircase, she noticed the boxes sitting at the end of the hallway. *I must try to find the key for that spare room, can't think where else to put those boxes. I wonder why it was kept locked. I will write to Lady Morton; she may want to keep Freddie's things.*

Later that evening, sitting at her desk, she prepared to write. She struggled for a few moments, trying to think. She looked at the paper before her. Grace dipped the steel pen in the inkwell. Her hand hovered over the page. *How to begin?*

~

The next morning, Grace visited the ward to watch the changeover of staff. 'How was everything last night?'

'All was fairly quiet, apart from the usual antics from Mr Six.'

'Quiet upstairs?'

'Yes. I found Percy asleep in an armchair. He had a book open on his chest. I encouraged him to get into bed. He's quite a charmer, isn't he?'

'Ahh, I'll have a word to him.'

'No, please don't, he's fine. It's nice to have a bit of chat now and again.' She blushed.

Grace finished her rounds on the ground floor and went upstairs. First, she visited the two officers and found all was well there, before tapping on Percy's door. 'Good morning, this is Grace, popping in to see if you slept well,' she said as she entered the room. Mr Nine lay with the sheet pulled up to his chin and his face turned away from her. She turned to Percy and whispered, 'How's everything?'

He pointed to the notebook on the bedside table and indicated for her to pick it up and read it. Meanwhile, he climbed out of bed, went to the patient's side, and said, 'Good morning, I hope my snoring didn't keep you awake. I'm just going to the bathroom.' He winked at Grace while she read his notes.

Day One:

Chatted for a while. No response, he avoided my eyes most of the time.

Decided to show the picture book. Pointed out a few places he would know. Showed no interest. Turned his head away.

Chatted a bit longer, still no response.

Decided to read him the 'Jungle Book,' finished chapter one. Nurse came in and took him to the bathroom, he seemed agitated when he came back.

After supper, I read some more of the book to him.

Middle of the night, the nurse came in, after she left, I heard him crying, just quietly.

'Well done,' she said, handing him back the notebook. 'Are you comfortable? Got everything you need?'

'Yes, all good, so far.'

~

On Thursday, Doctor Kirke discussed Percy's notes with Grace. 'There doesn't appear to have been any change so far. That's not a bad thing, as he hasn't had any negative responses to his move back here. I think it may be time to put a therapy programme to treat his needs into place.' Kirke opened a file. 'I recommend a course of hypnotism. I believe our patient is sufficiently emotionally stabilised to withstand the treatment.'

'I'm not familiar with it, are there risks?' Grace asked.

'I believe the benefits far outweigh the risks. Hypnotism shuts down the field of consciousness,' he explained. 'We are able to speak to the patient's subconscious in the hope of bringing up buried memories.'

'But aren't those memories the things the patient's nightmares are about?'

'Not really, using this technique, we can get the patient to view forgotten facts, study them, rationally tackle them and learn that the need for fear exists no longer.'

'I see.'

'It won't happen straight away, of course. The brain is a powerful, self-protecting entity. Hypnotism is a process we must begin cautiously and will need to be repeated numerous times over several weeks. We also need to plan for the patient's health and wellbeing. I have scheduled dental work and he may require some facial surgery to repair the broken jaw which was obviously left to self-heal. I'm not sure we can do much about the scarring on his back and legs. That might be something we can look at in the future.'

~

As the days passed, Grace concluded that Percy had slipped into a comfortable routine with his charge. The doctor would be back on Friday to start the hypnotism treatment. She could take advantage of this quiet time to organise the storage of Freddie's boxes. She still had not discovered the whereabouts of the key to the locked room.

Perhaps Lady Morton will know, she thought.

~

Friday morning, Kirke arrived to conduct the hypnotism. 'How is our patient today?'

Grace handed him Percy's journal. 'There haven't been any incidents. He is still withdrawn but calm, taking his food and getting plenty of sleep.'

Kirke read through the pages. 'These notes are helpful. I see he's been reading to him and showing the picture book, excellent. Well, shall we get started?'

'Good morning, gentlemen. I am Doctor Kirke, and this is Sister Phillips. We have come to visit you in your hospital room.'

'I'll wait outside,' said Percy, lifting out of the armchair.

'I'm sure Mr Nine will be pleased if you stayed.'

'Yes, I would like to stay with my friend,' he said, smiling reassurance.

'Now, Mr Nine, I am going to try to help you using hypnosis. There is nothing for you to worry about, I want you to completely relax and look at my watch,' Kirke said, swinging the pocket watch slowly from side to side. 'You are with friends. You are safe. You are feeling very tired now and you want to close your eyes and sleep ... sleep.' He nodded at Grace and pointed to the patient's eyelids as they began to flicker. He continued to talk slowly and calmly. 'That's right, you're safe, you can rest in this comfortable place. You are lying on soft, warm grass in a lovely summer garden. The air is balmy. A lazy bumblebee is buzzing around the blue cornflowers and purple lavender. A sweet aroma of honeysuckle wafts across the garden on a gentle breeze. It is very peaceful here. You are resting with the warm sunshine on your face. The fine and wispy call of a song thrush carries across the still air. Children are playing close by; you can hear their laughter.'

Kirke leaned closer to check the rapid movement was still going on beneath the patient's eyelids. 'Yes, it is so peaceful here. Can you see the children? Perhaps you know them? Can you move towards them? They are very friendly. They want to meet you.'

The patient blinked hard and seemed to be considering the question.

'You can talk. You can tell me what you see. You can tell me if you recognise the children.'

Grace reached for the patient's hand as he started to tremble.

Kirke continued, 'Will you tell me your name? Will you tell me where you are?' He stopped suddenly when Mr Nine let out a roar of terror.

CHAPTER FOUR

March 1919

*T**he first day of spring, the air is warming, and the days will start to get longer*, Grace thought as she gazed out of her window. *The garden is waking up, grass is appearing. I should take my tea outside and sit on the stone terrace to experience the magic of all these new beginnings.*

Over the last two weeks, some patients had been discharged from the repat hospital but there was always a constant flow of new patients to take their beds. The newspaper reported of the hundreds of thousands of men ... British, Colonial, American soldiers, many injured and in need of hospitalisation, still awaiting transport home. Grace wondered how the French hospitals were coping, especially as many of the military field hospitals had already been disbanded. She pondered on the state of the infrastructure when she and Freddie had left France last year ... the roads and railways lines were in such a state.

Her thoughts turned to the young men, recently discharged from Broadleigh. She and some of the nurses had lined up to wave them off; they were going home and yet their faces portrayed such trepidation.

Soon it would be her turn to go home. *Goodness knows what kind of reception I'll receive,* she thought. *I must write to my parents and let them know about my baby. I don't want to give Ma a shock.*

The crunch of gravel pulled her away from her reverie.

Leather squeaked as Lady Isobel Morton eased across the seat. Her fingers, cold inside black lace gloves, clamped onto Hibbert's proffered arm. She straightened her lace bodice and smoothed the taffeta skirt, which swished and swayed as she walked up the stone steps. Pausing for a moment, her cloche's ostrich feathers took on a life of their own, quivering as she turned to look along the expanse of formal gardens, where early snowdrops peeped through.

Grace opened the door and beckoned them in.

The lady's nostrils pinched as she sniffed carbolic and disinfectant. She stood blinking, her eyes adjusting to the dull hallway.

'Your Ladyship. Please come in.'

'You may leave us, Hibbert.'

'Yes, M'Lady.'

'May I offer you tea?'

Lady Morton inclined her head, taking a chair by the bay window. She examined Grace from the boots up. The fine lines around her mouth compressed into a tight fan.

Despite the coolness of the gaze, Grace recognised the same loved features; familiar eyes had looked into hers, only they had promised love. Those eyes belonged to Freddie.

'Perhaps you would care to visit one of the wards while you are here?'

'Of course not.'

'Milk, your Ladyship?'

Grace poured milk into the teacups. Her hands shook a little as she placed the tea strainer over the first cup and poured from the China pot. She summoned the courage to ask, 'You received my letter, my Lady?'

'Why else would I be here?'

'Yes, of course. Thank you for coming.' Grace sipped her tea. 'The boxes, mostly containing papers, some pictures ...'

'Hibbert will collect them.'

'Yes, and the locked room? I have not been able to find the key.'

Lady Morton stared disdainfully at Grace. 'Hibbert has brought the key. The contents of the room are of no importance to you. He will arrange for the items to be removed.'

'I see, thank you.' Grace's insides were boiling. *Why is she so horrible to me? Doesn't she understand how much Freddie and I loved each other?*

The front doorbell rang. Men's voices, including Hibbert's, could be heard, followed by footsteps climbing the stairs. Lady Morton turned her gaze to the gardens.

'Please excuse me,' said Grace. She followed the men upstairs. 'There are the boxes.' She pointed down the corridor.

Hibbert inclined his unsmiling head and looked at her through heavily lidded eyes.

'Hibbert, you have the key for the locked room?' Grace's voice quavered as she spoke.

'Yes, miss.'

Percy appeared from his room. 'Everything alright, love?' he asked.

Grace's heart began to pound. She felt hot and dizzy. *Why is this mysterious room so important?* She turned to look at Percy. 'I'm fine, thank you. May I have the key, please?'

Percy reached her side.

Hibbert handed it to her, and she opened the door. It was dark inside. Heavy drapes prevented daylight from entering the room. A sliver of light outlined where the curtains met in the middle. She walked in while Percy and Hibbert stood at the doorway.

'Careful,' Percy cautioned.

Grace pulled the curtains apart and light flooded the room, sending tiny particles of dust to spiral around. She gasped. 'It's a nursery,' she exclaimed breathlessly.

Hibbert called the men, 'Quickly, empty the room, take the crib first, then the chest of drawers, all the pictures. Come along, get on with it.'

Grace fought hard to regain her composure before returning to her office. She found Freddie's mother still looking out of the window. 'The room was a nursery ... I didn't know ... Freddie never said ...'

Lady Morton chipped in, 'That he was married? That he had a child. A wife that died in childbirth and took the child with her?'

'Oh, God, I'm so sorry.' Distracted by the unexpected discovery, words she needed would not come into her head.

'We must leave!'

Hibbert, who had been examining a wall hanging, turned to see his charge emerge from the office, his brows creased in concern, he moved quickly to her side, again proffering his arm. Without a backward glance, they walked down the steps and into the car.

Grace watched from the open door as the vehicle, its shiny black skin glinting in the morning sun, slowly departed. Gravel crunched in the car's wake, adding the last dreary touch to the scene.

I can never tell her that I am carrying Freddie's baby.

Percy called from the top of the stairs. 'Are you alright, love? Can you come up here? I've got an idea.'

'I'll be up in a minute,' she replied. She wanted a minute or two to herself.

'Here comes Grace. Let's see what she says.'

'What's all this?' Grace asked.

'I've been talking about my visit to the conservatory at the clinic. He'd like to see it, wouldn't you, Mr Nine? How about you, Grace? We could all go together. It's warming up a bit now. We've been sitting out on the balcony. But it would be nice to stretch our legs a bit and I couldn't think of a nicer place to visit. It's got a roof, in case it rains.'

'That sounds like a splendid idea. We will ask the doctor tomorrow.'

~

Later that evening, she set about reading Kirke's notes in preparation for his visit the next morning, when Mr Nine would receive the fourth hypnosis treatment. She took special interest in the closing paragraph:

> *The patient has made significant progress. Mr Nine is now speaking articulately and responding to questions without excessive distress ... I am hopeful of a breakthrough soon.*

Grace thought about the possibility of finding Mr Nine's identity. *Percy does seem quite confident this is his old school friend. If he is, it will be a wonderful thing to be able to inform his family that he is safe. Just imagine the pain and sorrow they have felt these last years. On the other hand ... Percy will be heartbroken if he is not.*

~

On Friday morning, Grace chatted to the doctor as they climbed the stairs. 'I noticed you wrote that you were hoping for a breakthrough today.'

'Yes, since that first upsetting result, I feel we have progressed, we just need to push a little harder today.'

As they reached the top of the stairs, Grace glanced at the open door of the nursery.

'Ah, I see you've managed to open the door,' said Kirke, walking towards it. 'Oh, this is very good. We should be able to fit two more beds in there; if we can purloin them from somewhere.'

Grace said nothing.

'Well, let's see to our patient, shall we?' He tapped on the door. 'Good morning, Mr Nine and Percy. Sister and I have come to visit you again.'

The patient was sitting on his bed, his legs hanging over the side.

Percy winked at Grace.

'Now, Mr Nine, please lie back and relax ...' Kirke continued the routine, '... and now you can see the door is opening. Please move closer to the door. Someone is standing there. Can you see who it is?'

'Mmm,' the patient replied.

'Good, do you recognise the person?'

No response.

'Please look again and tell me the name of the person waiting near the door.'

The patient's eyelids flickered rapidly. 'Mmm, Mrs C.'

Kirke wrung his hands together and took a deep breath. 'Yes, this lady is your friend. Now can you tell me your name? What is your name?'

'Tom.'

'I knew it!' Percy cried. 'Welcome home, my friend.'

Kirke brought Tom out of the hypnotic state. 'Percy, a word, if you please,' he said, motioning for him to follow. 'This is the breakthrough I have been hoping for. We still have a way to go but with his acknowledgement of name and your testimony regarding his identity, I believe we are in a position to contact the authorities. Now, will you confirm his full name, please?'

'Thomas Bellamy.'

'His date of birth?'

'Same year as me, 1894 ... August, I think.'

'Do you know his regiment?'

'Yes, Eighteenth Royal Hussars, Queen Mary's Own ... he was proud about it.'

'And he was born and raised in Hereford?'

'Yes.'

'Well done. Sister, we have much to do.'

Back in Grace's office, they put plans into motion. Kirke relayed the information Percy had given to the War Office in Whitehall. He then spoke to a doctor at the surgical hospital.

'So, we must wait for the investigation of Tom's identity and military records to be completed before we can write to his parents. I've spoken to Doctor Grafton, and he will have a bed for the patient on Monday.'

'Isn't that rather quick, considering his neurological condition?'

'With Percy at his side, I believe he will rapidly regain his memory. I also trust that surgery to correct his jaw and teeth will not only improve his features, but it will also enable him to masticate his food, which I'm sure he would currently have a great deal of difficulty with.'

'How long will he be in the surgical hospital?'

'Several days, it is not a simple operation. Grafton is an excellent surgeon; I have seen his work on similar cases. The operation is entirely carried out from the inside of the patient's mouth to minimise visible scars. A cut is made through the gum behind the back teeth to access the jawbone. The lower jaw is then cut with a small saw to allow it to be broken in a controlled manner. It is moved into its new position and held in place with small metal plates and screws. While anaesthetised, his teeth will be either removed or repaired.'

'That does sound complicated. Where will he convalesce?'

'Back here, where your brother can continue his work.'

'I imagine Percy is wanting to celebrate. He has suggested taking Tom to see the conservatory at the clinic. Would you consider that a possibility?'

'Most certainly, and you should go with them, my dear. It is a splendid facility. I'll send a driver. Saturday morning? How's that?' He checked his watch. 'I must go. Do enjoy the little outing and please make arrangements for the patient's transfer to the surgical hospital on Monday.'

'I will, thank you, Doctor.' She saw the doctor to the front door, slightly amused by the spring in his step.

CHAPTER FIVE

Ten days later, Grace supervised the movement of two patients from the general ward downstairs to the new room upstairs. Mr Six and another patient had already taken the beds of the two officers, now discharged. After settling the men into their room, she popped in to see Percy and Tom.

'Good morning, how are you both?'

'He's had a rough night. The nurse gave him a sleeping powder, and he was quiet after that.'

'The pain, Tom, is due to the stitches pulling on your healing gums and jaw. Doctor Kirke will be here later this morning; he will remove the bandages and examine the wounds. Please don't worry, I'm sure all will be well.'

Tom closed his eyes.

'How are you, Percy, love?'

He pointed to the door, and they walked out of the room.

'I'm fine … a bit worried about Tom though. I've talked about good old memories, but I can tell he wants to know more. I'm sure he's starting to remember more recent times and I don't know how to manage that.'

'Don't worry, the doctor will be here soon, I'll let him know. Are you feeling alright in yourself? You've been managing up here for several weeks.'

'I'm fine. A few of us meet out on the balcony for a smoke and a chat. It's a bit of a party atmosphere up here now, with all the rooms filled.'

'Don't lead them astray.'

'Whatever do you mean?'

Grace heard the doorbell. 'That's probably the doctor,' she said, ushering Percy back to his room.

~

Under Kirke's watchful eye, Grace removed the bandages from Tom's face. He leaned in closer to examine the surgery. 'Doctor Grafton has done a superb job. Now, let's take a look inside. I know this is painful, but I want you to open your mouth gently, that's it. Oh, this is excellent work. The gums have healed well. We'll get those stitches out and you will feel a lot more comfortable. Sister, if you please ...'

Percy held Tom's hand while Grace adeptly removed the stitches.

'All done,' she said. 'There is still some swelling and a little bleeding. Wash your mouth out with this.' She helped him to sit and rinse his mouth with salty water while Percy held a bowl for Tom to spit into. 'Well done, I'll get something to ease the pain.'

'Good man,' said Percy, examining Tom's face. 'There's a few bumps and bruises, but I reckon you'll have movie-star looks again before you know it.'

~

A few days later, Percy and Grace discussed future plans in her office.

'Tom seems to be doing well now; I think I will head to Hereford. I still have to take the watch to the Farringtons, and I must go and see Ron's mother as I promised. I've also written to Mr Cartwright to ask about getting my old job back at the cider mill and he's replied saying to call in.'

'I know how you feel. I'm ready to leave here now and

looking forward to getting home, although I must admit I'm feeling a little anxious,' Grace said. 'Ma replied to my letter, she is a dear, she told me not to worry, she and Pa will welcome the child ... just what I expected she would say.'

'She's right, love. We'll all look after you and the baby.'

'I know. I'm grateful but that's not what I'm worried about. It's what other people will say. In their eyes, I'm a *fallen woman*. I don't want to be treated with suspicion and subjected to demonising rhetoric about my behaviour just because I have no husband.' She blew her nose hard. 'I'm sorry.'

Percy wrapped his arm around her shoulders. 'Come on, Gracie. It'll be alright. We are all going home to face demons. I don't want to be accused of scaring children with this mug of mine. And Tom, well, who knows what scares him? He's still regaining his memory but has told me he's worried about the fact that he spent most of the last four years as a prisoner of war and that people may not understand. He's anxious and unsure how he will explain.'

'Poor Tom. No one could understand the hell he experienced. It's not surprising he said he thought his life was over, he'd lost hope,' she said. 'Oh well, at least we have each other.'

'Yes, we do. We're a bit like the Three Musketeers ... battered but not broken.'

~

The following Wednesday, Percy packed the last of his things into his suitcase. 'Righto,' he said, pushing hard on the lid to close the clasps. 'I've left you *The Jungle Book*. You'll be getting a new roommate soon, you never know, he might need a bit of cheering up too.'

'Thank you, Percy, you're a good friend. I can't thank you enough for all you did for me.'

'That's what friends are for. Now you look after yourself. Get well as quick as you can and hurry back home. I'll be waiting for you.'

'Percy, the car's here,' said Grace. 'Let me take that case. Mind how you go down the stairs.'

'Thanks, love. Bye, Tom.'

'Have you got everything?' Grace asked as she helped Percy to the car.

'Yes, I think so,' he replied, giving his sister a long hug. 'Well, here goes nothing.' He pulled his cap low and climbed into the rear seat.

'It will be alright. You'll be home soon. Tell Ma and Pa I love them. I'll be home in a couple of weeks and if Tom is well enough, he can travel with me.'

~

That night, Grace sorted through her belongings, packing away things she felt she would no longer need. In the weeks after the news of Freddie's death, she found it difficult to believe he was not coming back. Broadleigh was his house and it still felt like he should be there, she felt his presence, particularly in the apartment. Every corner was filled with his life. His photos and books, his furniture, and his clothes; a place for everything and everything in its place. She had meticulously boxed up his belongings, now in the care of his mother. But there were still small and painful reminders of his absence. She ached for him every day and reached for him at night. She whispered, 'I know he will never be back. How do I move past this grief?'

As she lay down to sleep, the familiar vision returned.

She watched from the window as he walked beneath the oaks. He stopped, turned and blew a kiss ... but this time, it was not Freddie's face she saw, but Tom's.

~

Meanwhile, in Hereford, Ellen Bellamy's thin fingers fretted at the frayed end of a ribbon on her bedjacket. She pushed her toes further down into the bed; the hot water bottle had slid just beyond her reach. Even with her woolly socks on, she felt the chill.

Outside, furry catkins of pussy willow, the early portent of spring, scraped against the bedroom window, drawing Ellen's attention to the garden. Veiled by the lace curtain, snowdrops and early daffodils edged the pathways through the long lawn. Beyond the privet hedge, a haze of green, like an aura above the stark orchard trees, implied renaissance.

Capt. R.B. Steele,
Southwest Medical Corps,
'Strowan'
Bridge of Weir
16th March 1919

9/5. Med.Cr/848 (M.S.3.Cas. T.F.)
Chief Inspector and Mrs Bellamy,
34 DeLacey Street,
Widemarsh,
Hereford

Dear Sir and Madame,

The officer referred to in the attached papers is undoubtedly Lt. Thomas Bellamy who was engaged in a cavalry assault with his Battalion in the battle of La Bassee on 16th October 1914. The brigade was ordered to drop back to the Brenicourt position on the Aisne. Lt. Bellamy was believed to have died in the attack; thus, you were informed on 24th October 1914 that he was declared 'killed in action'.

That report is now officially updated to 'missing in action, now returned.'

Your servant,

R.B. Steele

Captain for The Military Secretary

~

Soon, my love, you will be home. Ellen folded the paper and pushed it back under the pillow. She slid down into the warmth of her feather mattress, pulled the eiderdown up to her chin and closed her eyes.

~

A few days after Percy returned home, he telephoned Doctor Farrington to make arrangements to meet with him the following day at the Copper Kettle Café.

Tall trees flanked the roadway, their leafless limbs etched against the milky sky. A light breeze ruffled the handful of people going about their business, shrouded in overcoats, hats drawn down around their ears. Quiet figures, passing in and out of sight, captured for a few seconds in the bay window's dark wood frame.

A cheery fire crackled in the hearth of the Copper Kettle Café; occasionally, a damp wood hiss and spit sent tiny embers skittering across the sloping flagstone floor.

'Your tea, sir. Will there be anythin' else?' The waitress flinched as Percy looked up at her. A look of shock mingled with disgust crept across her face.

'No, thank you,' Percy replied.

With a swish of her skirt, she returned to the kitchen.

Percy looked at the wall clock. *Half-past ten o'clock.* He felt the flat round shape of the watch bulging through the coarse material of his flannel trousers. His hand shook as he reached for the teapot.

The little bell sounded merrily as the door scuffed open, a shot of chilly air crossed the threshold ahead of Doctor Farrington. He unwound his woollen scarf, removed the black Fedora, and joined Percy at the table near the window. Reaching out his hand, Farrington enquired, 'Mr Phillips?'

'Yes, Doctor, how do you do?' Percy instinctively raised his hand to conceal the left side of his face and winced as the effort to stand quickly brought a fierce pain to his left thigh.

The waitress returned. 'Good mornin', sir, what can I get you?'

'Tea, please.'

'We've got some lovely teacakes, fresh baked.'

'Just tea, thank you.'

'Mr Phillips; my son, you said you knew him?'

'Yes, Captain Farrington was in charge of our troop. We all respected him deeply. He was a brave and considerate officer. A man you were proud to follow.'

'Edmund was like that, always well respected. He was a teacher, you know, before the war, of course. We received a letter, but it didn't say much. Can you tell me more?'

A wave of nausea suddenly rose in Percy's belly. His mind raced ... *How we were all scared out of our wits. How the verey lights fell like stars, followed by the boom of cannon. How he was up the ladder, urging us on. Then the roaring, screaming, falling, bleeding. How your son died? Stretched on the wire like a puppet with all the strings cut. How we crawled in clay-mud, like grey ghouls, trying to reach him ...*

'Mr Phillips?'

A sudden rush of raindrops against the window aroused Percy. He reached into his pocket and retrieved the watch, the metal warm beneath his palm; he set it on the table.

'Doctor Farrington, your son's watch.'

The doctor picked it up and held it close to his chest. 'Mr Phillips, can you tell me how ...'

'We'd been in the trench for nearly a week. Lots of false starts. Snipers were a damned nuisance. We were so close to the enemy line we could hear them talking. Occasionally one of them would call over ... *"Hey English ... how you like this no bloody good weather?"'*

Percy took out his tin and started to roll a cigarette.

'D'you mind if I ...?'

'By all means, please go on.'

'Late in the day, the shelling got worse. We took turns to snatch a bit of sleep in the dugout, then the word came down the line that it was time.'

Percy poked the thin cigarette into the side of his mouth; the wiry strands of golden tobacco crackled and sparked in the match flame. He inhaled deeply, the sharp, sweet smoke searing his dry throat. He pulled a loose fleck off his tongue before continuing.

'We fixed bayonets and stood ready, waiting for the signal.

I can tell you that our guts turned to water and legs, well, you just wondered how they'd keep you up. Captain Farrington blew his whistle. Next thing we were scrambling up slippery ladders jammed against the slimy trench wall.' Percy took another deep drag of his cigarette.

They both watched the blue-grey smoke curling towards the window.

'Dodging bullets, mud holes and wire, we followed him as best we could through thick smoke. The next thing I remember, I was lying in a crater, shells exploding all around, earth shuddering; it was hell. Sergeant Howell and my mate, Ron, crawled out to find the wounded. They dragged as many to the trench as they could. Ron didn't make it. Neither did Captain Farrington. Later, Sergeant Howell shoved the captain's watch in my pocket and told me to bring it home to his family.'

Percy's cigarette burned down to his fingers. He took a last long drag before stubbing it out in the ashtray. 'I'm sorry, it took me so long. I was injured, you see.'

The rain drummed against the window.

'Thank you, Mr Philips. I am grateful to you. This has meant a great deal to me. You must excuse me; I have to get back to the surgery.' Farrington wrapped his scarf around his neck and pulled on his hat. He waited while Percy stood, shook hands, then hurried through the door, his head bowed against the weather.

Percy watched as the doctor's image dissolved into the wet landscape. *Give me strength. Now for Ron's ma.*

~

On the last day of March, Doctor Kirke arrived to collect Grace and Tom. 'Is that all the luggage you have, my dear?' he asked.

'Yes, this is all Freddie's stuff,' she replied, looking around the apartment they had shared for such a brief time. 'None of it belongs to me. I've taken a few bits and pieces that he gave me. The rest, I'm sure Lady Morton will appreciate being left here.'

'My dear girl ...'

'I will fetch Tom.' Grace left without a backward glance, her heart pumping hard in her chest. She found Tom saying "Goodbye" to his upstairs companions. 'Come along, Tom, we don't want to keep the doctor waiting. Goodbye, gentlemen.'

Soon, they were aboard Kirke's car and driving to the railway station.

'This is awfully kind of you, Doctor.'

'My pleasure, although I shall miss you, Sister. Do drop me a line when you get home safely. And Bellamy, please keep taking your medication and make an appointment to see your doctor. Farrington, isn't it? I shall forward relevant medical notes to him.'

'Thank you, I will.'

'Well, here we are.' They said their "goodbyes" and waved as Tom and Grace entered the station.

~

Tom pulled the collar of his greatcoat up and over his ears, glad he had listened to Percy's advice and selected the heavy weight khaki wool coat instead of the clothing allowance of fifty-two shillings and sixpence. He felt sure he would find some of his old clothes at home, but for now, the grey wool shirt and trousers Grace had found him would serve his needs adequately. He hoped they would not have to wait too much longer for the train. He glanced at Grace standing with her head bowed close beside him. *How small and fragile she seems,* he thought.

He watched people coming through the turnstile gather in small groups along the length of the platform. They seemed to huddle together for warmth and comfort while shreds of paper fluttered like swirling snowflakes in the cold wind. Tom pushed his hands deeper into his pockets.

With a hiss of steam, the train pulled into the station. Tom followed Grace up the steps. They walked along the corridor, hoping to find an empty carriage. 'Here we are,' he said, pushing open the sliding door to let Grace enter. 'Let me help.' He took her suitcase and placed it in the luggage rack alongside his.

'Thank you,' she said, sitting next to him.

The carriage door slid open, and people soon filled the carriage.

The train lurched forward. Tom turned his attention to the view past the station master's house and a few red brick cottages. Two boys painting the signal box turned to wave as the train rolled by. Slowly gathering speed, it rocked to the rhythm of the metal wheels on track. He glanced at his co-passengers as they took furtive looks around as well.

Tom returned his attention to the view of rolling pastures. Sunlight filtered through grey clouds scudding along the landscape, casting long shadows on the verdant scene.

A conductor entered the carriage. A paunchy man with a cheery smile. He stopped at each occupied seat and made polite conversation before checking the tickets.

I've been gone so long, this is somehow not real, this green, empty place, unspoilt. I never thought I would see it again. Tom checked himself, had he been thinking aloud? The thoughts were palpable, his mouth was dry. He coughed and pulled himself upright, resting his head against the back of the seat.

~

Grace looked at Tom, her eyes soft and sad, her thoughts far away. She pulled a book out of her handbag, *The Poems, of Emily Bronte.* She opened the front cover, gently tracing these words with her fingertips, '*For my dearest, something to distract you while I am away, Freddie.*' Grace turned the pages slowly.

~

The train emerged from a tunnel into greyness, raindrops slid along the grimy window blurring the goods yards and sidings. Couplings clinked; the engine hissed and chuffed as great puffs of steam billowed alongside the carriage.

Tom folded his arms, resting his cheek against the cold glass, lulled by the rhythm of the train. Insensitive to the occasional cough or dull conversation in the carriage, he breathed in the delicate fragrance of Grace, warm beside him, an unfamiliar sense of consolation soothed him to sleep.

~

'I think we're almost there,' Grace patted Tom's arm. 'Are you being met?'

'Yes, I believe so. My father said he would send a car for me.'

Tom stood with Grace on the platform while a porter retrieved her suitcase.

'Gracie.' Percy waved his hat in the air. People moved away and stared awkwardly at him as he made his way through the crowd towards his sister.

'Percy, it's so good to see you,' said Grace, hugging her

brother.

'Welcome home. How was the train journey?' Percy reached to shake Tom's hand.

As he was about to answer, a young woman threw her arms around his shoulders and took him by surprise.

'Tom, oh, Tom, darling! Sorry, did I make you jump? Here, let me look at you,' she said, her eyes wide with shock when she saw his thin, pale face. 'Oh, what have they done to you? Don't you recognise me? It's me, Alice, your sister.'

'Goodness me, Alice. You've grown up.' Her face, chubby when he had last seen her, was now slim and framed with red curls cut to chin length.

'Sir,' croaked a policeman. 'Sergeant Turley, here to take you home.' Turley, teary-eyed, a large lump raw in his throat, stood to attention and saluted Tom before picking up his case.

'Thank you, Sergeant.' Tom hugged Grace and shook hands with Percy. 'Well, here we go. See you soon, I hope.'

~

From behind a leafless elm, a sinister character watched the arrival of the police car at the railway station. Fearful of discovery, he was compelled to wait and see what transpired. He saw the police sergeant exit the station, followed by a tall, thin man arm-in-arm with an attractive young woman with stunning red hair. He licked his lips as they grew closer. Squinting, he returned his attention to the man and tried to make out the partially obscured features. 'It can't be, how did he survive that hellhole? I thought I'd got rid of him.' He squinted, trying to get a better look. 'Bloody hell, it is. It's Bellamy. Bloody 'ellfire. You owe me, pal, so lookout, cos now you're going to pay.' He pulled his collar up high and set off for his house, muttering as he stumbled, 'Fuck. Fuck.'

~

The housekeeper placed a tea tray on Ellen's bedside table and plumped up her pillows.

'Can you see him, Maisie? What's he doing?'

'He's sittin' in the sunshine. Got that big old coat on, a tammy on his head and a blanket wrapped round his shoulders,' she said, wiping a tear before blowing her nose. 'I'll take him some tea soon, but I think he might be dozin' at the moment.'

'Oh, don't let him stay out there too long, he mustn't catch a chill.'

'Don't you worry, M'am, I'll keep my eye on him. Anything else I can get you?' she said, pouring a cup of tea and handing it to Ellen.

'I didn't know what to say to him, Maisie. When he walked in, so pale, so thin. All these years, thinking he was gone from us.'

'I know, M'am. Praise the Lord for bringin' him home, safe. He'll take a bit of buildin' up, poor lamb,' she rubbed her nose hard. 'Yes, indeed.'

'Edward will be home soon,' Ellen said. 'Perhaps Tom should come in for a rest before he arrives?'

'Of course, M'am, but let's leave him in the fresh air and peace 'n' quiet while he can enjoy it. Speakin' of which, you should take a rest yourself. Don't you worry now,' she whispered as she collected up the tea tray and closed Ellen's door behind her.

~

Tom's elbow slipped from the arm of the chair, and he woke with a start as his chin dropped away from the cup of his hand. Pins and needles tingled in his fingers.

'Tom, are you awake?' Alice asked, sitting next to him on the garden seat.

He was surprised to see her dressed in corduroy trousers and sturdy shoes.

As if she read his thoughts, she stood up quickly and did a twirl. 'Would you like a cigarette?' She pulled out a packet of Woodbines from her hip pocket and offered one to Tom. 'Better not let Mother find us, she objects to it somewhat.'

'I'm not surprised,' said Tom, teasing. 'Not lady-like, is it? I don't like cigarettes but thank you anyway.'

She laughed. 'It's so good to have you home.' She pushed her arm through his and rested her head on his shoulder. They sat there for some time, warm against one another.

'It's gettin' a might cool out there now. Won't you come inside? Your father will be home any minute,' the housekeeper called from the kitchen window.

'Golly, I have a meeting tonight, I'd better get a wriggle on,' Alice kissed Tom on the cheek. 'See you later,' she said, scurrying back to the house.

Tom pushed himself out of the garden seat. His knees felt stiff, he steadied himself.

'Ah, there you are, my boy. I was just coming to look for you, Thomas.' Edward Bellamy offered his hand to shake.

Tom was surprised by the size and heat of his father's hand; his own felt cold and puny in the grip.

'Come, let's talk in the study. I could do with a drop of malt. How about you?' Edward led the way.

'Thank you, Father, I'd prefer tea.'

'I'll bring it in,' chirped Mrs Chadwick.

Edward poured himself a drink. Swirling the liquid, he

held it up to the light to admire its glistening golden lustre. He held the glass beneath his nose and breathed in the aroma of vanilla and spice.

Tom was relieved to see his father distracted by the malt. He was unsure what to expect from this conversation.

The housekeeper came in quietly with the tea tray and smiled at him reassuringly.

Edward placed his glass on the table and pushed his spectacles down across the bridge of his nose. He sat back in his chair, elbows resting on the arms, hands clasped, pressed his index fingers together and tapped his chin, a familiar pose. 'I can't begin to tell you how marvellous it is to have you home.' His voice broke and coughed to clear it. 'I wonder if you have any plans. Have you given thought to your future?'

'Not really, Father, it's all been rather anomalous.'

'Yes, of course.' He cleared his throat again. 'Well, you are home now. Safe and well. So, you must take your time. Get your strength back. No need for hasty decisions.'

'Thank you, Father.'

'Of course, there are many opportunities for you in the Constabulary. Changes have been implemented over these recent years, professionalising the officers, encouraging the adoption of innovative technologies. All of which I am sure you would find most interesting. There is also an emphasis on extended training for new recruits.' Edward waited, hopeful for a response, but none came. 'You realise, of course, that your grandfather and great-grandfather were respected members of the constabulary.'

'Yes, Father. I am aware of that.'

'Well, I must get on. Unfortunately, there has been a spate of violent crime afflicting our city.' Edward paused. 'The concern, of course, is that men trained in weaponry, brutalised in battle and inured to violence may well slip easily into crime. These concerns have not been unfounded.' Edward sipped his malt. 'Even here, in this last six months, we've had no less than twelve reports of robbery with violence. In one case, at Sutton Morton, a farmer pursuing the rascals who had smashed into his house, assaulted his wife and stolen a considerable amount of cash, was beaten so severely by the miscreants that he later died in hospital. These men are still at large.' Edward's face reddened, he continued. 'I fear some men have grown callous after four years of murderous activity. There are reports from other towns that battle-hardened men have murdered their own wives. Innocent women, raped and brutally murdered by their own husbands. To top it off, these dastardly perpetrators are claiming *the war made me do it,* or *it was the shell shock,*' he slapped the papers on his desk. 'We are opening a new Criminal Investigation Division and we'll be looking for good men.'

Tom felt anxious and wondered where this was heading. He rose quickly from his chair. 'Excuse me, Father. I must go to the bathroom.' Hurrying through the door, he nearly bumped into the housekeeper.

'Supper will be ready in an hour,' she said. 'I'm just going to check on your mother.'

Tom scurried down the hall, his chest felt constricted, and he wasn't sure if he would vomit. He sat on the edge of the bath and tried to calm his breathing, moistened a flannel and held it against his forehead. When his breathing returned to normal and the pounding in his chest diminished, he hurried upstairs to his room.

A light shower dampened the window blurring the image

of the orchard beyond. An impressionist painting of grey sky tinged with pink and endless green, framed by his bedroom curtains, captivated Tom for a while. Somehow it seemed unnatural, too clean, too fresh, too pure. *Things look the same as they were but it's different.*

He closed the curtains and lay on his bed. *What Father says about men committing violent crimes, affected by their experiences in battle, I don't get that. It's a different world. I must find a place in it, but first I must remember and try to understand.* He drifted into an uncomfortable sleep.

~

Something woke him suddenly. He felt sweat gather in his armpits and a sinking feeling in his gut. He squeezed his eyelids shut as every nerve alerted to the flood of memories that washed through him. His skin tingled and his pulse quickened as he encompassed the visions that appeared. Like pieces in a jigsaw puzzle, the cameos hung in a pale sky above a brown landscape that rushed past.

Part Two

WAR YEARS 1914-1918

CHAPTER SIX

August 1914

TOM

On fourth August, the Daily Mirror newspaper reported:

'Great Britain Declares War on Germany'

'Declaration made last night after 'unsatisfactory reply' to British ultimatum that Belgium must be kept neutral.'

During the ensuing week, Tom was busily employed completing preparations for war. Reservists were arriving at barracks almost hourly as the battalion had to be filled to war strength. He, and fellow Lieutenant D'Arcy, oversaw the intake of freshly acquired horses.

'Few of these are trained to carry men in combat. The farriers will have to look them over to ensure their suitability for cavalry,' said D'Arcy.

'And those rejected will be used to pull wagons and the big thirteen pounders. Poor devils,' Tom replied. He checked his watch. 'Look at the time, we better get in line for the medical inspection.'

'Bellamy, Thomas.' He stood to attention in the examination room, feeling awkward in vest and regulation underpants.

'At ease Bellamy,' the doctor studied Tom's medical record. 'Good, good. Stand over there by the chart, please.' He reached up to mark his height. 'Hand over one eye. Read the letters from here down,' he tapped the chart on the wall.

'S W P A ...'

'That'll do. Any medical conditions we don't know about?'

'No, sir.'

'Breathe in ... out. Quick jab. Righto, you'll do. Send the next man in if you please.'

'You're in D'Arcy,' he said as he reached for his pants and tunic.

A few days later, Tom attended Major Adcock's office.

'Gentlemen, you have been selected to participate in a special escort. Tomorrow, you will take the Colours of the Battalion, to be laid away in the Cathedral Church of St Michael and St George in Aldershot.'

Tom felt both pride and foreboding as D'Arcy whispered, 'Let the war drums sound, we take the fight to them.'

The following day, the special escort undertook their duties, ceremoniously handing the flags into the care of the Dean and Chapter.

The Dean accepted them in saying, 'Fear not, these flags, symbols of history and loyalty for the regiment, will be preserved in the Cathedral until the Battalion should next require them. God bless you and preserve you,' he called as the escort took their leave.

That evening, Tom folded and packed away his gold-braided, royal blue tunic, he thought back to the happiest times, sitting in Major Crabbe's parlour, by a warm fire. Hot crumpets and jam, sweet tea, photos of Crabbe in his blues and the table set with tin soldiers.

By the twelfth of August, the mobilisation was complete and now they stood fast awaiting orders, these were days of tense excitement and speculation.

Early next morning, the 2nd Battalion marched down to the government siding at Aldershot and entrained. D'Arcy, Pendle and three fellow junior officers shared Tom's compartment.

'So, we're finally on the way. Anyone up for a bet about our destination?' D'Arcy said.

'I'll wager we're bound for Le Havre,' said Pendle.

'More like Boulogne,' another offered.

'You're both wrong.' D'Arcy teased. 'We're on our way to Brighton. A bit of sea air and sunshine, that'll do us a power of good.'

'What d'you say, Bellamy?'

Tom considered before answering, 'I think it may be dangerous to speculate.' He was grateful for time to think, the men fell silent as the train rattled along

~

'Looks like we've arrived,' said Pendle, rubbing the window. 'What a calamity. A sea of khaki out there. God knows how many on each train.'

'The trains will be running from several locations, back and forth all day. I heard there are at least 500 men on each one, not to mention the horses,' said Tom. 'A huge operation.'

'All to be transported by sea,' said Pendle with a grim face. 'I hate ships.'

'And don't forget the ships will be loaded with lorries, motors cycles, big guns, petrol and oh, I do hope they remember my menu selection,' D'Arcy laughed.

Tom observed how slowly and methodically the loading took place. Two electric cranes hoisted the vehicles by their hubs; the horses, picked up by a sling under their bellies, were frightened and skittish, as soon as their feet touched down on the deck, they appeared ready to jump overboard. By half-past-ten that night, the first of the ships was escorted into the Channel. The primary wave of the British Expeditionary Force was deployed to France and put out to sea under sealed orders.

~

From the deck of HMS Formidable, Tom watched the dock lights become mere pinheads before vanishing. The salt breeze was cool and pleasant after the heat of the day. The regular rumble of engine propelled the darkened ship towards its destination. Countless vessels travelled the same course through the still night. Some were transport ships such as the Formidable, others, small Royal Navy vessels patrolling the waters of the Channel and along the coast of France.

White tipped waves, illuminated by a crescent moon, washed against the hull. Lulled into a rhythm, Tom let his mind wander.

'Got a light, Bellamy?' D'Arcy asked.

'Not here, chaps. No lights allowed.'

Pendle pushed the cigarette into his pocket.

They stared across the inky waters, watching the warships' shifting beams of white sweep the sea.

'Searching for German U-boats,' said D'Arcy, in a low voice. 'The German fleet won't wait for any declaration if they thought they could catch us napping. I fancy we're ready for them. We just want to get off this bloody water and into some ground action.'

Tom looked back to the shore, but he could only imagine the winking lights and looming cliffs. England seemed asleep. They had slipped away without notice.

In the early hours of the morning, HMS Formidable was towed and steered into Boulogne Harbour. Along the piers, flanking the waterway rang French cheers. Disembarkation began in earnest.

Several hours later, the 2nd Division of the British Expeditionary Force began its march. Along the roads, they were greeted by French civilians who went mad at the sight of them. In every village, girls threw flowers, ran alongside with gifts of fruit, and flung kisses at the men. Tom had never seen so many pretty girls. D'Arcy was in his element, lapping up the attention.

'*Vive les Anglais, A bas les Bosches.*' The cries continued as the men marched for three days under a hot sun over cobbled streets, resting at night in makeshift camps outside small villages en route to Mons.

October 1914

The third month of the war. The cavalry had performed brilliantly in scores of engagements with lance and rifle. However, the reality was now apparent that they were fighting with weapons and tactics that were antiquated and inferior to the enemy.

'Lieutenant Bellamy, the captain wants to see you, sir.'

'Thank you, Stevens.' Tom rose from an almost sleepless night to a crisp, clear autumn dawn. He pulled on his breeches and boots, pulled his greatcoat across his shoulders, and hurried to find Captain Marcroft.

'Coffee, Bellamy?'

'Thank you, sir.'

Marcroft pumped up the burner on the tiny paraffin oil

stove. He stirred dregs in a tin pot, sniffing them before shaking in fresh grounds. 'Reminiscent of coffee,' he said, handing Tom a cup of the steaming brew. 'I sent Swayne out on his bicycle last night to find Brigade HQ. He returned, sore-assed, at four this morning. We've orders to entrench a defensive position while we wait for the infantry to get here.' Marcroft spread the field map. 'Severe action here,' he tapped his finger on the map. 'There are slag heaps, furnaces and industrial villages lying between us and Mons. The local inhabitants are rapidly evacuating.'

'Where to?'

'God knows. The bloody roads are choked with civilians, a pitiful sight. Laden with great bundles, carrying children. On they come in the blind hope of self-preservation. French police are moving them along as quickly as possible but the sheer volume of civilian columns on the roads is causing obstacles. Slowed down the infantry brigade on its way here. They've made progress through the night and should be here soon and ready to deploy for action by mid-morning.'

'Sir, do you think there may be German spies amongst them?' asked Tom.

'Of course, there must be. HQ has set up blocks, but spies will be almost impossible to detect in such a massive swell of people.' They returned to studying the map. Marcroft traced a thin line with his finger. 'This canal is slowing the German advance. It reaches over twenty-six miles, all the way from Meurot to La Bassee. The ground on either side of the canal is treeless and undulating. The highest ground is to the east, near this town,' he bent closer to read the name, 'Le Cateau. This is where they will place the heavy battery, just north of here.'

'Excuse me, Captain.'

'Corporal Swayne, come in.'

'A message from HQ, sir.' Marcroft took the paper, 'Thank you, corporal.'

'The enemy is getting ready for a smashing blow. They've dug in along an eighteen-mile section of the front, surrounded by bloody barbed wire.'

'That'll tear the horses to shreds,' said Tom.

'The artillery will commence a heavy artillery barrage.' Marcroft looked at his watch, 'In one hour. Let's pray our nine-hundred-pounders blow enough holes through the Hun's barbed wire, not to mention a few of their guns. Grab some rest and breakfast. We'll meet back here at zero eight hundred.'

~

The earth shook and the sky was ablaze with fiery colours as the bombardment increased in intensity. Tom finished a hurried breakfast and stood watching the hordes of bedraggled men of the Fourth Battalion arrive.

The barrage ended as suddenly as it had begun; when the firing stopped, a moan filled the air. Tom decided to check on the horses. Troopers moved tenderly amongst the wild-eyed mounts, soothing and reassuring them. Above their whispers, all that could be heard was the creaking of saddlery and champing of bits. Tom sought out his mare, a powerful bay, standing at eighteen hands, one of the tallest mounts. He took a nosebag from a passing trooper and gently placed it over her head. 'Here you are, my lady.' Tom patted her neck, ran his hands over her shoulders, down her legs, feeling for signs of stress or strain. Satisfied that she was in good order, he left for his meeting with Marcroft.

'Ah, Bellamy, come in. Monck is just telling us about an

incident at Reumons last night. Carry on, Monck.'

'HQ warned us that a night attack might be imminent, even so, they nearly took us by surprise. At twenty-three hundred, we were picketing the north-west entrance to Reumons. We heard the infantry approaching. It was dark, but we held fire as we heard men singing French marching songs. We made out their blue uniforms as they got closer, so the lads started to ease back. Behind the men on foot, we saw four motorised lorries. That's when I started to get suspicious. I shouted to the men to prepare for attack. The bastards opened fire at close range with a machine gun hidden in one of the lorries. We got our field gun up and the third shot put out the German gun and the lorries.'

'The blighters. Casualties?'

'A barn we had been using for stores was hit by an incendiary, most of the equipment was out as we were preparing to deploy. It was pell-mell for a couple of hours until we chased them off. We counted one hundred and thirty of them dead; we lost forty-seven men plus a few badly banged up.'

'Thank you, Monck.'

'It's madness. Senseless, bloody lunacy.' Captain Faulkner continued. 'Bloody swords and rifles against cannon. Damned barbed wire everywhere, horses haven't had their saddles off for days. My men have marched through the night, they're exhausted.'

'Captain Faulkner, as matters stand now, we can't allow ourselves to be weakened by backbiting.' Marcroft checked his watch. 'Here's our plan. Our gunners will commence the barrage at precisely zero ten hundred. Under cover of fire, the infantry will move forward to these positions.' He tapped the map and the officers all moved in closer. 'The cavalry will charge from the right and left flanks, sweeping northwards to attack the German positions, here and there, rolling them up from the south. Any questions?'

There were none. 'God speed, gentlemen.'

The British guns began heavy fire. The saddle-up order came for Tom's brigade. They moved swiftly to the west, south of the road, avoiding the hard surface. For an hour or more, they cantered steadily forward, travelling two abreast through ruined villages, pounded by high explosives, burned to charred fragments by incendiary shells. Battered squares and crumbling churches. Unroofed, desolate farmhouses and dead livestock littered the once-verdant pastures.

A dismal rain fell as they approached an open field, Marcroft called a halt. Men were keyed up. Horses' nostrils flared. The sound of battle was close. The enemy artillery sent regular bursts of shell towards the approaching infantrymen.

Marcroft rode up and down the ranks calling, 'See that your swords are loose.' Men sat tense in their saddles, despite the cool morning, sweat soaked their armpits; their mouths dry with anticipation and guts churning, they waited for the order to go forward.

Tom turned to examine some of the faces he had come to know and trust. *Are they thinking the same thoughts? Will I keep my feet in stirrups in the charge or fall in the chaos?*

Marcroft and Tom exchanged a look. There were no words. This was the moment they had faced scores of times already. The die was cast.

'Half-sections right, walk march. Head left, wheel. Draw swords. Trot. Form column of half squadron. Gallop.'

Hearts pounding and wind biting into their faces, the great mass of men and horses surged forth. German artillery turned on them. Machine guns spat fire. Shells dropped before and behind them.

In the flash and smoke of burning shell, Tom's mare reared up. Shrapnel ripped her gut, her blood spewed in the air above and over him. Brought to earth by his dying mare, his world fell silent until an unremitting scream intensified in his head, and he lost consciousness.

Dead and dying horses dropped in their tracks. Some still living, a strange appeal in their eyes. Dust caked their thirsty lips and nostrils. Men, overcome by fatigue, dropped or lay where they had fallen. The retreat sounded; the spirit of duty bore them on.

Marcroft dismounted, shouting, 'Search the fallen, for those who can be rescued. Take the identity tags from the dead.' He watched his men drag the wounded up and across their saddles. Unknowingly, he walked past Tom's prone, blood-soaked body. 'Retreat,' he shouted, mounting his horse. Bringing up the rear, he urged men forward while he paused to survey the carnage.

A sergeant came riding alongside. a wounded soldier across his saddle. 'Captain? We must leave.'

Marcroft's throat was raw with emotion as he spoke. 'In the days to come, mothers will weep for their sons' sacrifice.' With that said, they galloped away.

~

Captain Eichel of the Twelfth Prussian Grenadiers watched as his men scoured corn stooks for British stragglers. They collected weapons of the fallen, occasionally turning a body or jabbing with their lances.

'He, hier - dieser ist noch lebendig.' *Hey, over here, this one is still alive.* Eichel picked his way carefully across the pockmarked field, avoiding carcasses, torn limbs and the wet fissures filled with rain and blood.

Tom's fingers grasped for a hold on sticky soil; pain and dizziness engulfed him; the only sound he heard was a high-pitched screeching. Gritting his teeth, he forced himself to open his eyes. He saw a pair of mud-covered boots and the point of a lance.

Strong hands dragged him to his feet and turned him to face the officer. Eichel's mouth opened and closed. Tom pointed to his ear and shook his head. Eichel's grey eyes looked suspiciously into Tom's. He ordered his men to take him.

CHAPTER SEVEN

'Take it easy, let me help. You were in a mess when they brought you in. Dougie did a pretty good job on removing shrapnel, considering he ain't a real doctor and we have no proper medical supplies.'

Tom felt tender hands raise his head to remove bandages from his neck and face.

'There you go pal, easy now.'

Suddenly a call. 'Snowy, the Huns are comin'.'

'Now look smart. Let's get you sittin' up.'

A guard shouted, 'Get up, stand up.'

A doctor walked with the guard, scrutinising the patients. 'This one is ready. This one, yes. How long has this one been here?'

Despite the chill, Tom began to sweat. Pain in his back, neck and right ear throbbed with every beat of his heart. He eased back the sheets, unsure if he would be strong enough to climb out of the bed. Within a breath, Snowy was at his side, helping him to stand before the doctor.

'Herr Doktor, this one's only come round today, no food yet,' said the orderly.

'Forty-eight hours!'

Snowy levered Tom back to his bed. 'Y'did real good. I'll be back with some grub soon. He's given you two days, so we better get you fixed up.'

Tom lay bathed in perspiration, visions of battle returned, his teeth chattered in his skull, hands trembled, and his fingers grasped and dug deeply into the sanctuary of the grey bed sheets.

~

Two days later, Snowy woke Tom. 'Here's your tunic and trousers. I did me best to get the mud and bloodstains out. Get dressed; the guards will be 'ere shortly. I found this in yer pocket,' he said, pushing the match case into Tom's palm. 'It might come in handy, and you don't want to get it pinched. Here's your boots, at least they're dry.'

'You're a good man, Snowy. Thank you,' said Tom.

'Oh, and here's a tin of baccy, the poor bugger that owned it won't be needing it now,' Snowy winked. 'Keep your pecker up. It can't last much longer, eh?'

~

Tom joined men standing to attention outside the ramshackle hospital building. None spoke, each looked around furtively. Like Tom, they were dressed in the remnants of their uniforms; some had great coats, most without; some wore sealskin waterproofs, most did not.

Tom whispered to the man on his left, 'Do you know where they are taking us?'

The man simply shrugged.

They were ordered to pick up a pack, bound with twine, holding a thin straw pallet, grey blanket and tin cup. As Tom picked up his pack, he felt the raw pain of his wounds, barely healed.

A dozen guards, with bayonets fixed, fell in on either side of the line of men, two abreast, they were ordered to 'March on.'

A gunmetal grey sky loomed heavily above, rain drizzled on the men gathered at the station, their breath steamed into a white mist that gathered low above their sodden heads. They stood on the cold concrete steps of the railway siding, silent, subdued, inwardly wrestling the fear of the unknown. Each bore the heavy burden of defeat. The engine steamed into the station, and the long train of carriages slowly crunched to a halt. Further down the platform, anonymous figures, screened from the prisoners, were hurried aboard. The train shunted along for fifty yards and came to a halt.

If there is any chance of escape, I must take it now, Tom thought. Abruptly, timber doors clattered open, guards exited and exchanged greetings with their compatriots. Tom realised escape was futile.

The prisoners were herded aboard. Windows, partially boarded, restricted the view and fresh air. The dank, rotten smell of foul timbers made men gag. The doors slammed shut; the engine dragged forward. Tom joined men at the back of the carriage. They stacked their packs together to form a resting place. Red and blue uniforms identified many of them as either French or Belgian. One man in khaki stared at Tom.

'British?' the man asked.

'Tom Bellamy, Hussars,' he replied.

'Ah, fancy cavalry, eh? Arthur Skaggs, infantry. Got a light?'

Tom pulled out his match case.

'Put it away, stupid,' said Arthur, his eyes darting around to see if anyone had noticed. He pointed to a young man, also in khaki.

Tom studied the face and form of the youth. He was tall like Tom but of slighter build. There was something about him, as though his shape was in shadow. *He's just a boy, can't be more than sixteen*, he thought.

The train clattered on, Tom closed his eyes and leaned

back to rest for a while. He woke to find Arthur talking in a low voice to the young soldier, who had moved next to him.

'His name's Hugh McTeele. He was with the Percys,' said Arthur. 'He came to grief at Ypres. Where did they get you?'

'La Bassee,' said Tom. He was relieved to find someone he could finally talk to. 'I don't know what happened after the first day of the battle at Bassee, we seemed to be gaining ground. I woke up in the field hospital. I haven't seen anyone from my brigade.'

Arthur spat a tobacco flake. 'They brought us down on London double-decker buses from Vlamertinghe. We was ordered to start digging trenches, but the countryside was flat, marshy and cut by so many streams. Bloody impossible. Us infantry were matched up with French cavalry, what a bunch of ... We captured Le Pilly but were pushed back by German artillery fire. It was chaos; that's when I got taken, outside Bassee.'

Something in Arthur's story did not ring true for Tom but he decided to let it go, for now.

'C'mon, lad, tell us what happened to you.' Arthur said.

'They brought out this bloody-big cannon, blasted us to hell. We had been pushing forward all day. Our corporal ordered us to stop and rest, he had the squits, so we dug in, just for a bit. Then we heard this noise, it kept getting louder and closer, then this almighty bang! Blood, bits of bodies, flew around me. Blood and smoke in the air. Corp fell on me, top of his head and his arm was gone, I couldn't get up.' Hugh's voice faded to a whisper.

Tom leaned back, lulled into an uneasy rest, and slept until a change in the engine's rhythm and the clatter on iron rails slowed. His back and shoulder had grown stiff during the long journey. He grimaced as he stretched out his arm, tried to raise it above his head, reawakening the rawness of wounded flesh and muscle.

'What's happening?' Hugh cried, wakening suddenly.

The train ground to a halt, the carriage door scraped open. A shock of cold fresh air blew along the carriage. Men struggled to stand. Four guards with bayonets fixed, shouted, 'Back, back.'

A young woman appeared in the doorway. She wore a grey woollen uniform and a white tunic bearing a red cross and carried a basket covered with a linen cloth. Guards pushed a bucket of water and ladle towards the men, who greedily grabbed it and began to drink deeply. The young woman followed silently, handing out bread and round biscuits. She arrived at Tom's end of the carriage. The nurse stiffened as she looked at the khaki uniforms and refused to give the bread. 'Englanders? No, not for Englanders!' She walked back to the guards, who lifted her down to the platform.

The train trundled on until, once, again, it began to slow. Arthur climbed on a sleeping man to reach the small window.

'Where are we?' asked Hugh as the station buildings came into view.

'Saabrücken. Looks like we're in Germany,' Arthur replied.

Suddenly the doors opened, cold air was sucked in, and the clear light of early afternoon pierced the dimness of the carriage. Guards shrieked their orders, 'Get out!'

Men clambered to collect their packs and exit the carriage as quickly as possible. They jumped down onto the platform and formed into lines, two abreast.

Tom pulled Hugh into line next to him, with Arthur behind. He estimated around eighty men on the station platform and observed that less than a quarter of them were wearing khaki. The first five rows were ordered forward. Tom watched as posts and beams, unloaded from the train, were lifted by pairs of men, some with apparent ease, others struggled under the weight; however, all balanced their load while clinging to their pack roll. The next five rows moved forward. Now it was their turn. Tom urged Hugh to the front as the long rough-cut beams were lowered to their shoulders. Both grimaced beneath the load, Tom stepped closer to Hugh to take the bulk of the weight. Sweat stung their eyes as they staggered forward.

Fifty yards on, Hugh's legs began to buckle. Tom encouraged the boy. 'Keep going. We're nearly there, it's not much further.'

Hugh staggered onwards clinging desperately to his pack, one arm locked onto the beams, the timber grating into the flesh of his shoulder, driven on by Tom, who steered the cargo from the rear.

'That's it, Hugh, drop it here.' Both men fell to their knees, the beams dropped, vibrating with the hollow sound of raw timber on cold ground.

Arthur and another man were directly behind. They too dropped their load. 'Fuck,' Arthur swore and spat.

All too quickly, the guards were upon them, shouting orders, 'Move forward.'

Tom grabbed Hugh by the collar and dragged him up. Together they entered the compound at Saarbrücken.

Hereford, December 1914

Police Constable Greenaway knocked on the Chief Inspector's door.

'Excuse me, sir, there is an officer wishing to speak with you.'

'Show him in, Greenaway.' Edward swallowed the last of his tea, ignoring the biscuit which lay, soggy, in the saucer. 'You wish to see me, Officer?'

'Bradbury, sir. Reservists. It is my painful duty to inform you ...'

Edward felt his chest tighten.

'Please, sir, won't you sit down?' Bradbury reddened, this was the first notice he had delivered, and although he desperately hoped, he knew it would not be the last.

Edward noticed that the usual buzz of conversation in the Constabulary had ceased.

'Give me the paper please,' Edward said. He read:

K ... 144 Army form B 108-42

If replying, please quote above number

Household BN Record Office Worcester

2nd November 1914

Sir or Madame

It is my painful duty to inform you that a report has been received from the War Office notifying of the death of: -

    Number: 1507 Rank: 2nd Lieutenant

    Name: Bellamy, T

    Regiment: 18th Hussars

    Occurred: In the field, France

> The report is to the effect that he is KILLED IN ACTION
>
> By His Majesty's command, I am to forward the enclosed message of sympathy from their Gracious Majesties, the King and Queen. I am at the same time to express the regret of the Army Council of the soldier's death in his country's service.
>
> I am to add that any information that may be received as to the soldier's burial will be communicated to you in due course. Currently, the soldier's person is listed as 'not found'. A separate leaflet dealing more fully with this subject is enclosed.
>
> I am,
>
> Your obedient servant
>
> P.F. Gray
>
> Lieut. Colonel
>
> Officer in charge of records
>
> Folio: 988271

Bradbury mumbled some words, attempting condolence, before leaving.

Edward retrieved his hat and coat from the rack; without a word to anyone, he hurried out of the building.

As soon as he left, the Constabulary came to life.

'Cor Blimey, that'll be bad news.'

'That'll be about young Tom. D'you remember, he came in here looking for his pa? When was that, August?'

'Aye, I remember, looking really smart in his uniform.'

'Alright, you lot, haven't you got work to do?' Sergeant Turley steadied himself on the timber counter.

~

Edward found his wife in the front parlour. She slept, a blanket wrapped around her shoulders, the Book of Common Prayer lay open on the table at her side. He coughed and she stirred.

'Edward?'

His throat constricted and unshed tears stung his eyes.

'What is it? Has something happened?'

'Devastating news, I'm afraid, my dear,' he choked as he handed her the notice.

Ellen's hands shook as she read. She read it again. 'Oh, God, NO!' she cried, clutching at her chest.

Edward fell to his knees, threw his arms around his wife, and kissed her on her forehead and cheek. Then he stood, steadied himself and rushed out of the parlour, calling for the housekeeper. He marched up and down the long hallway past photographs of long dead relatives and dreary paintings until he caught sight of himself in the hall stand mirror. He marvelled how his eyes bulged and the veins in his neck stood out like thick vines against his high white collar.

'Whatever is the trouble, sir? Is something wrong with Mrs Bellamy?'

Edward gripped the edges of the hall stand and stared at the reflection of his reddened features. 'Please take care of Mrs Bellamy,' he spluttered.

'Beggin' your pardon, sir, may I ask ...?'

'Thomas ... killed ... in France.'

'Oh, it's terrible news, sir. Oh, poor Mrs Bellamy,' she said, hurrying to the parlour.

'M'am!' Mrs Chadwick found Ellen slumped in the chair; her face was ashen and her hands icy to touch. 'Lor' love us. Sir, Mrs Bellamy needs the doctor, she's fainted.'

Edward was already on the telephone. 'Bellamy ... Widemarsh Common ... it is urgent ... tell him to come immediately.' Next, he dialled the station. 'Put Sergeant Turley on. Turley, send the car to Withnell to fetch my daughter. Tell her she must come home without delay.'

Doctor Farrington expressed his deep condolences to Edward as he left, issuing instructions that Ellen should not be left alone and that Mrs Chadwick ensure she took the prescribed draft regularly every four hours for the next two days.

The housekeeper sat by Ellen's bed, desperately trying to stifle her own sobs. Ellen reached out and took her hand and that is how they remained until Alice arrived.

All the while, Edward's footsteps were heard pacing backwards and forwards upstairs.

Turley waited by the front door until he saw Alice safely inside.

'Mother?' Alice opened the door quietly and peeped in to find Mrs Chadwick still sitting by Ellen's bedside. She carefully slipped her hand from beneath Ellen's, trying not to disturb the sleeping woman.

'Miss Alice, thank goodness you're here,' Mrs Chadwick whispered as she motioned for Alice to follow her out of the parlour.

'Whatever's happened? Sergeant Turley said he couldn't tell me and that I had to come home at once.'

'I'll fetch your father.'

'Please, Mrs Chadwick. You must tell me.'

'Oh, my dear, it's your brother ...'

Alice gasped.

'Alice,' said Edward, carrying a large bundle wrapped in a sheet. 'I'll be with you shortly; stay with your mother.'

~

Later that afternoon, smoke rose from a bonfire. Books, clothes, shoes, tennis racquet. Slowly and meticulously, Edward fed the hungry flames. Finally, a bicycle, wheeled from the garden shed, was set atop the blaze, smouldering rubber tyres filled the air with pungent black smoke.

'Father, whatever are you doing?' Alice cried.

'My son, my boy ...' Edward sobbed.

In Tom's bedroom, a single book remained on the mantle above the fireplace. The Oxford English Dictionary. Inscribed in boyish handwriting inside the front cover, the words *'this book belongs to Thomas Bellamy, Lord Scudamore School, 1908'*. Alice took the book and placed it under her pillow.

~

Late November and the first frost had left its mark on the last vestige of autumn. Ellen sat rigid as the iron frame of the old park bench. She gazed across long rolling lawns, her breath a fine mist in the cold air. A red squirrel chattered after his mate high in the boughs of an oak, which framed perfectly the grey river flowing briskly below the bank. Fluffy clouds scudded along in a swift easterly breeze, bringing the musty perfume of composting leaves. Ellen breathed in the scent. She lingered, motionless, like the statues in the centre of the Castle Green. Austere Victoria, ribboned in regal pose. Sir Arthur Scudamore, adorned in tutorial robe, a pigeon perched nonchalantly on the brim of his stony cap.

This was the first time Ellen had left the house alone. She slipped out while Edward was at his office and Mrs Chadwick attended the grocery shopping.

The pigeon suddenly lifted from the stone brim of Scudamore's cap, leaving a small white trail behind, a kiss of remembrance. The bird's wings made a whirring sound as they flapped quickly and carried it higher into the grey sky.

Across the river, in St George's Meadow, schoolboys gathered on the hockey field, their laughter resonated, followed by the hollow sound of stick against ball. A whistle blew, boys cheered in celebration of the goal.

A copper-coloured leaf spiralled slowly to the ground and landed near Ellen's shoe. 'Thomas,' she whispered. She stood, her feet were so cold she could hardly feel them, and her knees stiff from sitting so long. She walked to the centre of the Victoria Footbridge; her steps echoed on the timber decking. She leaned on the rail and peered into the fast-running water beneath. A sudden gust of wind caught her cloche hat. She watched it fall and sail away, bobbing and bouncing along the speedy current. 'My hat!' she cried.

~

Sergeant Turley twitched nervously as he knocked on the Chief Inspector's door.

'Enter.'

'It's Mrs Bellamy, sir.'

Edward rose from his seat. 'What about Mrs Bellamy?'

'She's been brought in by Constable Greenaway.'

Edward hurried into the waiting room to find Ellen sitting, head bowed, revealing a tangle of windswept hair. 'Sergeant Turley, some tea for my wife if you please.' He knelt by Ellen's side. 'My dear, where have you been? You should be home in the warm,' he rubbed her cold hands until Turley arrived with a tray of tea. 'Constable Greenaway, my office, please.'

Ellen sat silently, listening to the muffled voices of her husband talking with the constable until the door opened and Edward commanded. 'Bring the car, please.'

'Come, dear, let's take you home. Sergeant Turley, I will be away for the rest of the day,' Edward said as he escorted Ellen to the waiting car. They travelled in silence.

Later that evening, Ellen reached for her Book of Common Prayer, but the words appeared desolate. She opened the bureau drawer to search for photographs or old letters. At the back of the bureau, she found a small box, a gift from her grandmother. She opened it and cupped the delicate rosary in her hands. She studied the Ave's of pale coral, Paternosters of silver filigree and the fine splinters of wood embedded in the tiny silver cross. She remembered the words her grandmother had said when she pressed the gift into her hand. 'Let it speak to your heart. The heart prays, the beads count.' An owl hooted in the distance and the window rattled as cold wind hurried past. Ellen folded the rosary into a handkerchief and placed it beneath her pillow. She pushed off her slippers and climbed into bed.

In her dream, the sky is the colour of pale peach. She nurses her infant, a little girl with golden curls and long ginger lashes. A second child plays at her feet, his spinning top spiralling in vibrant colours. The housekeeper sits beneath the porch, elbows rhythmically working, knitting needles click-clacking. Ellen looks on the face of her child; he is pale and his face dirty. She looks again but now it's not the face of her little boy, it's a man who lies in her lap, his face blackened and bloodied.

~

Ron Clune leaned his bicycle against the station master's brick fence and studied the posters freshly pasted on the ticket office wall.

'Bye, Ma,' Percy called as he followed his father through the front door. 'Hello there, Ron. Ready to go?'

'I was just looking at this new poster. I haven't seen this one before.'

'Let's see. "WOMEN OF BRITAIN SAY: GO!" I can't see my ma saying that. Can you see yours?'

'I dunno, Perc.'

'Come on, we'll be late.'

The pair rode off, wheels skidding on the frosty pavement.

~

Sarah Phillips stoked the ashes in the fireplace, added a couple of pieces of coal before sitting in her chair. This was her moment of indulgence, time to sit for a while before the warmth of the fire. Settling into the familiar embrace of the old armchair, she felt the ache in her bones begin to ease. She uncoiled and stretched her fingers, rubbed her reddened, swollen knuckles, the skin on the back of her hands creased into a myriad of lines and folds. *And such fine hands I had when I was a girl.* The kettle whistled, she warmed the pot, spooned in the leaves, poured the steaming water, and then left the brew to rest beneath the cosy.

A click of the latch heralded Matthew's return.

'Heavens, Matthew, that took you a while, tea will be stewed, I'll make another pot.'

Matthew did not respond.

'What is it, Matthew?'

'Not good news, I'm afraid. I bumped into Reg Turley.

Where's that ten o'clock from Birmingham? I must see the newspaper.'

'Come now, Matthew, you're talking in riddles. Have your tea; the train will be here soon enough.'

'Chief Inspector Bellamy's son has been killed. They sent those boys out on horseback with lances to fight big guns! There's bound to be more of them. God help us all! Here's the train now; I'll be back for my tea.'

Sarah placed a saucer over Matthew's teacup, whispering, 'Oh Lord, that poor family.'

'I'm home.' Grace walked into the kitchen to find her mother looking distressed. 'Whatever is it?'

'Your father's just come home with dreadful news. Percy's friend, young Mr Bellamy, he's been killed.'

Grace gasped. 'Oh, no. How dreadful. He was such a nice young man.'

~

That afternoon, Percy took one final look around the engine before turning it off.

'So, you got the old thing working again, eh Percy? Boss will be pleased.'

'Hello there, Ron. Yes, she's a cantankerous old girl, but I think I've got her measure.' He took a rag from his belt and rubbed the grease off his hands. 'So, Ron, what's on your mind? Fancy a pint on the way home?'

'It's those posters on the wall near the ticket office.'

'They're everywhere. Right now, I reckon our cider factory needs us. How's Caldecott going to get this old girl going without me to keep her turning? C'mon, it's knocking off time, let's get a pint.'

They put on their caps, scarves and jackets, collected their bicycles and rode towards town. As they pedalled, the sound of drums, bugles and marching feet grew louder. They turned the corner and saw a band converging outside the Butter Market. Tom and Percy joined the crowd.

A dozen soldiers dressed in scarlet uniforms, with highly polished brass buttons and black boots, stamped to a halt. Their sergeant major climbed onto a timber box, tucked his stick under his arm and led the throng in singing 'God Save the King.'

The crowd cheered.

In a commanding voice, he called for the attention of the people. 'Ladies and gentlemen, may I have your attention, please?' He waited for the crowd to quiet. 'I am here this afternoon to ask you all a simple question. A question that you will no doubt not need to consider for too long before giving an answer in the positive. Who do you wish to see marching through the streets of your fair city?'

A murmur buzzed through the crowd, but no one answered.

'Come now, ladies and gents. It's not a difficult question to answer, is it?' The sergeant major narrowed his eyes and scanned the crowd. 'Let me put it to you this way. Would you rather see His Majesty's troops or … the Hun?'

Still, no one answered.

'You mark my words, ladies and gents, if we don't stop the blighters in France, then we're next.' He scoured the crowd again. 'So, I'm asking you, do you want the Hun marching through your streets?'

'No!' a resounding roar.

'Ex-actly!' he pointed his stick at the men in the crowd.

'Your country needs you. Your King needs you. And the brave lads already in France need you.'

With that, the band struck up again and led by the sergeant major, the soldiers marched off to another part of town. Behind them followed a small group of young men and women. The crowd dispersed.

'How about that pint?'

They parked their bicycles outside the King's Head.

'Afternoon, gentlemen. What can I get you?'

'Two pints of cider, please,' Percy replied.

As the landlord poured the drinks, he asked, 'Did you hear the band playing? What was all that about?'

'They're on a recruitment drive. It was all I could do to stop Ron here from joining up.'

The landlord laughed. 'Better hurry up then, they said it will be over by Christmas.'

'I don't think that's the case now,' Ron said. 'Things are not going as well as they thought. You heard what the sergeant major said.'

'Well, shooting people isn't a good thing to do, is it? I mean, you might shoot a rabbit because you could eat it. But shooting people?' Percy said.

'I dunno, Perc. What that sergeant major said was convincing. I, for one, don't want the Hun marching through our town.'

'Obviously, me neither,' Percy replied.

Ron drained the last of his pint. 'There might come a time when we don't get a choice about signing up.'

'On that note, I'm heading home before it gets dark. See you tomorrow.'

The house seemed unusually quiet when Percy arrived home. 'Hello, anyone home?' he called as he walked in through the back door.

'In the kitchen,' replied Grace. 'Come in, love, you must be cold.'

Percy took off his damp coat and warmed his hands near the hearth. He looked from Grace to his mother and back again. Their faces portrayed apprehension. 'What's going on?' he asked.

'Percy, it's bad news, I'm afraid,' said Grace. 'Pa heard that Tom Bellamy has been killed.'

'What? When?' Percy exclaimed.

Matthew Phillips came hurrying down the hall. 'It's true, I'm afraid,' he said, opening the Hereford Times newspaper. 'Here, in the second column. Bellamy, Thomas.' He spread the paper on the kitchen table.

'Oh, God. It can't be true,' said Percy, tears stinging his eyes.

CHAPTER EIGHT

1915 – Drawn to War

December 1914

Somewhere on the Western Front, German, British, French, and Belgian troops joined their voices to the chorus of 'Silent Night'. But there was no such truce for the prisoners of Saabrücken.

Exhausted, Tom slept. Hunger gnawed at his stomach, cold ached through his body and the tiresome screech in his damaged ear echoed in his head. He woke as the first light of pre-dawn crept through the cracks in the timber walls. Soon it would all begin again. '

'How long have we been here? It must be seven or eight weeks at least. What comes next?' a man whispered from his bunk.

His neighbour responded, 'They won't keep us all here now, surely? We've built their bloody stockades. What more do they want?'

'Hardly enough rations to keep us alive. I swear when I get home, if the wife ever tries to give me cabbage and peas for dinner, I'll ...'

'You'll what?'

Hugh lay curled on his mattress, tuffs of red hair the only part of him visible above the dark stained blanket.

'Hugh,' Tom spoke barely above a whisper and moved closer to him to avoid having to raise his voice any higher.

'Hugh.' Tom's guts began to rumble and cramp, *Oh Christ.* He pulled on his boots, wrapped his blanket around his shoulders then headed for the row of four tin buckets which served as latrines. Tom lifted the lid on one of the buckets and retched as the stench filled his nostrils. He lowered himself over it, effortlessly the loose faeces dropped away. He dipped his hands into the icy water of a wash-bucket, rubbing vigorously in the vein hope of cleansing them. He tried to be as quiet as possible, but now men stirred.

'Bugger off, you noisy sod.'

Tom returned to his bed. He glanced across to Hugh, who had not moved. He knew the boy was in a bad way and wondered how much longer he would last. *He needs medical attention. I don't know what I can do for him.* A few days ago, Hugh suffered a severe beating. Tom begged for mercy for him and was rewarded with a blow from the guard's cudgel.

Hugh's thin hand appeared from beneath his blanket. 'Mumma, is that you?'

'Hugh, it's Tom, I'm right here.'

The boy's hand dropped. He made a gurgling sound.

'Shite, man, he's a goner, that's a death rattle,' hissed Arthur from his bed in the row behind.

'Yes, I believe so.'

Daylight stole into the camp. Men scrambled for their boots, whistles shrieked, dogs barked, guards cursed.

'C'mon man, gather your wits, there's nothing you can do for him now.' Arthur grunted and headed for the muster.

~

The Bellamys

Christmas was a desolate event at the Bellamy family's residence, not even the coal fire which burned generously in the parlour could warm the atmosphere. The family prepared for their walk to All Saints Church to take the Holy Communion.

'When I survey the wondrous cross
On which the Prince of Glory died ...'

The Very Reverend Ormond Snell surveyed the congregation from beneath his huge eyebrows. *A poor turnout indeed,* he thought. His facial muscles tightened as he restrained a potentially large interruption to the hymn. *Humph, those pickled onions are repeating on me again, I must ask Mrs Davies to refrain from serving them with my late supper.* He continued the hymn in his deep rumbling baritone.

~

How much longer can this go on? I feel I shall burst with exasperation if Reverend Snell doesn't end this sermon soon, Alice thought, holding her mother's limp hand. *My poor dear mother. How frail she looks. Dressed in her new velvet cloche, not even the lace veil can hide the despair in her face. Her skin seems like fine alabaster, almost translucent.*

~

Edward's eyes fixed on the ancient, stained-glass window above the altar. The Bellamys had occupied this pew almost every Sunday of their thirty-two years of marriage, as had Edward's parents before them. *A good marriage,* he thought. *Why are we condemned to such sorrow?* His thoughts wandered to the early days of their courting. Ellen was three years older than he, from a privileged background. He had won her despite the odds against him. He remembered her father's outburst. *A commoner? A policeman?*

'God has spoken through the word incarnate ...' Snell rumbled on.

Edward had worked hard to impress her. He had purchased the house on Widemarsh Common. He rose through the ranks. *I made her happy, didn't I? But then the tragedy, the death of our first child, I nearly lost Ellen as well.* He trembled; it was all he could do to contain himself. *And now my son, my boy.*

The last hymn sung, Reverend and choir–with great ceremony–left the nave and walked to the rear door of the church.

'Mother, the service is over.' Alice gently shook her mother's hand to rouse her.

Snell stood waiting to farewell the faithful few. 'Mrs Bellamy ...'

Ellen nodded, propelled along by Alice, 'Thank you, Reverend,' she said.

'Edward, my good man. How are things? Err-um, improving I trust?'

Edward grunted but did not reply. He hurried to catch up to his wife and daughter, muttering, 'Fool of a priest.'

~

The Phillips

Pots of every size and description bubbled and spat on the hearth. The sweet aroma of goose, ham, and earthy vegetables roasting permeated throughout the house of Matthew and Sarah Phillips.

Percy brought in a large bucket of coal and stoked up the hearth. 'Nipping out for a smoke,' he said.

'We're just going to have some tea,' Grace called.

'Save me a cup, I won't be long.'

'My dear girl, how would we manage without you?' said Sarah,

'How are you, Ma? How are your hands, is the arthritis bothering you?'

'I'm fine dear, a little tired now and again,' Sarah sipped her tea. 'Grace, we are so proud of you. Ward sister now! And isn't it wonderful that you could get the time off over Christmas, especially with all that's going on.'

Grace took her mother's hands in hers and gently massaged the joints of her fingers. 'Ma, I've something to tell you and I wanted to be sure to speak with you while it is quiet. I don't want to spoil Christmas for everyone, so can we keep this to ourselves for now?'

'Good heavens, what is it, dear?'

'I've left the infirmary. Please don't be concerned; I left with Matron's blessing. I've joined the Red Cross. I know this is going to be hard for you to understand, but I leave for France on the fifteenth of January.'

Mother and daughter rose from the table, their chairs scraped on the tiled floor as they stood. They reached across, cupping one another's faces in their hands, drawing together, cheek to cheek in a silent embrace.

CHAPTER NINE

1915

January

Grace was first to arrive in the parlour. *Brrr, it's chilly in here.* She took paper spills from an old cider pitcher and bent to light the coals, neatly stacked in the grate. A small flame emerged, she took the poker and adjusted the coals. Warming herself by the fireplace, her fingertips resting on the carved mantle, she looked wistfully through the fine net curtain to the small patch of garden beyond. She had rehearsed a speech in her head but now that the moment for the announcement had arrived, she felt lost for words.

Her parents entered. Matthew led Sarah to sit on the sofa.

Grace watched her mother unconsciously twisting her handkerchief.

'Well, let's hear this news of yours, Grace,' Matthew stood with his back to the window, chin raised, and head cocked to one side in anticipation.

Grace took a deep breath. 'I'm not returning to the Infirmary. I've joined the British Red Cross Nursing Service. I leave for France on Saturday morning.'

Matthew gasped, 'What nonsense is this? War is no place for a woman; your place is here, at home, with us, your family.'

'Please try to understand. This is not a decision I have taken lightly. I'm a trained nurse and I am needed there.'

'But you have an important job at the Infirmary.'

'Matthew, please,' Sarah reached for his hand. 'It is a brave decision that Grace has made. God knows, my heart is breaking and yes, I'm filled with fear at the thought of the danger she will find. But we should not turn her from this path. We must find the strength and courage to support her, to let her go.'

The laughter of young men interrupted the conversation.

'By crikey, it's cold out there! Come on in and shut the door, man. Let's find some tea.' Percy led Ron to the kitchen. 'Where is everybody? We're going to make a pot,' he called. 'Will you join us? Ma?'

Matthew took Grace into his arms and held her close. 'My dear girl. Your mother and I are so proud of you. You have given us immense joy in our lives. You are so dedicated, courageous and brave. Your mother is right. We must not turn you from your decision. We will pray every day for an end to this war so that you will come home safely to us.' Matthew paused. 'Come, my lovely,' he helped Sarah out of her chair. 'Let's go and talk to Percy.'

The kitchen was warm and cheery. 'Is there any of Grace's lovely Christmas cake left? Aha!' grinning, he returned with the cake tin. He pulled out a chair for Sarah, 'What is it, Ma?'

'I'll be off,' said Ron, noticing the serious looks on the family's faces. 'I'll see myself out.'

'Grace has some news.' Matthew took Grace's hand and kissed it, motioning for her to speak.

'I leave for France on Saturday morning.'

Percy stood up, pushing the chair away, its legs scraping on the tiled floor. 'Grace, are you mad? You can't go to France! You're a woman. This isn't right! Pa, tell her she can't go. Do you have any idea what it will be like in France? Look what happened to Tom.'

'Percy, being a woman will not be a hindrance. Doing what I feel I must do … what I feel called to do, is important to me. I am a trained nurse. I will be of use. Nothing will make me change my mind.'

'What? But …' Percy threw his arms around his sister. 'You are so bloody brave.'

~

GRACE

Grace watched from the deck of the four-funnelled steamship, HMS Forrester. Earlier that morning, seventeen nurses had arrived by train from various locations and boarded the ship at eleven o'clock. It was now two o'clock and the embarkation of men, horses, pontoons, ambulances, wagons and various machines of war continued relentlessly. 'Oh dear, those poor horses, their handlers really are struggling to get them on board.'

'I'm not surprised, I've never been on a ship before myself, and I must say, I feel a little nervous and queasy. How are you feeling, Grace?'

'I feel the same, Lily. I do wish this were over and we could get going. I've heard that motion sickness is not so bad once the ship is actually moving.'

Lily waved again to her father standing amongst the crowd of relatives and friends on the quay. 'I do wish my father would leave. It saddens me to see him standing there.'

'Yes, my brother Percy is still there too, I asked him to stay home, but he insisted on travelling with me. He's not looking our way, though. He seems transfixed by the embarkation. I wonder what's he's thinking, seeing all those men in uniforms, hugging mothers, lovers and children before lugging their kit up to the gangways?'

'Mmm, it's quite a stirring sight, isn't it?' Lily replied. 'Oh, look, Grace, here come the doctors.'

'Yes, I met Doctor Anderson in Hereford when she came to talk to a group of us nurses last November. Who is the other doctor, I wonder?' Grace said.

'That is Doctor Murray. She's lovely, she came to Worcester Infirmary. I believe they have been overseeing the outfitting of a military hospital. I wonder how many nurses they managed to enlist?' Lily said, looking around the deck.

'We'll soon find out, I expect,' replied Grace.

'Ladies, may I interrupt? Good afternoon, my name is Morton, Medical Corps. The supplies have now been stowed and the doctors ask that you kindly join them and the other nurses for introductions. And then we can set to work, sorting supplies and organising your personal arrangements for the voyage.'

'Thank you,' said Grace. 'We'll follow you.'

Grace waved her arms vigorously and blew kisses to Percy, but hands-in-pockets, he was busy watching the embarkation. 'Oh dear, he's not looking. Come on Lily.' Together they turned from the ship's rail.

~

PERCY

A chilly rain interrupted Percy's thoughts as he watched men boarding the ship. They appeared to be in jovial spirit as they teased and encouraged each other in the queue to board. A sharp wind whipped up spray. Percy tasted salt on his lips; he tugged at his cap, pulled the rim down over his forehead and drew his collar up to protect his ears. He scanned the ship for a sign of Grace, but she was no longer in sight. The crowd on the quay began to thin. *Time to go, heaven knows how long I've been standing here. God speed, Grace.*

He walked along the cobbled streets leading away from the quay, the wind and rain strengthened and lashed at his back. His trousers soaked within seconds and stuck uncomfortably to the back of his legs. Ahead, he saw the welcoming lights of a pub, the *Chain & Anchor*. The pub offered warmth that his bones ached for and the anonymity he craved. He made his way through the crowd to find a spot at the bar. A cacophony of unfamiliar accents filled the space as men competed for vocal dominance.

A huge bear of a man, sleeves rolled up displaying tattoos, barely visible between the thick black hairs on his forearms, scraped the froth off the bar with a beer-soaked cloth and asked Percy, 'Wot's yer poison lad?'

'A pint, please.'

'Yeah? What's yer brew?'

Percy looked along the bar to see men cradling long glasses of dark ale with a thick creamy top. 'I'll have one of those, please.' He felt a tinge of trepidation as the barman lovingly coaxed the dark brew from tap to glass, turning it gently from side to side as the thick ale slowly filled the vessel. He held the glass up to the light to admire his handiwork, the creamy top less than half an inch thick. By now, Percy's thirst was getting the better of him and his stomach growled with hunger. He drained the brew quickly. The air, thick with smoke and smells of beer and sweat, filled his lungs. He ordered another pint.

~

Percy woke to the sound of the bustling port city. He tried to lift his head from the pillow but failed. His eyelids seemed glued shut, but finally, he managed to open them and looked around the dimly lit room. A thundering headache thumped in his skull. 'Where in hell am I?' Percy rubbed his head with his right hand; he could not feel his left arm. Looking at his chest, he found he was wearing his woollen vest but no shirt. A stained satin eiderdown covered him. Slipping his hand beneath the covers, he nervously investigated the depths of the bed. His fingers gingerly inching down over his curled vest, he discovered his gut was bare, he felt the fine hairs around his belly button. He gathered courage and continued the exploration, down towards his groin. 'Agh! Oh no!' The hair stood of its own volition. A sticky mess had stiffened the normally smooth bush.

Percy's left arm tingled with pins and needles.

Another body in the bed roused.

His immediate instinct was to pull his arm away and leap from the bed, but the weight of the body on his arm, coupled with the pain in his head and dread of what had transpired the night before, immobilised him. He turned to look at the person lying by his side. A single ringlet of red hair trailed across an ample shoulder, speckled with small freckles or pimples. Percy found it difficult to judge as the thick curtains across the window let through a limited amount of light.

A deep rattling sound erupted from the back of the bed mate's throat. Her arm moved as she reached to scratch her buttock.

Percy held his breath.

The woman's knuckles brushed against the skin of his thigh. She tensed for a second, continued to scratch, stopped, then slowly, her hand explored Percy's hot and sticky upper thigh.

'No, get off, get off!'

In one swift movement, Percy yanked his arm free and leapt from the bed, dashing for the curtains, he dragged them back to reveal the cold grey Liverpool morning.

''Ere, where's yer manners?' The woman sat up, tousled red hair falling over her face and naked shoulders.

Percy, dressed in his woollen vest and one black sock, searched around the room for the rest of his clothes. Speechless, his stomach churned, and he dry-wretched, doubling over with the cramp of nausea.

'I'm sorry,' he mumbled, wiping the spit from his mouth.

'Bloody 'ellfire!' The woman stared through soporific eyes, then piqued, slumping on her back.

Percy struggled into his trousers, turned to apologise again, but was momentarily mesmerised by the sight of the woman's breasts as gravity pulled them apart from the breastbone to sprawl solidly at her sides.

'I'm so sorry, I'm late. I've got to be somewhere.'

'Oh, piss off.'

Percy, minus one black sock, hastily pulled the door closed behind him. He hurried down the winding stairs, hoping not to disturb any residents, and particularly keen to escape without being noticed.

'Wotcher, whack!' The barman rolled a barrel across the passageway, winked and grinned through broken teeth.

Without responding, Percy pulled open the door and rushed out into the cold, damp morning.

Two hours later, he sat in the carriage, head against the window cooling his aching skull, comforted by the rhythm and roll of the train on track; he tried to fathom what had happened the night before. *How much of that ale did I have? I remember the first two pints.* Try as he might, he could remember little more of the night, and each time he pressed his memory, a chill came to his skin and caustic bile burned in the back of his throat.

Hours passed before the train pulled into Hereford Railway Station. Percy had slept for much of the journey, a fitful sleep, haunted by glimpses of salacious deeds and hints of men's ribald laughter. *I've never felt so glad to be home.* The carriage door swung open; he stepped down on the platform. There, near the ticket office, he saw his father.

'Why, Percy lad, what on earth have you been up to? You're looking green around the gills, boy.'

'I'm alright, Pa, just something I ate.'

'Humph.' Matthew appraised the dishevelled appearance of his son. 'So, tell me, did you get Grace safely to the ship? Your mother and I thought you would be home on the seven o'clock last night?'

'I missed the train. I stood on the quay watching the embarkation, it took hours.'

'Let's get home, your mother is anxious to hear all about it, and it'll do us no good standing here.'

February

Two weeks passed since Percy returned from Liverpool. In that time, his mind was consumed by thoughts of Grace in France. Large posters of Lord Kitchener had been placed outside all the municipal buildings. 'We want you!' Percy felt it was always pointing at him. After work, he went to the stables to look for Ron. He found him whistling as he worked, rubbing down the horses. 'Hello Ron, got time for a half on the way home?'

'Aye, why not.' Ron grinned. He washed his hands in a bucket of water and flicked the droplets at Percy. He pulled on his cap and jacket. 'Dyin' for a drink, me.'

They walked in step, turning the corner into High Street, and arrived at the King's Head.

'I'll get 'em; half-a-cider?'

'No, I'll have half of stout, thank you, Ron.'

Percy found a table at the rear of the smoky room. He looked through the greasy pains of bottled glass at the passing crowd, who resembled liquid figures. His thoughts returned to the image of Grace boarding the massive steamship in Liverpool. He visualised the colossal embarkation of men and machines, which had rolled along for hours on that cold January day. A growing sense of dissatisfaction had been mounting within him, disturbing his normally happily-go-lucky disposition. In these quiet opportunities for reflection, his mind occasionally drifted to the unpleasant memory of the vulgar night in Liverpool. He shivered with disgust.

''Ere we go.'

The two men raised and clinked their glasses, each took a good mouthful.

Ron swilled the sharp, sparkling cider around his mouth before swallowing. 'Arghh ... that's good.'

Percy closed his eyes; the dark brew left creamy foam on his top lip; he enjoyed the tang and bitterness as it slipped slowly down his throat. 'I'm glad we found this chance for a drink, Ron. Might be the last one we'll have for a while. I've decided to enlist for Lord Kitchener this Friday morning.'

Ron reached across the wet table, shook Percy's hand and said, 'Good man. We'll go together. Friday it is.'

The two men laughed and slapped each other on the shoulder. Percy took the empty glasses to the bar and ordered a second round.

~

One week later, they lined up at the Brecon Barracks QM's store with young men, each as eager to do his bit for King and Country. They found men they knew. Bert Haines, a foreman at Cartwrights, Peter Jones, whose mother owned the knitting store in the Butter Market and Samuel Dawkins, star of the King's Head skittles team. Boots and uniforms were issued with little attention to size.

'These boots are awful. Bloody stiff,' Percy complained.

'Put two pairs of socks on, they'll soon soften up and you'll save a few blisters,' said Ron.

'What about this tin hat?' Percy stomped around like a circus clown, the helmet so big it covered his eyes and rested on his nose.

On the second day at camp, men were instructed how to wear and care for their uniforms; this included pressing the creases, darning socks, and polishing buttons and boots. On the third day, the drills began. Marching up and down the parade ground; saluting officers; about turns without colliding with their teammates. They wondered when the serious business of training would begin. On the fourth day, it was back to the QM's store, this time to receive rifles, packs and trenching shovels. They learned the basics of movement in the field and were introduced to night operations and route marching.

After two weeks, advanced training began; weapons handling, marksmanship and the serious business of how to shoot straight. Ron proved to be the best shot by far and received a red marksman's badge.

As the days passed, the training intensified. They learned how to run up and down the hill carrying their heavy packs. The peak of the training was the attack with bayonets. Straw figures were secured to posts and the young men, in full battle uniform, trained to run at them, shout obscenities, thrust the bayonet into the dummy, twist the blade and pull it out.

'Stop poncing around with the shoulder, man. Go for the gut!' yelled the sergeant. They learned to dig trenches. 'Deeper. Faster. You'll get your bloody head blown off at this rate! Dig, you useless buggers! Dig for your lives!'

Finally, the recruits received a day's leave-pass to London.

'London?' Ron exclaimed. 'I never thought I'd see it.'

With a rush of steam, like a great sigh, the train pulled into the station. Men descended to the platform, eager for the excitement of the city following three weeks encamped in the bleak Brecon Beacons. They emerged from the station like ants on a mission.

Enchanted by the rush of traffic and grand Victorian buildings, Ron and Percy made their way past jostling commuters. They were astounded as horse-drawn carriages vied for road-space with bicycles, motor cars and omnibuses and fascinated as shopkeepers extolled their wares.

'Best pies in Lambeth. Come 'n' get 'em.'

'Ecco un poco!'

'What the heck's that?' Ron pulled Percy to see what the vendor offered.

'Antonelli's famous ice-cream and biscuit cone, just tuppence a pop, gents.'

'We'll take two,' laughed Ron.

'C'mon, this way to the river,' Percy said.

Elated, they sprinted down York Road and turned into Westminster Bridge Road. 'Look, there it is, the Thames.' They ran to the centre of the bridge, dodging the busy traffic. Beneath, boats and barges sailed along the brown water. Conspicuous landmarks, which they had only seen in picture books, loomed before them.

'Big Ben, the Houses of Parliament. I wish we had more time to see inside.'

'We'll see it again next year, eh?'

''Ello there, ducky, fancy a good time?'

''Ere, Tommy, want a bit o' 'ow's yer father?'

'No thank you, ladies,' laughed Percy. 'I'm starving, let's see if we can find a pasty or a sausage roll.'

'Look, postcards. What's this? Piccadilly Circus, and this one's Saint Paul's Cathedral. My ma would love these,' said Ron as he collected a handful of the cards.

CHAPTER TEN

March 1915

Matthew heard the squeak of the letterbox flap. 'I'll get it, dear.' He found a brown envelope with an official stamp. *Lord, don't let it be bad news,* he thought. He hurried down the hall calling, 'Letter from France!'

Sarah's hands shook as she turned the envelope over, finding an opening in the flap.

'Well? What does it say?'

She began to read:

4th February 1915

Dearest Mother and Pa,

I hope this letter finds you well, you are constantly in my thoughts.

Much time has passed since my departure from Liverpool; I have a lot to tell you.

The journey by ship started out to be most exciting, for there were warnings of enemy attack. Our ship was escorted by two small destroyers running one in front and one behind us, then sometimes round and round like little dogs chasing a ball.

The passage was not terribly smooth and before long both Lily and I succumbed to seasickness and found ourselves quite unable to remain standing.

We joined members of our group, collapsed on mattresses in the cabin.

We arrived at dawn to a very wet and inhospitable port station. There was much ado with the disembarking, and we were left to our own devices to sort and repack. Huddled in the waiting room, we spent the night on cushions borrowed from the train carriages.

The following morning, we woke to the sound of vehicles; our transport consisted of five cars with Tommy drivers and in charge was Captain Morton. Along the way, we passed through little villages and at each place the villagers lined the streets waving caps and handkerchiefs calling 'Vive les Anglais!' to which we all shouted in return 'Vive les Francais!' Many offered hot coffee and sandwiches, for which we were grateful.

My first glimpse of the war I encountered a taut group of men, grim faced and clad in dark blue overcoats. They marched with determination and stern features, as though they would surely crush all in their path. Later we met a troop of our own Tommies who waved and whistled as we drove on. The journey took the whole day, and we were quite ragged by the time we arrived.

The following morning, we were thrust into our work. I was quickly to learn of the dreadful conditions as wave after wave of men were brought in. The first I saw was without a foot, the second with only one leg. They told terrible tales of the mud and wet in which they stood for hours on end, often up to their waists.

Our accommodation is simple but clean. Lily and I and four other nurses share a dormitory room with a cosy sitting room attached. We work in shifts as the operating room is going all night, so there is space for us all.

Tiredness is overcoming me. I must close now and will endeavour to finish this letter soon.

9th February 1915

Dearest Mother and Pa,

Finally, a chance to finish my letter. These weeks have been hectic. The hospital is dreadfully overcrowded and of course we are under-staffed. Yet with all this work, we try to remain merry and bright. Occasionally we snatch a short time away from our duties. Lily and I have managed to find a little café in a nearby street where they serve us English tea and patisseries, as they call their cakes, they are quite divine!

We have found a fine friend in Captain Morton, who escorted both Lily and I to tea yesterday.

I am called. I must leave now and will write more very soon.

15th February 1915

Dearest Mother and Pa

I write in haste; last night, our doctors told us that this place is to be re-classified as a clearing hospital to cope with the growing number of casualties. The able patients will be sent to a hospital in London.

We are to be escorted tomorrow by Captain Morton, and our destination will be Arras. I must hurry now and pack, we leave without delay. The captain has assured me that he will place this letter in the dispatches for immediate delivery to you.

Do not fear for me, I am well cared for and under the protection of the good captain.

My love and blessings to you, my dear Mother and Pa, please kiss Percy for me.

Your loving daughter

Grace

Sarah folded the letter and held it to her breast. 'Oh Lord, please protect them all.'

~

Bellamy Household

The period of mourning continued in the Bellamy's house. Edward spent much of his time at the Constabulary or in his home study. Ellen slipped into a deep depression and nothing it seemed would pull her out of it. The housekeeper crept quietly around the house, trying to keep out of everyone's way.

Alice sat at her dressing table, looking at her bedraggled image in the mirror. *Is this what Tom would want you to do?* she thought. *Sit here, moping around, feeling sorry for yourself? Indeed, he would not.* Wrapped in a dressing gown and slippers, she went downstairs.

'Oh, you startled me, Miss Alice. Can I get you something?'

'I need a hot bath and a hair wash. I'm going out.'

'The water's on, I've had the boiler going this morning. Will you have breakfast before you go? I've got some porridge on the stove,' Mrs Chadwick asked as she went to run the bath. 'Better dress up warm, there's a real chill in the air this morning.'

An hour later, Alice arrived at the Town Hall. She entered

the vestibule where posters adorned the panelled walls. One grabbed her attention:

> Lady Volunteers Required for
> The Army Remount Depots
> No experience necessary
> Enquiries: Lady Elsenham
> Culverston Park, Malvern

She took the information pamphlets that caught her attention and hurried home with a lighter step and hope in her heart. On arrival, she tapped lightly on Ellen's bedroom door. 'Mother, I've just been into town.'

Ellen sat despondently, looking out at the winter garden.

'Mother, please look at me.' Alice knelt in front of her. 'Tom wouldn't want this. He loved us. He was always full of life and so brave. What are we doing, hiding away like this? The grief will destroy us.'

The housekeeper called out, 'Is everything all right?'

'Yes, Mrs Chadwick. Please come in, I want you to hear this too.' She waited for the housekeeper. 'I went to the Town Hall. I found something interesting. It's called "the Army Remount".'

'Remount? What is that? Something to do with horses?'

'Yes, Mother.'

'But you can't, Alice. Horses are dangerous. You can't ride.'

'I can't ride yet. I can learn. Tom learned.'

'Alice ...'

'Please don't worry Mother. What's the worst thing that

can happen? This is a way I can help. Tom would be proud of me.'

'But whatever will your father say?'

'Surely he'd be impressed to know that Lady Elsenham is involved. Anyway, look what else I found.' Alice unfolded a flyer and read: 'Queen Mary is urging ladies throughout the land to set up needlework and knitting groups to provide our fighting men with socks and vests and ... Why, you could start a group here.'

'Knit? Sew? I have no idea how to do that.'

'I do, Ma'am, if you'll excuse me for butting in. I can knit and sew; I'll teach you if you'd permit me.'

'There you are, Mother. I'm sure Mrs Chadwick would be happy to show other ladies how to do that too.'

The housekeeper smiled and nodded approval.

'That's very noble of you, Maisie. I don't know what your father will say about bringing strangers into the house.'

'I'm sure he will understand. There's a war going on and we have to do our bit. Queen Mary herself has invested her name in the sewing guild.' Alice stood defiantly. 'Anyway, I'm going to find out more about the Remount. I shall write to Lady Elsenham at once.'

'Maisie, dear,' said Ellen. 'I believe we have preparations to make.'

March

TOM

The morning air was fresh, a watery sun rose in a pallid grey sky. The promise of fine weather, a change from the howling sideways snow and bitter cold winds that beleaguered the land over the last few weeks.

Men stood to attention in the quadrangle. In front of Tom stood Arthur, straight and square, a good six inches shorter, and certainly older as his greying crop of hair stubble suggested. Tom noticed that Arthur's ears were weathered and scarred; *he's either a rugby man or a fist fighter,* he thought.

He took stock of his surroundings. Four prisoner barracks ten yards long by five yards wide, constructed of rough timber, tar applied to the walls, iron roofs. Of similar construction were the guard's barrack, commandant's hut and admin building situated next to the camp kitchen, the guardhouse next to the gate. Barbed wire, three yards high, wooden posts every three yards, an impenetrable mesh around camp. *A couple of months ago, there was nothing but mud and canvas strung over poles. In any other time or place, we could be proud of this achievement.*

'Sie bekommen die vier eimer scheiße.' *You four get the shit buckets.*

Four men were directed back to the hut, led by two guards. The first supervised the men, the second strolled around the hut poking and lifting mattresses with the point of his bayonet.

Good luck finding my stuff, you bastard, thought Tom. He felt the weight of his match case deep inside his pocket, next to his heart.

Men emerged from each hut, struggling to carry the

buckets without slopping the contents. The stench was sickening as they emptied them into the open drain.

Tom looked again at the barbed wire fence and the armed guards posted either side. Beyond the wire, he could see no outbuildings. A single road led to the gates, with no significant vegetation on either side of it, no trees or bushes within one hundred yards of the fence. *Endless, flat terrain with no cover.*

'Alle treten diejenigen, die Ingenieure sind, heraus!' *All those who are engineers step out!* A number stepped forward and were marched off.

'Alle treten diejenigen, die Gärtner sind, heraus!' *All those who are gardeners stand out!* More men advanced and were marched off.

'Männer, die mit Tieren arbeiten.' *Men who work with farm animals.*

Horses? Yes, this must be me. Tom stepped forward along with Arthur.

'Eat, drink. Schnell.' They were hurried through the line and served bitter coffee and coarse black bread. 'Schnell!' the guards shouted.

A lorry pulled up at the prison gate, its exhaust pipe belching out black smoke. Guards ordered the men to board. Within minutes, the tail gate slammed shut. A small, armoured vehicle drew up behind. The gates opened and the vehicles moved forward.

Tom gripped the metal bars on the tail gate to steady himself as the truck rolled and lurched over the uneven surface of the road. *There's hope yet!*

~

The lorry lurched and bumped over the pockmarked surface of the dirt road. Tom tasted exhilaration nourished by the thrill and anticipation of escape. Adrenalin coursed through his body. His fingers gripped the metal rim of the truck, determined to secure footing on the rutted floor. Using his skills of observation, he proficiently calculated his strategic situation. *I must measure the distance as we travel. Heartbeats, seventy-two times per minute.* Tom felt his heart racing. He took a deep breath and willed himself to composure. Placing his forefinger and middle finger on his inner wrist, he began to count. The truck rolled on.

We're about three minutes out of camp; I can still make out the fence line, heading in a south-easterly direction. No sign of any cover, the occasional tree, nothing else. Hell, no chance for concealment here! What's that over there, a line of trees? Could be a river. Tom strained to focus on the dark smudge way to the east.

One driver and two armed guards in the front of this lorry, two guards in the following vehicle plus their driver. Tom diverted his eyes from the landscape and scrutinised his fellow passengers. There were ten men in the lorry, most were standing, others resigned to the journey, rested at the rear against the wall. A couple of men appeared intent on analysing their status; a brief glance of mutual resistance passed between them.

Tom returned his attention to the armoured vehicle twenty feet behind, which drifted across the road from side to side, avoiding potholes and the smoke belching out of the exhaust, however, close enough for Tom to see the expression on the faces of the guards. *They're not taking too much notice of us! Cock-sure we won't jump out of this vehicle. Fair enough, nowhere to run and no cover for at least fifty yards on either side of the road. They're laughing, or perhaps they are just as glad as we are to get out of that hell hole for a while?* As if in response to

Tom's thoughts, the guard near the passenger door held out his hand, fingers splayed, to stroke the cold air whispering past.

Tom counted a further nine minutes when the lorry slowed at a fork in the road. To the right, the land abruptly dropped away, large boulders and piles of smaller stones littered the landscape. *Good, that's more like it; those boulders are big enough to hide a man.* To his left, the environment had also changed, small, fenced fields, clusters of bare trees, scattered ramshackle outbuildings. *We must be near the farm, so that's about a twelve-minute trip. How fast were we going? Say, 15 miles an hour? That's about five miles from the prison to this point.*

As the lorry suddenly lurched forward, men lost their footing and bumped into one another. Tom continued his observation of the topography. *We're moving to the south. A fence-line follows the line of the rocks heading east, I imagine that is the perimeter of the farm. I wonder what's at the base of that rocky outcrop. Could be a stream? Perhaps it leads to the river I saw earlier?*

The road narrowed beneath broad reaching boughs of dense fir trees. The impenetrable branches wore a thick swathe of green needles and swept graciously towards the ground; the men in the truck ducked to avoid collision with the lower branches. *This is good. Quick as a flash, I could reach into one of these trees. If only those bloody guards weren't so close behind.*

The lorry slowed to a crawl, lurching as it negotiated the tree roots extending across the road from both sides. It stopped and the driver shouted, 'Erhalten sie das gatter.' *Open the gate.* He looked down at the man at the gate, briefly their eyes met, the guard glowered at him and thrust his rifle menacingly.

As they approached the hub of the farm, Tom breathed deeply. The air was heavy with the rich aroma of organic compost and animal excrement, he closed his eyes, and for a moment he was back in the stables at his home barracks. The driver slowly manoeuvred the lorry in an arch across the cobbled courtyard, chickens squawked and scattered in the wake of the vehicles as they came to a halt, the armoured vehicle pulled in front. The guards formed a semi-circle at the rear, one loosened the bolts to the tail gate and the men ordered to jump down.

'Aus der lkw-sie hunde.' *Out of the truck you dogs.* 'Machen sie eine linie, schnelle.' *Make a line, quick.*

Tom felt his pulse quicken again as he weighed up the risk of making a dash for freedom. As Tom calculated the risk, the canvas screen at the rear of the armoured vehicle jerked open to reveal the second driver now positioned behind a machine gun pointing directly at the prisoners. *With patience, luck and careful planning, I will make my escape! I must hold this hope fast.*

CHAPTER ELEVEN

The Western Front

 *May 1915*

PERCY

Percy watched the campfire flames dance in tune with a light breeze. He saw Ron stir and wake with a snort. 'Back from the Land of Nod, eh?'

Ron stretched. 'Did I miss anything?'

'Uh, no.'

A third man grumbled and sat up, rubbing his eyes.

Percy reached into his pack and found hard cheese, biscuits, and cocoa. 'Got any of that tinned milk left, Ron?' he whispered.

'Here,' Ron replied.

'Smoke?' asked the third man. 'You Welsh?'

'No. Hereford. Name's Ron, this is my pal, Percy.'

'Norman,' the man replied.

BOOM!

They instinctively ducked. Three more earth cracking explosions followed before stillness returned.

'Poor bastards. That'll be us tomorrow.' Norman finished rolling the cigarettes then passed one each to Ron and Percy. He pulled a stick from the fire and lit the cigarettes and stared at the two younger men. 'I ain't seen you around. When 'd'you get here?'

'We marched up from Rounierres last night,' said Percy, pulling a strand of tobacco from between his teeth.

~

Sergeant Howell peered out from the cover of sandbags at the edge of the wood. The last three explosions stole the small chance he had for rest. He squinted across the darkened landscape, listening and watching as calmly as one would watch an apple falling off a tree. His steel helmet pulled low over his eyes; the grimy cracks of his face creased further as he willed his sight towards the trenches of his battalion. His concentration was interrupted by movement behind him; he turned to find Captain Charnley clambering towards the lookout point.

'Evening, sir.'

'Sergeant Howell.'

'Not long now, sir. I was hoping we'd have the weather on our side, but looking at that, it will be raining within the hour.' The moon, partially hidden by clouds, was bathed in a milky haze which blurred its appearance, a sure sign to Howell that rain was on its way. 'Right sir, I'll go and relieve the lads on watch.'

The heavy fire slackened; only the whine of bullets and occasional rattle of machine guns continued.

Howell found the men on watch. 'Good lads. Go and get yourself a bit of shut-eye while you can.'

'Thank you, Sergeant; there's an open tin of milk there and some cocoa,' said Percy.

Howell watched as the three men sloped off to the nearest vacant bivouac. He squatted before the fire and poked the embers; a timid flame ignited the fresh ends of sticks. He rolled himself a thin cigarette, lighting it from a glowing cinder. Feet towards the fire, he slumped back into sandbags, listening to the snores and murmurings of the young men in his charge. *What I wouldn't give for a hot bath, a good soak and a bit of Ma's boiled pudding.*

~

Pearl-grey slithers of dawn pierced the night sky. A steady rainfall filled puddles and settled into the folds of the waterproof bivouacs. The ground was wet and sticky underfoot. In the melancholy light, a mass of men emerged from the battlefield. Bedraggled men, clothes and hair covered in yellow clay; their uniforms ragged. Like zombies, they traipsed exhausted, spines bent, heads bowed, they staggered on in silence.

Sergeant Howell went about the task of waking his men. 'C'mon lads, grab your things. Time to go.'

'Oh, bugga! There she was, right on top o' me, tits fillin' me face ...'

'Aw, stick a cork in it, Lumley. Just another one of yer bleedin' wet dreams. We all 'eard ya! Oooh, ahhh, I'm comin', I'm comin'!'

'Get a move on,' growled the sergeant.

The men stirred, buckled on their waist belts, gathered knapsacks and blankets, and emerged from the bivouacs. They collected weapons, shovels and congregated to report.

'Right lads,' Sergeant Howell shouted above the din. 'Get over to the cookhouse quick as you can and get some grub in you.'

The men hurried off to join the queue for breakfast. Raindrops hissed into balls of steam as they fell on the lids of hot billies, bubbling over the smoky fire.

'Move along, keep it moving,' yelled Howell.

'Gorblimey wha' d'ya call that then?' asked one of the men.

'That my good man is porridge. Why was you wantin' somefin' special today? Ows about a nice bit o 'gammon then, eh? Some nice tomatoes fresh out me garden? Move along, ya silly bugger.'

Breakfast finished, the men restocked their packs with rations of bully beef, tea, tinned milk, and hard biscuits from the QM's store.

Sergeant Howell and Captain Charnley studied a chart.

'Right, so we enter here through Parkes and then make our way down to Leicester. We'll be billeted here, at the junction of Leicester and Orchard.'

'Right, sir, looks like we got about a half mile run to get there.' Howell instinctively looked at the sombre sky to gauge the weather. 'No lettin' up of this rain and no wind to blow it away. The ground will be hard going.'

'Indeed,' Charnley replied, checking his watch. 'It's nearly zero five hundred. Time to go.'

'Fall in,' Howell inspected the men. 'Stow those spades like I showed you. Check rifles.' He moved amongst them as they completed their task, murmuring words of encouragement. 'Permission to address the men, sir?'

Charnley nodded to Howell and continued his study of the chart.

'Right, lads, once we leave the wood, we've got some bad ground to get across before we reach the cover of the trench. So, stay alert and keep moving. We've got one hour 'til daylight, let's make the best of the dark. Watch out for the wire and look out for potholes.'

Thirty pairs of frightened eyes fixed on him. His guts wrenched as he looked back at the young faces.

'Thank you, Sergeant Howell, let's go.' Led by Captain Charnley, they marched on, beneath the scant cover of remnants of trees, splintered, most torn up by the roots. At the edge of the wood, the fields opened before them, beyond lay the entrance to the nearest trench. A tangle of wire and churned earth stretched for as far as the eye could see.

Under the cover of darkness throughout the night, stretcher bearers carried an endless stream of wounded men to the dressing station at the edge of the wood. Ambulances departed with their cargo of human suffering.

'Oh Christ, Ron, I'm scared rotten.'

'Me too, Perc.'

'Ron, if anything happens to me, you know what I mean ...'

Within seconds a bombardment was issued from British guns. Howell signalled for the men to crouch low. Above the din, Charnley shouted, 'Forward!'

In unison, the men ran from cover into the field. To begin with, the ground, although dampened by the overnight rain, was still solid underfoot, but soon they came upon earth churned by exploding shells and tangled wire, before long they were ankle-deep in mud. Their wet greatcoats heavy on their shoulders, but heavier still were their packs, fifty pounds in weight.

'C'mon lads, keep moving,' Howell roared as he dropped back a few paces to urge the men on. 'We're nearly there, look fifty yards to go. Double it up!' Howell pointed ahead to the ridge of a small rise, the entrance to the trench. Zip! There was no mistaking the sound; the first bullet whistled past his right ear.

'Argh!' Howell turned to see Bradley had caught the bullet in his neck. He fell face forward in the mud. A man slowed nearby and bent towards him.

'Leave him. Pick up his rifle and get going. Run!' Howell waited until all the men had passed him, taking up the rear position he urged the men on. Moments later, another man was down. Ron slowed his pace to help the injured man. It was Norman.

'You can't help him, keep going.'

Together Percy and Ron leapt the last few paces to reach the entrance of the trench. They slid down the muddy bank to the wet duckboards. Sergeant Howell landed heavily behind them.

'Two down, Captain. Bradley and Jenkins.'

'Right, thank you, Sergeant. Keep the men low for a few minutes to get their breath, then we must move along.' Charnley moved ahead of the men.

'Cor, Percy, it stinks in here, doesn't it? What is it? Bloody latrines? Something else though as well.'

'I think it's creosote, stuff to stop diseases spreading. That and rats, I can smell them.'

'You heard the captain. Make way. Move along. Keep yer heads down and watch how you go; these boards are a bloody disaster waiting' to happen. Corporal Trotter, bring up the rear.' Howell pushed past men to take the forward position. The trench was narrow at this point. The walls glistened with recent rain, trails of water and grey mud slid down, making the surface of the boards dangerously slippery. A foot or so beneath, a well of murky water emitted a nasty sulphurous odour.

'It's quiet in here,' whispered Percy.

'Yes, not a sound out there either ... perhaps the Hun's gone home?' Ron grinned.

'We should be so lucky. Listen. The digging has started.' The echo of metal spade on solid ground reverberated along the line as foes and comrades alike took advantage of this brief respite to repair the ravaged trenches.

Howell signalled the men to halt. 'Here we are, lads, home sweet home. Corporal, take those four men with you, get that pump going, use buckets if you have to.' He winced at the sulphurous smell. 'Clune, take two men and check out the stores in that dugout. Sparkes and you three, see if you can find some timber and nails to repair these duckboards, they're a bloody disgrace!'

'Sergeant Howell, a runner please, meeting at HQ at seven hundred hours.'

'Yes, sir. Phillips, go with the captain.'

Percy followed Charnley as Howell continued to issue orders. 'Lumley, Fitch, check out those latrines.'

'Bloody typical, isn't. Me, always get the good jobs I do.'

'What's that, Lumley?'

'Nothin' Sarg.'

'Good, well, clear it out, get on with it. Harris and Watts, you get that brazier going. We'll get this place sorted in no time.'

Percy struggled to keep up with Charnley, who hurried along negotiating the slimy duckboards; his tall thin frame bent beneath the summit of the trench wall, he moved confidently and with purpose.

Arriving at HQ, Charnley pulled aside the hessian curtain and entered the dugout.

Percy stood outside wondering whether to follow or not.

'They'll be in there for a while. Fancy a cuppa?' The voice

came from a man sitting on a ledge outside the dugout.

'Thank you,' Percy took the mug and sipped the strong sweet tea. The two men appraised each other silently.

'First time?' asked the older man.

'Yes,' Percy responded.

'Fourth time for me. Yer gotta keep low. See? Keep low, that's it.'

Half an hour passed before the hessian curtain opened, the officers appeared, grim faced, they returned to their junctions.

'Sergeant Howell, a word please,' said Charnley.

'Yes, sir. Good lads, stow some of that old timber in the dugout, we may be glad of that later tonight,' he followed the captain into the officer's niche.

~

At ten hundred hours, a brutal roar like wild thunder sounded. The earth shook, a flaming curtain erupted as shells exploded in and around the trench. From the east, artillery fire cracked and flashed, tossing dirt and debris into the air. Men dropped, riddled with splinters of shrapnel. All through the afternoon, the bombardment raged. When it finally stopped, Howell moved swiftly amongst the burned and bloodied bodies of men lying in the trench, applying what first aid he could and comforting the injured and dying. 'Steady lad; soon as it's dark, they'll get you to the dressing station; then you'll get your ticket to Blighty.'

Percy rolled a cigarette as he and Ron crouched down on their haunches amidst the debris. He took a long draft then handed it to Ron. They watched Howell apply a bandage to a gaping wound on the left side of Lumley's face.

'Stoke up that brazier Clune, let's have hot water.'

'Right Sarg,' said Ron, rummaging around for scraps of timber from the dugout. Soon the fire was burning brightly. He filled two billies and placed them over the flame. A bullet whistled past his left ear.

'Keep down, lad. There's a sniper got you in his sights, he's a goodun.'

'Report please, Sergeant Howell,' called the captain.

'Yes, sir. Willis, Fitch and Clarkson, all dead. Half a dozen lads there badly scratched and shaken but they'll do. Lumley ...?' Howell screwed up his face, 'I'm not sure he'll make it.'

'Thank you, Sergeant. Get half the men in the dugout, see if they can snatch a bit of rest.'

'Excuse me, sir, new orders from HQ,' a runner said.

Charnley read the dispatch. He folded the paper neatly, placed it in his breast pocket, and then turned to face his men. 'Take what rest you can, eat, clean yourselves up. At eighteen hundred hours, we are going over the top.' He took out his field glasses and climbed the parapet. Behind the sandbags, bent figures, working like demons, cut through barbed wire. Machine guns chattered, and occasionally, a great gun boomed, yet all the while, during this brief parallel truce, men on both sides of no man's land flitted here and there, fetching, carrying, digging.

Howell tapped on the captain's boot and offered up a mug of steaming tea.

'Thank you, Are the men fed and rested?'

'As far as possible, sir.'

'Give them another half hour, then we must rally them.'

The two men sat on the ledge next to each other, sipping their tea. Minutes passed without conversation, then Charnley tipped the dregs of his mug into the murky water below the duckboards and Howell moved off to rally the men.

'Right, lads, let's be having you.'

Charnley read through the orders one more time; the men stood ready to receive their instructions. 'Shortly, the artillery will continue with a bombardment, the mortar detachments will fire smoke rounds in front of the forward trenches. Once over the top, our orders are to regroup, attack and capture the forward redoubt and the immediate area behind it. Is that clear? Any questions? Have courage, God Speed. Sergeant Howell.'

'Right, lads, you heard the captain. Check your gear. Fix bayonets. Gas masks ready? Get those scaling ladders in place, good lads.' Howell walked along the line of men, checking kit and equipment, exuding reassurance and encouragement. Nervous eyes looked at their sergeant, counting down the minutes and seconds waiting for the captain to blow his whistle.

The British artillery began their bombardment; German guns retaliated. The whistle blew. Captain Charnley led the way, Howell in hot pursuit. Up the ladders, the men climbed and in unison, there rose an inarticulate battle cry. Rifle and bayonet fixed in one hand, spade in the other, bullets cracking past their ears like hailstones, on they forged. A smoke cloud partially obscured them as they reached the first tangle of wire, desperately searching for free passages cut earlier by the forward platoons, men hacked their way through.

Despite the confusion and chaos, Percy and Ron managed to keep together and close behind the sergeant. As they approached the edge of the enemy parapet, Howell hurled a grenade over the sandbank wall. Screams erupted from behind the fortifications. He threw another into the dugout and blew the door out. 'Get ready, lads,' the sergeant barked.

Screaming men, blackened by fire, burst through the smoking ruins. Howell, followed by Ron and Percy, leapt into the trench with bayonets at the ready. The fighting was fast and furious. Stabbing and slashing, with trench knives and bayonets, they overpowered the enemy and took control of the trench.

~

That night and for many nights to come, Percy remembered, with cold shivers down his spine, the blackened face of the first man he had killed.

CHAPTER TWELVE

GRACE

The nurses arrived at a small hamlet, a few miles from Arras. Morton helped them from the train.

Grace was transfixed by the desolate landscape. 'Oh God,' she shouted, above the pouring rain and din of a continuous rumble and roar, like an immense factory of vibrating machinery. 'This place is a quagmire.' A crash of big shells burst at no great distance away.

'Captain Morton?' Called a young man with a shock of red hair, which poked waywardly beneath his tin helmet. 'George Cooper, I've been sent to find you. Please follow me. Watch out, the mud's bad here. Let me take your bags, ladies.'

Cooper led them to a huge city of canvas, batteries, and ammunition dumps. 'Here we are,' he said, pointing to the casualty clearing centre tents and huts, camouflaged by sheets of canvas, splashed with brown, green, and yellow paint, to mimic autumn leaves. 'The nurses' tents are just there. They look a bit odd, but don't worry, they're in dugouts, so the bell tents look short, and they're sandbagged all around; cosy inside,' he said, with a twinkle in his eye. 'Doctor Fiske and Matron are in the HQ hut, they're expecting you.' Cooper saluted and left.

'Ah, Captain Morton and nurses, welcome,' said Fiske, extending his hand to Freddie. 'May I introduce Matron Halse?'

Grace, Lily and the matron exchanged nods of acknowledgement.

The doctor continued, 'It's been absolute mayhem here for the last few weeks, particularly since the recent assault started. Thousands of shells exploding, torrential rain with no let-up, the battlefield looks like Armageddon. The land is swampy, and craters filled with water deep enough to drown a man. The bodies of soldiers killed earlier have started to rise to the surface; soul destroying for even the hardiest man out there.'

'With your permission, Doctor,' interrupted the matron. 'Shall we leave the men to talk? Let's find you a hot drink, then I will show you around the wards.'

Grace and Lily followed Matron to the kitchen.

'You haven't been this close to the Western Front before, I believe. This is a casualty clearing station, hence its location near the railway, so we can facilitate the movement of casualties from the battlefield and onto the hospitals. Of course, the location has added dangers, we are so close to the battleground as to occasionally become the target of a shell or bomb dropped by German aeroplanes. Arras is a tragedy. It was such a beautiful city. I visited in my younger days.' Matron's neck stiffened. 'A terrible cost. Ready? We'll start with the Pneumonia Ward.'

They followed her through a series of wards, finally arriving at 'the nursery'. 'Unfortunately, the serious nature of many wounds defies our medical facilities. The danger of infected wounds due to men covered in filth and mud at the time of injury means that many casualties end here, with no hope of recovery. The nurses do their best to comfort these poor souls. Ah, Nurse Dixon,' she waved to a young woman. 'Here are Sister Phillips and Nurse Price, please show them to their accommodation. Do excuse me, nurses.' Matron nodded and left without another word.

'Hello, I'm Winnie. Follow me. Do you have any luggage?'

'Yes, we left it in the HQ hut.'

'Fine, let's swing past there and collect it.'

The HQ hut was empty when they arrived. They picked up their bags and followed Winnie to the nurses' quarters.

'Watch your step here, these duckboards are slippy. Over there is the nurses' latrine. Only cold water, I'm afraid, but we have a tin tub in the kitchen and take turns once a week to have a nice hot bath. Here we are, this is our tent. Take your boots off and leave them on the stakes. That gives them a chance to air, and we don't tramp mud into the tent. Here we go.' Winnie opened the tent flap.

'Oh, it is quite cosy,' said Lily.

'Hahaha, home sweet home. Those are your beds, mine is here, that's Tilly's, she's Australian and over here is Mary's, she's a sister too and Canadian. We don't have ranks here. We're all nurses, apart from Matron, of course. Oh, and here are your sleeping bags,' Winnie unrolled the padded bags consisting of a sheet folded to contain a wool blanket and held together with large safety pins. 'There are a few bullet holes, don't let that worry you, it happens often when we put the washing out to dry. My shift starts shortly, when does yours start?'

'I don't know, Matron didn't say.'

'Well, come back with me, and we'll see if Matron has updated the shifts on the noticeboard. You must be starving too. Come on, we'll look for your shift and then I'll show you to the canteen, can't have you fainting from hunger on your first day. Don't forget your gas masks and tin hats.'

Outside the tent, they pulled their boots back on and headed for the notice board.

'You're both on the midnight shift on the Acute Surgical Ward,' said Winnie, tapping the notice board. 'Just as well you get something to eat now and take a rest while you can. The canteen is this way.' They followed Winnie through a labyrinth of passageways. In the far corner of the canteen, she spotted Matron in deep discussion with several men, including Doctor Fiske and Morton.

'Mmm, handsome. Do you know the new captain?' Winnie teased.

'Yes. I mean, we travelled here together.'

Lily chuckled.

Suddenly they fell to the ground. There was a shrill sound followed by an enormous bang that shook the earth beneath their feet. Dust and darkness descended on the canteen.

'Grace, are you alright? Lily, quick, get up, we have to get out of here ... the patients.' Lily grabbed Grace's hand and pulled her up. They ran out of the canteen.

'Tilly,' called Winnie. 'What happened?'

'Thank God you're alright,' Tilly answered. 'Who have you got there?'

'Grace and Lily, the new nurses.'

'Shells burst on two sides of us, not fifty yards away. I've just come from the Advanced Abdominal Ward. No direct hits but black smoke and hot shrapnel flying everywhere. One poor chap caught some in his cheek. It's made a mess of some of the nurses' tents. Thank God there was no gas. Anyone hurt in the canteen?'

'I don't know, we high tailed it out of there.'

'Ted,' called Tilly, as a young orderly came running towards them. 'What's happening back there?'

'No injuries, just a big mess. We're all heading to the wards.'

They reached the wards to find so many wounded coming in that every available space held a stretcher.

'There's no more room in here,' Tilly shouted above the din. 'You'll have to keep the stretchers outside until we can make some space.'

'It's bloody raining out there and these men are in a bad way,' one of the stretcher bearers replied.

Winnie grabbed some ground sheets. 'Here. Put these over the men.'

~

The boom of guns shook the earth continuously day and night, week after week. The Battle of Arras had begun in earnest.

~

A boom followed by a high-pitched squeal increased in volume and intensity until it became unbearable. Grace put her hands over her ears and knelt on the ground. There followed a massive blast, then all was silent for a breathless second.

'What on earth was that?'

'I don't know but it was close. I was getting a clean tray of instruments. Everything rattled and shook, and I dropped the lot. Now I'm shaking.' Lily held out her hands.

'Come on, Lily, buck-up. The rush will be on now. We already have two wards full of patients. We'll have to work fast to get them dressed and off to the evacuation tent as there will be more to take their places.'

Lily slumped on a chair. 'Just give me a minute, please. Grace, I feel quite helpless. I don't know where to turn to next. I'm worried I'll make a mistake.'

Grace hugged her friend. 'I know, I feel the same, we are so busy here with the procession of wounded coming and going all the time. But this is what we signed up for. We are British nurses. The men look to us for support and care. We've got to keep our heads.'

Lily took a deep breath and said, 'You're right, of course. Let's go.'

Wagons pulled up at the door. The injured carried on stretchers, while those who could walk were supported by less injured men. One or two of the stragglers fell up the steps from fatigue and lay there.

A grim-faced Morton appeared, supporting a young soldier. 'Most of these men have been for three days without food or sleep in the trenches,' he said, lowering his charge to sit on the ground. His eyes met Grace's. 'You're safe, thank goodness.'

'We must clear some of the patients to the evacuation tent. How many injured do you estimate?' Grace asked.

'I don't know. I'll find out. There are lots more outside.'

Grace followed Morton and was shocked when she saw the number of men lying on the ground, blood thick over their uniforms, flies settled on the torn flesh. Orderlies laid the injured in rows and sorted through them, pinning labels to their covers. They lay perfectly still.

The French and English guns bellowed a continuous resound, like the roar of a train in a tunnel. Wind skimmed over their heads, bringing air filled with dust, ash, and the cries of men.

Grace felt stunned. 'It's like an endless nightmare,' she said. 'I must get to the ward.'

The flood of injured streamed in, the nurses examined

them while still on stretchers, cutting away uniforms to access the injuries. Soon a pile of clothing reached from the ground to the canvas roof. Corridors were crowded with stretchers lined up against both walls. In the surgeries, as one operation finished and the patient removed from the table, blood was wiped away and the floor mopped before the next man was placed on the table.

In the early hours, the rush over, Grace made her way to the nurses' ablutions tent. She stripped off her bloodied uniform and scrubbed her hands clean, poured water into a bucket, not caring that it was cold, and washed herself from head to toe. She wrapped herself in a towel, placed her clothes in the bucket, left them there to soak and went to her tent to find clean clothes. Her bed looked tempting, but she needed something to eat and drink, so dressed in her pyjamas, she walked back to the kitchen. *A cup of tea and a biscuit, that's what I need. Then perhaps I can sleep, if when I close my eyes, I don't see the endless bandages, rolling and winding and staining red.* She filled the kettle and put it on to boil.

'Sister Phillips, is that you?'

Grace gasped with surprise. 'Captain, what are you doing here?'

'I could ask you the same question,' he said, a smile creasing the corner of his mouth.

'It's nearly dawn,' she blushed and turned to the kettle. 'I'm going to have a cup of tea. Would you care for one?'

'No tea for me, thank you. Grace, may we talk for a minute?' he asked.

'What is it you want to talk about?'

'That's a good question. I admit I am a bit lost for words at the moment.'

'I'm not surprised, I expect you are exhausted. How did you know to find me here?'

'I saw you in the ward several times through the night but when I brought the last of the men in, you were gone. So, I … ah … Yes, I am tired, and you must be too. It's just …'

She took a biscuit from a tin. 'Yes, it's just … what?'

She smiled, and in that moment, a joy rose within him, and words bubbled forth. 'I've been wanting to tell you how much I admire you. Oh, that sounds … I love you. There, I've said it. Before you tell me how stupid you think I am, let me say … I know this is a most inappropriate way of approaching this, um, topic …'

Grace laughed but deep inside, she felt her heart pounding in her chest. 'Captain Morton …'

'Oh, please, call me Freddie.'

'Freddie, I don't know what to say. I'm flattered, of course.'

'But?'

'No, I'm more than flattered. I'm thrilled.'

'I must kiss you. May I?'

'Yes, please.'

The kettle began to whistle.

Their lips touched, gently at first. His arms drew her closer. She clung to him as his mouth parted her trembling lips; she felt a warm rush as she yielded.

'Oh, gosh, excuse me. I heard the kettle whistling and thought no one was here,' Lily exclaimed.

'Ah, it is I who should apologise, nurse,' said Morton.

The three started laughing.

'Well, ladies, please excuse me. It's been a hell of a day and night. You should get some rest. Goodnight, Grace.'

'Goodnight, Captain ... Freddie.'

~

The usual hot, dry weather of July had turned to cool and wet in the beginning of August, drenching canvases, and turning dust into swirling pools of mud.

'Have you heard the news?' Drops of water spat on the hot hearth when Tilly burst into the kitchen and shook her waterproof.

'What news?' Grace asked.

'They're moving us. Shifting the whole clearing station.'

'God, not in this weather, surely,' said Winnie.

'Apparently, there's been a big breakthrough by our forces. They've pushed the Germans back, they're on the retreat.'

'Hooray!'

'Nurses.' Matron Halse stood stiffly, waiting for their attention. Her eyes settled on a puddle of water steaming from the heat of the hearth.

Tilly grabbed a rag and mopped the water.

'Nurse Barnes is correct. The patients who can be evacuated immediately will board the hospital train in the next hour. Others will follow, some may have to remain. You, nurses, will accompany the patients on the trains. The first train will travel to the hospital in Rouen, the second to Wimereux. Once we have the patients on the trains, the demolition of the clearing station will commence. Please take it in turns to pack your belongings, you may store them in the kitchen until you leave.'

'Matron, what will become of the patients who can't be moved?' Winnie asked.

'Doctor Fiske and I will take care of them. Hurry now,

Captain Morton will take charge of the evacuation, he will be along shortly.'

'Grace and Winnie, you've been on shift all night. Why don't you go and pack first? Mary and I will start preparing the patients. Oh, I can hardly believe we're finally getting out of here!' Tilly hooted with delight.

Grace and Winnie hurried to their tent. 'I hope we get sent to Rouen, I remember it fondly,' Winnie winked. 'Lily, wake up, love, we're on the move again, we have to pack quickly.'

They packed and returned to the kitchen.

'Sister Phillips, may I have a word?'

'Yes, of course, Captain.' Grace followed him into the corridor.

'Grace, I want you to go with the first hospital train to Rouen. I have orders to go there myself and will follow in one of the later transports.'

'Oh, yes, of course.'

'I know this is all a bit sudden. I hope you weren't offended, by our kiss, I mean.'

'Not at all, it was wonderful.'

'Alright, well, Corporal Cooper will accompany you. I have given him a note and some cash and asked him to secure lodgings near the hospital for us. I'm afraid discretion has flown out of the window.'

'I don't care. Just to be together for a while.'

He kissed her softly on the lips. 'I must get on now. The faster we get things moving, the sooner we can be together.'

~

At eleven o'clock, the first train arrived at the siding. Grace, Lily, and Mary were in the troupe of nurses assigned to Rouen.

They supervised the boarding of the patients.

'Gosh, this train must be half a mile long,' said Mary.

'Just as well,' replied Lily. 'Look at the number of patients we have and I'm sure there will be more joining as we journey along. Oh dear, I think this could mean a nightmare for some of the men. The bunks are so small and there's not much space between each one. I think they may feel claustrophobic.'

'Men with broken bones will probably feel every jolt. Be prepared for some cries,' said Mary.

'Nurse, please help. I can't raise my knees to relieve the cramps because the bunk above me is only a few inches away.'

'What did I tell you?' Lily said.

The nurses did their best to comfort the men but the cries for help were endless on the long journey to Rouen.

~

'Ah, ladies, found you at last,' Corporal Cooper grinned. 'We're almost there. Have you been before to the *pot de chambre de France*?'

'What?' exclaimed Lily.

'I know what he means,' said Grace. 'The hospital was erected on the racecourse and, as Rouen is in a traditionally rainy area, the sandy, gravel-covered ground of the racetrack provided the best drainage, hence the *chamber pot of France.*'

'Charming,' said Mary, rubbing her tired eyes. 'I'm exhausted.'

'When the train pulls into the hospital siding, there will be nurses and volunteers on hand to escort the patients to their wards, so please stay together and wait for me and I will show you to your accommodation. And the good news is, you all have two days' leave. I'm going to find the rest of the nurses now.'

'And probably crack the same joke,' sighed Mary.

~

They followed Cooper past a village of bell tents, illuminated by candle lanterns until they reached a series of wooden huts inside a protective barrier of paddock fence. Grass covered the ground between the huts and flowers bloomed here and there.

'Here we are, ladies.' Cooper announced the names of the nurses allocated to each hut.

Grace and Lily were in the last group of four nurses.

'Nurses Price, Tierney and Blare.' Cooper pushed open the door.

'What about Grace?' Lily asked. 'Oh, I see ...' She hugged Grace. 'Enjoy, my dear. See you later,' she whispered.

Grace blushed.

'Follow me, Sister.'

They walked along cobbled streets, lit by soft gaslight until they arrived at a small stone building in a lane, *La Maison De Jeanne.*

'Do you mind waiting in the foyer while I see the manager?'

Grace nodded.

'Your room awaits. Let me carry your bag, the stairs are rather steep and narrow.'

'Oh, my. This is lovely,' she said, admiring the cosy bedroom. A double bed adorned with colourful quilt and plump pillows along with the perfume of lavender made her heart sing.

'I'll leave you to it,' Cooper smiled. 'The captain should be here by late tomorrow afternoon. Your breakfast has been organised. Have a nice rest,' he said, closing the door.

'Madame?' An elderly woman, wearing a white cap and pinafore, entered the room. 'Pour Madame. Serviette de bain,' she said, handing Grace a warm bath towel. 'S'il vous plait, suivez moi.' She beckoned Grace to follow her along the hallway. 'Ici le bain.' She smiled and pushed open the bathroom door.

Grace gasped with delight. Before her was a green enamel bath filled with hot water. She stepped out of her boots and let her clothes fall to the floor, then eased her tired body into the soothing water.

~

The sun was low in the sky when the final hospital train pulled into the siding near Rouen's military hospital. Morton disembarked and found Cooper waiting for him.

'Good man, Cooper. Everything set?'

'Yes, sir.'

'HQ first.'

'Yes, Captain, this way, close to the main pavilion, in the old racetrack office.'

Cooper waited outside while Freddie presented himself to his senior officers. 'Hello there,' he called to two pretty nurses, one of whom was Lily. 'Enjoying time off?'

'We've had such a lovely day, haven't we, Mary?'

'Indeed, we have. We walked around the Cathedral, very 'gothic', wasn't it? Then we found the square where Joan of Arc was burned at the stake.'

'Oh, it sounds like you've had a really fun day,' laughed Cooper.

'It was interesting, and I love all the medieval buildings,'

Mary replied. 'Best of all though, we found a dear little café where we had the best pastries I have ever tasted.'

'I didn't think much of their coffee, though.' Lily laughed.

The office door opened, and Freddie appeared, looking grim.

'Goodbye, ladies,' said Cooper. 'Ready, sir.'

'Show me the way to my lodgings, please, then take some free time. I must be back here by two o'clock tomorrow.'

~

Grace sat at a table in a small room off the foyer to the hotel, where she could watch the comings and goings of guests. Each time the door opened, she hoped it would be Freddie. She had borrowed a book from the hotel library and tried to amuse herself by reading but it was really a sham as the book was French and her knowledge of the language was limited. She peered through the leadlight windows to the wet street scene where, occasionally, weak sunshine broke through and highlighted the bejewelled raindrops.

Once more, the door opened. She recognised the familiar footsteps and his voice as he addressed the receptionist in perfect French. It took all her will to restrain herself. She walked calmly into the foyer and their eyes met. She nodded to him before climbing the stairs. Grace left the door ajar and sat on the edge of the bed, heart pounding.

Freddie mounted the stairs two at a time. He dashed through the open door and fell on his knees before Grace. 'My darling.'

Instead of answering, Grace stood and pulled Freddie to stand before her. She reached up and put her hand on the back of his neck. She lifted her lips to his and they kissed, at first lightly, then more urgently.

Freddie pulled away. 'Wait, my darling. I must wash. I stink and the mud still clings.'

'Of course. Here is a towel. I'll show you to the bathroom.'

In the minutes Freddie took to wash, Grace undressed and climbed into the soft bed. She peeled off the quilt and lay naked beneath the thin sheet.

Freddie returned with the towel wrapped around his middle. He threw his soiled clothes into the corner of the room. His eyes fixed on Grace's form beneath the sheet, her chestnut hair spread across the pillow, the appeal in her eyes. He dropped the towel and climbed in beside her, pulling her close. 'I can never bring you close enough. I want to fold you inside me. I want to keep you warm, keep you safe, keep you with me always.'

Grace tilted her hips against his. Her breasts pressed against his chest.

Freddie traced the line of her cheekbone with his lips. The sensation sent wild tremors through her nerves and made her body tremble.

'Grace ...'

His words were lost in her mouth as she pulled him closer to her, her fists knotted in his hair. Freddie positioned himself above her, she locked her legs around the small of his back. She groaned lightly as he entered her. They built a rhythm of long, sliding strokes. Their sweat mingled and the pace intensified, accompanied by muffled cries as Grace pressed her fist to her mouth to quell the sound of her passion. Until together, they reached elation, and they began to breathe normally, enmeshed in each other's arms.

After a while, Freddie asked, 'Are you hungry?'

'Hahaha. Starving!'

'Shall we find some supper?'

'Yes, let's.'

They washed and dressed before going down the narrow stairs.

'Bonsoir, Monsieur, Madame,' called the manager from behind a small bar. 'You would like dejeuner, wine perhaps?'

'Yes, please, merci,' said Freddie.

'S'il vous plaits,' responded the manager, leading the pair to a candle-lit table near the bar. 'Ce soir, we 'ave the soup of onions avec baguettes and le Camembert, c'est tres bien.'

'Oui, merci, monsieur,' Freddie replied.

'Vin rouge ou blanc?'

'Rouge, s'il vous plait.'

'Red wine for us tonight, darling?'

'Yes, Freddie, wonderful.' Grace sighed deeply. 'This is so lovely. I wish we could stay here forever.'

'Vin rouge,' said the manager, placing two glasses on the table, he uncorked the bottle and poured a little wine for Freddie to taste.

'Bien, merci.'

They clinked glasses and sipped the wine. Soon the supper arrived. The hot soup, deliciously flavoured with beef stock, the crusty baguettes, soft inside, were a perfect accompaniment to the rich, salty Camembert.

Finishing the wine, Freddie said, 'Darling, I feel quite done in, shall we go upstairs?'

They rose from the table, the manager said, 'Bon nuit.'

Exhausted, they slept, Grace couched, safe in Freddie's embrace.

~

The next morning, they breakfasted on warm rolls with jam in the hotel's courtyard.

'We were given two days' leave, so I suppose that means I must go to the nurse's quarters tonight.' Grace hoped Freddie would say she was wrong and that they could stay longer at La Maison De Jeanne.

He did not respond, continuing to stir his coffee.

'Freddie?'

'Grace. The war is changing. I would like you to go home.'

'I don't want to leave. Not without you.'

'Let's walk for a while.' Freddie took Grace's hand and led her into the cobbled street. They walked in silence, deep in their own thoughts, oblivious of people passing by, of street sounds and aromas from the small cafes. Eventually, they arrived at the lofty and imposing Notre Dame Cathedral. 'Would you like to see inside?' Freddie asked.

'Yes.' Grace replied.

Their footsteps echoed on the marble slabs as they walked together beneath the massive ceiling of the nave. The church seemed to stretch on forever. They continued to walk in silence until Freddie slowed, pointed to a small chapel and whispered, 'This chapel is dedicated to Joan of Arc.'

Grace did not respond.

'Come, darling. Let's get out of this dreary place.'

Outside, the air was warm, and sunlight filled the square. Pigeons fluttered about, looking for crumbs.

'I understand that you want me to go home. But I simply can't. I am committed to being here. I know the dangers. I'm prepared to take the risk.'

'Somehow, I knew you would say that. I just want you to be safe. It was foolish of me to expect you to agree. We can stay together tonight but tomorrow I must leave. I have to oversee the setting up of a new clearing station near Tilques.'

'Then I shall come with you,' Grace said, her face determined.

They returned to the hotel and lay on the bed, hand-in-hand, staring silently at the ceiling. It seemed no words could fill the void.

CHAPTER THIRTEEN

TOM

After a few months of travelling daily to the farm, Tom had every bump, turn and twist of the road etched clearly in his mind.

Gone the cold maw of winter, the landscape revealed itself more each day, and the sweet hint of spring whispered in the air as the lorry hurried along the dirt road, passing fields now vibrant, blissfully at ease and ignorant of the ravages of war.

The lorry pulled into Steinke farm. The guards released the bolts from the tail gate. Men jumped down to the cobbled ground. Some were taken to tend the animals; others to haul coal or harvest timber. Tom and Arthur walked to the forge.

Lars De Smet uncoiled himself to his full height, stretched to relieve tension in the taught muscles of his neck. His skin, like tanned leather, was glazed in perspiration. His hands, as broad as shovels, flexed while his sharp gaze appraised Tom and Arthur. 'We work.'

Tom pumped the bellows while Arthur stoked shovelfuls of coal into the hearth. Soon the forge glowed brightly, and a surge of heat filled the draughty building. They made way for Lars as he carried a lump of iron in the grip of tongs. From the fierce heat, the iron radiated a yellow-orange glow. He lifted the metal to the anvil, signalled for Tom to pick up the sledgehammer and indicated where to strike. Tom delivered the heavy blow; sparks flew from the glowing bar. The day's work had begun. The ring of hammer on anvil sang throughout the morning.

They stopped their labour when Henrietta De Smet appeared in the doorway. She carried a large steaming stew pot and pulled, from her grubby apron, three tin bowls and spoons. 'Eat,' she said.

Lars rubbed his hands on a rag and bent to kiss his wife. 'Danke Liebling.' He filled three bowls with the steaming stew made from vegetables and smoked meat. The men sat together on timber stools and ate in silence, savouring every mouthful of the salty fare. Lars cleared his throat, set down his bowl and focussed his steely gaze on Tom.

'My son, like you. Tall, strong. Blacksmith, like me.'

'Where is your son?' Tom asked.

'Hergel, they forced him to go to war. Dead!' Lars spat.

~

Later that night, Tom lay on his mattress, intrigued by his conversation with the smith, who had shown a distinct loathing of war.

'Arthur, are you awake? I think there is a chance we may have an ally in the blacksmith. I think he's vaguely offered his help. He said I reminded him of his son.'

'It all sounds a bit bloody vague to me.'

'Maybe, but there's a chance he can help us escape.'

'We may get out but what then? I can't speak the fuckin' language for a start, can you?'

'No, but I've picked up a few words. I agree there are obstacles but where there's a chance ...'

'Get some sleep,' Arthur retorted, pulling the blanket over his face.

~

A few days later, Tom swirled black bread in his coffee.

Today's the day, he thought. The last months of labour at the forge had hardened not only Tom's muscles but his will to survive and determination to escape. He and Arthur had discussed their plan and now they were ready.

'Rouse, rouse!' shouted the guards.

Arthur fell in on his right. They did not exchange even the remotest glance, however, the tension and anticipation resonated between them. Despite the cool morning, Tom's palms were wet with perspiration; his breathing was taut, nevertheless, he directed his gaze forward.

The guards performed a routine head count, then signalled for the lorry. The tail gate opened, and the driver sounded the horn. Men climbed aboard; seconds later, the lorry surged along its familiar route. Tom leaned his forearms on the rim of the truck, feeling the vibrations rattle through his body as the wheels negotiated the rough road to the farm. He was on edge, trepidation swelled in his gut. *This is it. I can almost taste it. Freedom.* He caught Arthur's eye as the tree-lined banks of the river appeared on the horizon.

Arthur acknowledged Tom's look and squinted his eyes as he registered the importance of the landmark. He retreated to the other side of the truck and feigned boredom as he studied the passing vista. As they neared the farm, men ducked to avoid the sting of low branches. Arthur chuckled to himself as he watched Tom stoop. 'That's one advantage of being a short bastard,' he cackled. Tom straightened as the lorry passed beneath the trees and came to a halt at the farm gate.

'*Now, the next part of our plan, Johan must come through for us.*' Tom had not wasted a second of his time over the last months of labouring in the forge. He had gathered information, assembled intelligence which would make or break his chance of escape.

The men disembarked. Tom strode ahead towards Johan's forge, his heartbeat with renewed vigour, he breathed in the imminent oxygen of freedom. He felt taller, lighter, like a wild beast about to leap into the unknown.

Johan bent over the furnace, coaxing the fire to life. The previous night's rain darkened the walls of the old forge, the dampness gathered in gloomy corners, steaming as the fire in the furnace gained momentum.

Tom bent to enter the beamed entrance of the forge and his eyes met Johan's. They shared a moment of empathy. He felt Johan's gaze on him as he stood silhouetted in the entrance. He thought the man might reach forward to embrace him. *Hergel is beyond embrace, he is dead, killed in a war which makes no sense*, Tom thought, his face conveying the message. Arthur followed behind.

Johan spat into the furnace, it sizzled and bubbled for seconds before vaporising.

Outside, the familiar routine was taking place. Men, accompanied by two guards, led cattle to a field, collected pats and tilled the land. Four guards led a larger group to the woods to cut and collect timber. Two guards remained in the courtyard. They lit cigarettes, laughing, distracted by a pretty dairymaid.

Johan wiped the sweat from his brow with his sooted forearm. 'See there,' he whispered, pointing to a pile of rags. 'You have little time. You must do it now.'

They let go their shovels and rummaged amongst the rags, finding two old grey jackets, trousers, and caps. They hurriedly pulled the clothes on over their khaki.

'Thank you, Johan.'

'Come, you must do it now! Hit me. Tie me.'

At this crucial moment, Tom froze.

'You must!' hissed Johan.

Thwack! The sickening thud of metal shovel against flesh and bone brought Tom back to the moment.

'God, man, why did you hit him so hard?' Tom bent to Johan, who was bleeding profusely from the blow to the side of his head.

'Quick, help me tie him,' Arthur insisted.

Tom grabbed a handful of rags and, tearing them into strips, bound Johan's wrists and ankles. He gently pressed the back of his hand to Johan's cheek.

Johan rasped, 'Go, flee.'

Arthur pushed the last handful of rag into Johan's mouth.

Tom crouched near the entrance and peered out. The guards were nowhere in sight. He reached behind and grabbed a handful of Arthur's jacket; pulling him forward, they ducked and crept around the side of the forge. Before them lay small outbuildings and sheds. Hearts pounding, they darted from the cover of one building to another until they came to the last. 'There's no more cover between us and the orchard up ahead, about twenty yards. Straight over the wire, then we head east. Ready?'

The fence was knurled, twisted, and choked with weeds, they surmounted with relative ease. They ran beneath the cover of fruit trees in full leaf, wet from overnight rain, underfoot the ground was soft and moist, well-trodden and grazed by resident stock. Tom paused to get his bearings, peering through the trees which grew so closely together; it was hard to see far ahead.

Arthur grimaced; a glaze of sweat smeared his upper lip.

Together they ran, branches whipped their faces,

scratching skin and cloth. Tom's long stride placed him yards ahead of the shorter man. Sheep scurried away in the wake of the fleeing pair, their bleating, a constant cause of concern should the sound alert the guards. Finally, the eastern boundary of the orchard came into view. Tom paused behind the last tree and caught hold of Arthur as he staggered to a halt. Gasping, they stopped to catch their breath.

'Look, there's the lower fence, it's in better condition than the other, barbed too. Not so easy. There's a plank of timber that might help. Once over the fence, we're moving down the hill. See the boulders? They will give us cover. Then down to the stream.'

Swiftly they heaved the timber on top of the fence and climbed over. Arthur's trouser leg caught on a barb. Cursing, he tore it away, blood spilled down his right thigh and a three-inch flag from his trousers waved in the breeze on the barbed fence. On they ran. Fear was their powerhouse, the energy that forced them into flight. Legs pounded turf and skittered over gravel. The exertion tore the air from their lungs and their leg muscles screamed.

Tom arrived at the huge boulders; Arthur dropped beside him. They dragged themselves up to a sitting position to rest their backs against the cool stone.

'We can't stay here. Got to keep going.' Tom took hold of Arthur's coat and dragged him up. He pointed down the steep descent. 'Christ, it's steeper than I thought.' They heard the first shrill whistle. 'They've found Johan.'

They hurled themselves down the bank. The ground, littered with small stones, sent an avalanche of shale before them. Gravity dragged them on as they fell from boulder to boulder, hearts pounding, pain forgotten in their frantic bid to reach the stream in the gully below. They tumbled against thorny bushes. Tore themselves free and rolled down the bank to the sweet music of clear water gurgling and splashing over mossy rocks. The sunlight pierced through the dense tree-lined banks to dance on the rippling stream. But this was no time to rest and play beside the water's edge.

Tom strode in first, his foothold tenuous on the slippery rocks, Arthur followed. Both cupped their hands, scooped up cool water, drinking deeply before moving into the middle of the stream where the water was cold and deeper, it covered Tom's thighs and came to the middle of Arthur's chest. Underfoot, the stream bed was treacherously slippery.

'Reach for the branches. Pull yourself along.' Tom shouted.

They were beyond Arthur's reach. He lurched and slipped; the weight of his wet clothes dragged him down. He came up gasping for air and spewing water. The stream widened and a floor of pebbles offered an easier route, they gained speed.

Suddenly Arthur stopped. 'Hear that?'

'They're catching up.'

They struggled forward through the rushing water. 'Hold on,' Tom shouted, grabbing Arthur's sleeve as the torrent swept them downstream. They emerged in a deep pool of calm water. 'Keep low. Look, there's the river.'

Beyond the shallow banks, mud flats spread before them. Bright green and red-brown carpets of sphagnum moss glistened on the surface between them and the river.

'Keep moving.' Tom pulled Arthur over to the bank with him. They slipped into the bog, bent low, their eyes stinging from the stench of partially decomposed plant material and acidic water. The cloying mud made progress difficult.

'We'll sink in this stinkin' stuff. Bollocks ...' Arthur slid sideways in the mire. The first bullet pinged past his ear.

'We're fucked!'

They raised their hands and turned to face their captors. Just two hundred yards away, the river flowed wild and free.

~

Tom remembered little of the punishment he received on returning to camp after the first few savage blows smashed his jaw. Mercifully, he descended into unconsciousness before the guards' boots broke his ribs. Hours later, he managed to drag himself to the wall of the cell, slowly climbing into a sitting position. It was pitch dark. He held his hands in front of his face and could just make out their shape. His fingers nervously traced his jaw, he winced with pain. Dried blood blocked his nose, he blew it out and a fresh trickle seeped out of his left nostril. Hesitantly, his tongue explored the inside of his mouth. Several teeth felt loose, partially congealed blood filled the cavity between teeth and jaw.

'Tom. Can you hear me?' Arthur persisted. 'There's a Red Cross lorry just arrived. They're gettin' all the blokes to line up fer inspection. Wait on ... I'll get someone.'

Metal studded jackboots struck the concrete outside Tom's cell. Fearful of another beating, he tried to stand and brace himself.

'I asked you, what is zis place? Who do you keep in here?' the voice was insistent. 'Open this door, now, I insist.'

Sunlight streamed into the murky cell, dazzling Tom. The light shimmered through a fine halo of white hair on the head of a short man, his face obscured by darkness. He bent to look at Tom, 'Bring zis man immediately, he needs medical attention.' The guard protested. 'I said, bring him now.' Arthur and a second prisoner lifted Tom onto a pallet and carried him across open ground, every bump sending shockwaves of pain through his body. He blacked out.

Arthur pushed through the tent flaps, waiting inside the Red Cross doctor busied himself organising instruments.

'Leave him here.' Peering over horn-rimmed glasses, he bent close to Tom. 'I am Doctor Schaffs, Red Cross. I am going to examine you now.'

Under the doctor's gaze, swiftly yet carefully, the nurse removed Tom's filthy clothing and washed his wounds. 'Deubel, come in here please,' Doctor Schaffs called. 'You have no identification tag? Why not? Your name and rank?'

Arthur stuck his head through the tent flaps and gathered up Tom's shirt and tunic. 'I'll get these cleaned up.'

'You know zis man? Ah, Deubel, make notes, please.'

'Yes, his name's Bellamy, I think, first name, Tom.'

'You think? What about his rank? Get out!'

Tom regained consciousness. He groaned as the doctor applied firm bandages to his rib cage.

The nurse gently lifted Tom's head and tipped a cup of warm salt water to his lips.

'Rinse,' ordered Schaffs. 'Repeat.'

Tom spat congealed blood and gunk into a metal bowl.

Finally, the nurse applied salve and bandages to the wounds on his face, bending as she finished, to whisper words of comfort in a language he did not understand.

Returned to his bed in the hut, Tom pulled the thin grey blanket up to his chin and settled into the familiar profile of his straw mattress. It felt strangely consoling to be back in the hut. Whatever the doctor had given him to ease the pain was certainly working; he was asleep within minutes.

~

Hours later, Arthur patted Tom's shoulder. 'Wake up, pal. Take a sip of this, it'll do you good.' He put the tin bowl on the floor and tucked his clean clothes under his head. 'Look what I found when I was washin' your tunic,' Arthur held Tom's match case up for him to see. 'Lucky, eh? Got something written on it,' he held it close to his eye and squinted, 'pro rege ... pro le ... I dunno, looks double-Dutch to me.' He tucked the matchbox under Tom's clothes. 'Come on, try this,' he said, soaking black bread in the broth of potatoes, black peas and turnips. He spooned some into Tom's mouth. 'Good man. Try some more. Look what else I gotcha, socks and baccy,' Arthur held up the gifts. Tom nodded.

'Red Cross have taken all our names, rank, regiment where we got captured. I did me best to tell 'em about you.' Arthur continued to spoon more broth. 'The Kommandant's not a happy man. That Swedish doctor gave him a right bollicking.'

Tom's stomach growled as the food stimulated his appetite. He rolled the soft bread pieces between his tongue and the roof of his mouth,

'You hang on to these,' Arthur pushed the woollen socks into Tom's hand. 'Somebody's lovely mam knitted them; shows they're thinking of us, eh?'

Tom squeezed the woollen socks, bringing close a vision of his mother. Tears stung his eyes.

CHAPTER FOURTEEN

1916

Beyond the wire, tiny white daisies with yellow hearts quivered in the gentle breeze. They gathered in small bunches between the posts, inquisitively turning their faces into the camp.

In the six months since Tom's attempted escape, things had changed in the camp. Arthur had secured a job in the kitchen and often managed to secret a morsel of meat-fat, codfish, beans, or some other useful extra into Tom's daily soup ration, dropping it into his bowl with a wink and a nod.

Although grateful for the treats, a shadow of suspicion had been growing in his mind. He tried to push it back, but it often returned. *How did Arthur avoid a beating when we were both caught trying to escape?*

Red Cross parcels arrived over recent months, but none addressed to him. Arthur was among the group of prisoners charged with sorting out the packages in the kommandatura. Everything was divided ... tins emptied, chocolate bars broken into pieces, sausages cut lengthways, knitted items separated. Arthur worked his way into favour with the guards by putting some choice items their way, particularly tobacco and papers; he also managed to hide away a tidbit or two for himself, some of which he later shared with Tom.

The number of prisoners doubled; the barracks overcrowded to the point where men argued for a reasonable space to lay out their mattresses for the night; there was always a long wait for the toilet, which consisted of a simple board on blocks with a hole in the middle above a pit. The heavy rain overnight turned the clay soil to mud and caused the latrine ditch to overflow.

Tom viewed the line of men queueing for their meagre breakfast; black coffee and hard black bread, hardly sufficient to sustain a man expected to work a ten to twelve-hour day. The lorries queued in, waiting for the labourers.

Kommandant Friedrich von Klaus appeared on the deck of the kommandhutte, followed by his second in command, 'The Clog.' So named by the prisoners because of his wooden leg. Klaus hurriedly pulled a handkerchief from his pocket and held it firmly over his nose. The Clog screwed up his face, effectively pinching closed his nostrils. KIaus paced, legs strutting in black-red-striped trousers, his Iron Cross catching a flash of sunlight. The Clog followed, bending to catch the words of the smaller man and scribing rapidly as Klaus gesticulated towards the queue of men and waiting lorries; his face reddened with anger and eyes bulged as he spat out his rhetoric.

Tom had picked up a few words of German here and there over recent months but was unable to hear much as guards hurried him and the crew along. They wheeled their barrows to the ditch, rags tied tightly around their mouths and noses, eyes stinging and watering from the toxic atmosphere. The guards stepped away, pointing their weapons, the men began the toil of shovelling shit to barrow.

Hours they toiled, occasionally slipping from the crusty edge to knee-deep in mire, one by one dragged back by the handle of shovel wordlessly offered by companions, they continued the task.

At the end of the shift, they scrubbed with pumice and carbolic, tipping buckets of cold water over themselves from head to toe; it seemed nothing would remove the stench. Marked men each of them. Men who violated the rules, men who answered back, refused to toe the line, and the long-term punishment for the worst of the bunch, the men who tried to escape. A moribund crew, they went their separate ways without a word.

~

Tom sat on the back step of the kommandantur, curling paper carefully around crispy-dry strands of tobacco, deftly pushed into a narrow tube. He rubbed his chin to coax moisture, licked his dry lips before hanging the fag into the corner of his mouth. He looked at his hands, brown and scarred, deep clefts of grime, nails broken and toughened by labour. His fingers curled, the veins dark and raised from taut, dry skin stretched across his bony hands.

A weak sun had already started to set. Dark skeletons of trees in the distance lined up in a slow dance along the horizon. Squinting, he thought he could see the pale shadow of the road disappearing into the firs that lined the scarp towards the deep gully where he and Arthur had been recaptured. He thought of the blacksmith and wondered what had become of him.

'Here you go, chum.' Arthur struck a match to level at Tom's cigarette.

He sucked as the end crackled and spat in the light of the match; the intake of smoke seared his lungs and filled his belly with a foul delight. '*Phgggh,*' he coughed.

'Look what I've got fer yer.' Arthur looked around to ensure he wasn't being watched and pulled a bundle from his breast pocket. 'Go on, take it, it's yours, don't worry, they won't miss it, there's a whole box brought in for the kommandant. That fat little shit isn't going to notice. Go'orn!'

Tom peeled back the rag to reveal a square of yellow Hartkäse cheese. His stomach rumbled and a sharp burst of salt filled his mouth. 'Are you mad?'

'Don't muck about, eat the bugger,' Arthur said, looking furtively around.

'We've got to get out of here. We need to plan. Have you heard anything? The bloody place is bursting at the seams. I watched Klaus this morning yelling instructions to Clog, but I couldn't get close enough to hear what he was saying. Something's up.'

'So, you don't want it, no problem, I'll 'av it m'self! Fuck you!' Arthur grabbed the cheese out of Tom's hand and stormed off.

'Wait …' but he was gone. *Things have changed between us; I'm still desperate for escape, but Arthur seems content with his job. Something's up, I can feel it.*

~

In the early hours, barking dogs and the grumble of engines roused the men from their sleep. Tom listened, trying to interpret the shouts of the guards. The man nearest to the door peered through a loose plank.

'Christ, there's gotta be a dozen lorries out there.'

'There's dogs 'n' all. What's goin' on?' said another.

Men peered through cracks in the planks; some hurriedly gathered their clothes and boots, retrieved small treasures hidden in the straw of their pallet.

Tom thrust his hand deep into his mattress to retrieve his silver match case. It was not there.

Arthur pulled his blanket a little higher over his head and sunk deeper into his bed.

The hut door burst open, 'Schnell, Schnell!' the guards yelled, threatening their weapons, ordering men out into the crisp pre-dawn air. A sliver of pink-grey light reached through the darkness as men mustered. Despite being torn from rest, the prisoners quickly formed rows and stood to attention.

The kommandant stood on the deck. Clog barked orders. The atmosphere was electric. Yowling dogs, eyes white and distended, strained against chains held tight by their handlers. From the left, the first ten men in each row were herded towards the waiting trucks, Tom amongst them.

'Off. Strip to waist. Boots off. Schnell!' the guards yelled.

'No, you can't take our things.'

'Not the boots for Christ's sake …'

'The Geneva Convention. We are prisoners of war. We have rights!' A rifle butt silenced the man.

At bayonet point, shirtless and bare footed, they climbed into the back of lorries. Men sweated, despite the cool morning; it was the sweat of fear, causing an acrid smell that filled nostrils and caught sharply in the back of dry throats. It gleamed on their faces and slipped down their cheeks. It gathered in the pits of their arms and aggravated their groins. They shared furtive looks as the lorry lurched forward.

Tom peered through a crack in the canvas. He saw Arthur standing on the steps of the kommandantur, his elbow bent, hand raised in salute, or perhaps just shading his eyes as he watched the trucks' trek eastward. The figure waved and a glint of flame sparkled for a second.

A feeling grew in Tom's gut, a sense of losing something. The grey buildings dissolved into the horizon; the ribbon road disappeared in a haze of dust. *There was nothing here when we first arrived. We slept under bloody rags for the first cold months of winter until we built it, all of this, the huts, everything. It's like leaving home!*

With each passing mile, the prisoners' trepidation grew. They spoke in hushed voices. Hours passed until the lorries slowed. They pulled up at a railhead. Pushed and jabbed by rifle butts, men crammed into the rail trucks. Forced against each other, they struggled for air.

~

Two days later, with no food or water during the journey and stinking from the lack of toilet facilities, they arrived at their destination, deep inside Germany. As the door was heaved open, the men shielded their eyes against the glare of sunlight. Guards swore and spat at the men. Herded, whipped and screamed at, they were force-marched along a road lined by old men, women and children who jeered cruelly at the hapless prisoners. The massive, fortified gates of Hochfenitz Prison Camp loomed ahead.

As they passed through the gates, whips cracked, steering the men into a quadrangle. Without warning, pressure hoses turned on them. Buffeted, slipping, and sliding into mud puddles, they desperately tried to catch some of the water in their mouths to slake their dreadful thirsts.

Oh God, what is this place?

The men were ordered to pick up a pair of wooden clogs and a canvas shirt from heaps piled against a wall before marched into a compound.

Tom stared at the huge chimneys and slag heaps beyond. He took in a deep breath. *Whatever this is, I must stay strong. Please give me strength.*

1917

PERCY

By autumn 1917, the landscape of north-eastern France had changed. Once, warm sunlight flooded the wide yellow cornfields and lines of poplars edged the green fields. In that bygone autumn of frosty nights and sunny days, birds frolicked in wooded hills, brilliant with foliage. Now, like long abandoned tombstones, blackened shards of ancient woods dotted the flanks of that once bountiful countryside. Trenches crisscrossed the Valley of the Somme to the fields of Flanders, carving through villages, farms, roads and railway lines.

Day after day, the misery of trench life, exhausting marches and weariness of inaction taxed the endurance of men in the trenches. The cycle of four days in the front line, four days in reserve and four days at rest began again for Percy and Ron in the second week of October 1917.

A stream of exhausted men dragged themselves past the barrier to the cleaning station. Percy thought of the lice inhabiting his clothes and twitched involuntarily. The queue moved slowly towards the bath house. Four men at a time were hurried in: their woollen tunics, jackets and trousers taken away for de-licing with naphthalene powder. Their filthy underwear and socks destroyed, they would be issued clean ones after a five-minute bath.

'Ron, over here,' Percy called.

Ron pushed past the men to reach his friend. 'Look at this bloody queue.' He scratched at the skin beneath his collar. 'How long's it been since the last bath?'

'Four weeks I reckon. I've heard of a place where we can get a proper bath. Hot water! It's just outside the village.'

Ron shrugged. 'How far outside the village?'

'Not far.'

'I don't know, Perc. I don't want to get there and find there's no bath. It's not worth the risk.'

'Well, I'm going. We'll be there an' back before you know it. Otherwise, we'll be in this queue for at least another hour.'

Last time ... you know ... that woman. I can't get her picture out of my mind.'

'Yes, that was a mistake.' Percy thought back to the time he and Ron had been confronted with a terrible scene. They had walked to the edge of the town to get away from packed bars and cafes, hoping to find a half-decent meal or a chance to wash themselves and their clothes. They came across a small house, the only one left standing at the edge of a muddy brown field. A boy stood at the gate, his bony arms draped over the top bar, his chin hung forlornly over the edge. He perked up when he saw them approach. 'Bonjour, Tommies,' he called, waving. 'Come, come.'

Percy answered, 'Hello, there. Parlez English?'

The boy cocked his head to one side. His hair was dark and dirty and plastered to his forehead. He pulled open the gate and beckoned them in. His torn pants were too big and hung on his thin frame, held up by string tied around his waist. His bare feet were black with dirt.

They followed him down the pathway.

'Where's he taking us?'

'It's alright, Ron. I expect his ma's inside.' Percy tapped the boy on the shoulder. 'Hot water er bain?'

The boy did something which took Ron and Percy by surprise. He laughed. He led them into a dimly lit room; it took a few seconds for their eyes to adapt to the light. On the table stood a jug and several chipped cups. The boy held out one hand for payment and pointed to the cups with the other.

'It don't feel right,' Ron held onto Percy's shoulder.

'Bain, hot water?' Percy asked again.

The boy shook his head. He pulled back a ragged curtain to reveal a bed. A naked woman, resting on her elbows, stretched across filthy sheets. Ron recoiled instantly and pushed past the boy. Percy stood for a while before filling a cup from the jug. The woman sighed as she lay back. He drank the sour wine, pressed two decimes into the boy's hand and said, 'Merci.'

Percy ran to catch up with Ron. 'Wait for me,' he pleaded.

'God. What's to become of us?'

'So, are you coming?' asked Percy.

'No, you go on. I'll keep you a place in the queue.'

Percy passed through the checkpoint and out to the dusty street. He walked past men brushing cloying dirt from their jackets. The first red lamp shone, and men crushed forward, vying with one another to be first to enter. Percy walked on. He wanted to walk, to feel the stretch of his legs and to get away from this crowd of people, the noise, the stench. Already the bars were overflowing. Up ahead, he saw a battered, white bucket atop a gatepost. He walked through the gate, past desolate gardens overgrown with weed. The door opened before he had the chance to knock. A grey-haired woman bade him enter.

'Bain?' Percy asked.

'Oui,' she replied, pointing to a chair beside a tin bath.

A dishevelled old man shuffled into the room carrying a mug. He stared at Percy, his eyes rheumy and lids heavy. Deep lines etched his mottled face and dragged his mouth into a sorrowful snarl. Dried spittle caked his thick lower lip, which trembled as he tried to speak.

Percy pulled out his tobacco tin and held it up to the old man, who blinked in response. He rolled two cigarettes, put them both in his mouth and lit them, offering one to the old man.

The woman carried in two buckets of steaming water. 'Cinq decimes, monsieur.'

Percy placed the coins on the table and undressed. He pulled out his pay book and identity card and placed them on the table with his tobacco tin. As he tugged off his boots and puttees, caked mud fell to the floor. Percy grimaced as he smelt the stench of his socks.

The woman scooped up the coins and placed them in a pocket in her skirts. 'I take? Cleanse, oui?' she said, collecting his jacket mud-stained puttees and trousers.

The old man added broken fence pieces to the fire and stabbed the embers with a metal poker. Soon the flames licked at the wood.

The woman returned with two more buckets of hot water, a long handled scrubbing brush and soap in a jar.

Percy peeled off his filthy underwear. He held the bundle in front of his groin, embarrassed and unsure of where to put it.

'Vite, vite,' the woman wagged her finger, indicating that he should drop the clothes in an empty bucket and get in the bath.

He climbed into the hot water, which stung his skin in the most delicious way. He sighed as the steam rose around him, lowering himself as deeply as he could before closing his eyes, comforted by the crackling fire.

The old man propped his boots against the fender and

stared at him with sad, bewildered eyes.

Soon the woman returned carrying Percy's uniform, which she spread out over the fireguard. The clothes instantly began to steam, and the pungent aroma of naphthalene hung in the air. The old man lighted a thick wax candle with a spill from the fire. He took Percy's jacket, turned it inside out and laid it across his knees. Slowly and carefully, he ran the lighted candle up and down the seams.

The woman carried another bucket of hot water and set it down by the side of the tub. She picked up the long-handled brush and thrust it into the bath water, surprising Percy, who pulled himself quickly into an upright sitting position. She poured oily soap over the bristles. 'Lavage,' she said, scrubbing at Percy's head and neck. When she finished, she banged the head of the brush into the water, picked up the bucket and poured hot water over his head. Percy's eyes smarted with the stinging soap, which smelled of camphor oil. She worked quickly, scrubbing away at his back and torso, arms, hands, then down his legs to his feet. She then handed the brush to Percy and pointed to his groin. 'Monsieur.'

When he finished, she took away the soap and brush. 'Fini,' she said, handing him a thin towel.

As he climbed out of the tub, he noticed the surface of the water was thick with grease, grimy dead skin flakes and hundreds of tiny pale seeds. He stepped out quickly and rubbed himself dry.

'Clothes?'

'Non. Fini,' she pointed to the empty buckets by the bath and then waggled her finger towards the door.

'Yes, of course.' He tied the ragged towel around his waist, dragged the bath outside and bucketed out the bathwater onto the garden. The air was cold outside, but he felt invigorated, the cleanest he had felt for as long as he could remember. He came back inside to look for his clothes. The old man had finished waxing the seams of his trousers and hung them next to the jacket and puttees.

The woman pointed to the table. Folded neatly was a grey woollen vest, a pair of long-johns, a serge shirt and, on the top of the pile, a pair of green socks, neatly darned at the toes.

'Pour vous.'

'For me?'

'Oui. Ils etaient mon mari.'

Percy picked up the socks and held them to his cheek. 'Merci, madame.'

~

The next day they were back to the trench. 'Ah, Christ,' Percy groaned as he climbed down onto the wet duckboards. 'My guts. Latrine, Sarg?'

Howell nodded. 'Clune, take first watch. Lads, get that brazier lit. I'm going to find the officer in charge.'

Percy returned to find men huddled around the brazier; he pushed his way in to get near the heat. 'Here we go again then,' he said, rubbing his hands to bring the warmth into his cold fingers.

'How much longer is this bloody nightmare going to last?'

'Think yourself lucky, Jones, you're still here to moan about it!' Taffy scoffed.

'Lucky's not a word I'd choose to describe this stinking, bloody shit of a life.'

'For King and Country,' another man added.

'Fuck that.'

'So, we've got a new officer in charge,' Percy said, shifting the conversation. 'Heard anything about him?'

'Just another toffee-nosed-git,' Jones grumbled.

'I heard he's been in the thick of it. Come down from Ypres. I think he's from our neck of the woods, Perc,' added Taffy.

'Look out, here he comes now, with the Sarg.'

Grim faced, Captain Farrington appraised his men as they appraised him. He was tall, wiry. A ragged scar extended from his right cheekbone to the tip of his thin moustache. 'Men, we face an ordeal of the most critical kind ahead of us. Sergeant Howell tells me you are all experienced, therefore, I assume you have all endured long months of fighting and wasted time in these appalling trenches. I applaud you for your perseverance. I ask only that you follow me with the same strength and determination that got you this far. Are there any questions? No? Alright, Sergeant.'

The captain and sergeant left.

'You're wrong, Jones. I do know him. We went to the same school,' Percy said.

'Haha. You and that nob never went to the same school.'

'Well, it's true. He was head boy. Really popular ...'

'Fuck off, Phillips.'

~

On watch, through the grey dawn mist, Ron scrutinised the landscape for any sign of movement. A light breeze wafted the stench of mud and decay towards him, and damp mist settled on his cold cheeks. He focussed one hundred feet away, where the breastworks of the enemy trench stood out as a dark line in the grey mud.

Hiss. Ron squinted, unsure whether he had heard that

sound or imagined it. *Hiss.* Louder now and then, the unmistakable greenish-yellow cloud emerged from no man's land. 'Gas!' Ron shouted as he slid down the parapet steps. He hit the duckboards with a thud, grabbed his gas mask and shouted again, 'Gas!'

Men standing around the brazier dropped their tin mugs and hastily donned their gas masks. The chlorine veil like tendrils wisped and curled towards the British trench. Men cried in fear; others closed their eyes and shielded their faces as the gas sank onto them and drifted through the trench. Ron returned to the parapet to keep watch; he anticipated an attack, but it did not come.

Half an hour later, the sound of a hammer on an empty shell sounded the all-clear.

Howell came striding along the duckboards towards the dugout. 'Those dirty bastards,' he spat.

~

GRACE

Grace was alone in the ward when three wounded soldiers were brought in by orderlies.

'These lads got left behind, the ambulance has just dropped them off. No idea how long they've been stuck out there,' said the orderly.

Grace checked the three men. 'This man has a stomach wound. Orderly, please fetch the doctor, quick as you can.' The next man had a label attached to his shirt. He was conscious.

'Nurse, I can't feel my legs. I can't feel nothing. Am I going to be alright?'

'The doctor will be here soon; he will take a good look at you. Try not to worry.'

Next, she knelt by the bedside of a soldier. Bandage covered his whole face from forehead to chin, including his ears. The gauze was taut with blood and dirt. 'Hello,' she whispered close to his ear. 'You're safe now, in hospital. I'm a nurse, my name is Grace.'

There was no response. She was glad to find he was unconscious, as he would not feel pain when she cut and removed the dressing. Her hands moved quickly working, gently pulling away the binding. She controlled a gasp of surprise when she found the greenish-yellow flesh and foul odour of gangrene. *Poor boy, he will surely die,* she thought.

He murmured something.

'What are you trying to say?' Grace asked. 'Can you say it again, so I can hear you? Do you want something?' She watched the boy pull his arms out from beneath the blanket and hold them up in the air. She thought she heard him whisper, 'Mumma.'

~

Grace pulled her cape tightly around her shoulders and hurried through the courtyard to escape the wind that howled across the flat fields and rattled windows of the stone sanctuary. She pulled the heavy door closed behind her just as the rainstorm broke in fierce gusts upon the ancient convent walls. Apart from the rattling glass and creaking window sashes, all was quiet. She lit a candle and placed it inside a lantern, then sat at her desk to read the ward notes.

'Blesses!' Lily was startled. 'Grace, I didn't expect to find you here, I thought you were taking a rest? You've only been gone just over an hour.'

Grace smiled at her friend, 'Sorry, didn't mean to startle you. I couldn't sleep with this wretched wind blowing, so decided to come back early.'

'Pippa and Mary are stoking the fires and filling hot water bottles for the men. The others have gone off utterly exhausted. Are you sure you're alright to start again?'

'Yes, I'm alright.' Grace removed her cape and put on a clean apron. 'I'll go and help Pippa and Mary.'

The scullery was warm and cosy, despite all the draughts. Pippa's cheeks glowed as red as the coals in the twin stoves. Steam belched from six kettles set on the stove tops. 'Can you give me a hand?' She handed Grace some of the metal bottles. 'Bugger!' Pippa spat as she scolded her fingers, trying to get the stopper into the narrow neck.

Mary popped her head round the door. 'Ready?'

'Take these four. God, I've done my dash,' Pippa sighed.

'Sit down by the fire for a bit, I'll fill those last few, then I'll bring them out, Mary.'

Grace caught up with Mary with the last of the hot water bottles. They walked down the corridor together. Above the snores and groans of the men, one cry alerted Grace. It was a long, incessant monologue.

'He wants his wife so badly,' said Mary. 'Says he would die happily if he could only see her for a minute. I've written a letter for him, and he kissed it before I wrote his wife's address. He keeps calling out her name.'

When they returned to the scullery, they found Pippa asleep in the big wooden chair by the fireside.

'C'mon, love, let's get you to bed,' Mary said, taking Pippa's hand. 'Will you be alright for an hour or so, Grace? I could do with a break myself.'

'Absolutely. Off you go.' She pottered around for a few minutes, tidying up some dishes left on the sink, then put the kettle on to boil. She sat back in the chair and dozed until she was awakened by a sudden blast of chilly air and the noise of beating rain, followed by footsteps on the flagstones along the hall. The scullery door creaked open. 'Freddie. What are you doing here in the middle of the night?'

'It's a wild night out there. I'm soaked,' Freddie said as he shook off his oilskin.

'Here, let me get you a hot drink.'

'No, my love, I can't stop. I just called in to tell you that we're on the move again. The news is that the enemy has unleashed an air attack on the hospital in St Omer. Nineteen dead, nurses and patients. The Abbaye is to be evacuated. Can you fetch the nurses and tell them to pack quickly? I have some men on their way to help.'

'Oh no, why in the middle of the night? We've just settled the men down. Some of the patients can't be moved.'

'I know it seems unreasonable. There is no option, I'm afraid. Please, quickly fetch the others.'

The sound of the outside bell jangled as men hurried through the door. She heard the ambulance wheels crunch on the gravel drive as she ran to the nurses' quarters. 'Wake up. Quickly. We're being evacuated.'

'What ... uh?'

'Pack your things. The Medical Corps are here already. They've brought ambulances for the men.'

Quickly and efficiently, the nurses packed their belongings into bags, pulled their waterproofs on and gathered in Grace's office.

'There has been an attack on St Omer hospital. So, this is an emergency evacuation. The most severely injured troops are being loaded into the ambulances; ambulatory patients will travel in lorries. Off you go and help. Lily, please stay and help me empty the contents of the medical cabinets, here I have sacks.' Grace shoved the ward notes and other records into a briefcase.

With all the patients loaded, Freddie took charge. 'Righto, ladies, let's go,' He ushered the women out through the door. 'One nurse in each ambulance; Sister Phillips, with me, please.'

Freddie drove the lead ambulance. The wipers battled against the pouring rain as he squinted through the windscreen past the piercing headlights.

'Where are you taking us?' asked Grace.

'To the base hospital at Wimereux. You will be safer there.'

~

Oh, Freddie, safer? How can you be sure? She looked at his strong, stalwart face. *He gains courage from every experience. In every emergency evacuation, he is there, confident, unfailing. But here we are again, a vulnerable caravan of injured men and nurses, trundling towards another destination. Can I be relied upon to take the next thing that comes along? Can I look fear in the face and come to grips with it? Well, I can but try.*

CHAPTER FIFTEEN

1918

PERCY

'Right, lads, smarten up, Captain Farrington wants to address you,' called Howell.

The men pulled themselves together and lined up against the trench wall.

'We've fought together for over a year, and I wanted to take this opportunity to say that I'm damn proud of you.' He looked at the faces of his men before continuing. 'By now, most of you will understand that a great blunder has occurred over recent months. Each side has achieved stalemate, each fumbling its way towards a solution. Well, we are going to put an end to that stalemate. It is vital to press forward at all costs regardless of whether units on our flanks are held up or delayed. Do I have your understanding, men?'

'Yes, sir,' snapped Sergeant Howell.

'Very well, continue with preparations. Sergeant, join me, will you?' With a final look at the men, Farrington withdrew.

The two men climbed into the parapet, Farrington raised his field glasses and Howell squinted to take in the scene.

'The unit to our left will attack at dusk and occupy that large crater,' Farrington pointed. 'We are to create as much of a diversion as possible. Have the men prepare and place the trench mortar ten yards to the right. See that the men are fed and rested and get some rest yourself.'

'Yes, sir.'

The men in the trench spoke in low voices.

'Well, what're you lot waiting for? You heard the captain. Let's get some of the rubbish cleaned up. You two, sort out the rations. Becks, Harris, and Davies with me, we're moving the trench mortar. Check your weapons and ammunition. Jones, relieve Clune on the lookout.'

~

It was Ron and Percy's turn to take a rest in the dugout. 'Cor,' said Ron as they entered. 'Move over, you buggers.' Ten men rested on their groundsheets.

'Shut up, you blokes,' Jones complained, lunging past Percy at a scurrying shadow. 'Filthy beasts,' he cursed. 'Big as bloody cats.' The rat squeaked loudly as it squeezed through a gap in the dugout boards.

Percy rolled over and slept while Ron searched in his pack. 'Ah, one left. Oh, she'll love this one, St Paul's.'

Dearest Ma,

I'm sitting here in our dugout; it's quite cosy

Percy's fine, sleeping right beside me, snoring his head off. Me, I can't sleep. Every time I close my eyes, I just see your dear face and think of being home.

How's young Stanley behaving? Tell him he'll have me to answer to if he's not being good.

Well, pet, I'll write more soon.

Your loving son, Ron

Ron folded the postcard and pushed it into his top pocket.

~

Farrington returned to his quarters where a fellow officer

occupied the bed.

He quietly retrieved his knapsack and dropped it near the table. He cranked up the heat on the camp stove and set the billycan over the pale flame. As he waited, he stretched out his hands to warm them and noticed his left hand was shaking more than his right; for a moment or two, this fascinated him. The water boiled, he made tea, took his mug and a small tilley lamp to the table, pulled up a stool and began to write:

Dearest Mother and Father,

The order has come so don't expect to hear from me for some time as there will be lots to do. The fine weather of the last few days has come to a sudden end and rain is falling.

In a few hours, I shall take my men back to the front to do our bit once more for King and Country. I ask that you look on my endeavours as an honour given to your son. I never really wished for this, but I have to say that now it is upon me, once again, I shall not recoil from it nor leave my men in need of command or guardianship.

I wish I had time to write more, but I must close now.

Fondest love to you both and all those I love so deeply.

Your proud and devoted son,

Edmund.

~

Farrington reached into his breast pocket and retrieved his father's watch. The metal felt warm and solid and in his palm. A memory filled his mind of a warm summer's evening, the echo of a young woman's chatter, the thwack of tennis ball against racquet, young men in baggy white trousers laughed and shook hands across the net. He remembered his father saying, "Take this for luck and God bless you, my dear son," as he pressed the pocket watch into his hand.

He turned the watch over in his palm until the flickering light reflected on the face and he could see the time. He curled his fingers around the watch and squeezed it before returning it to his pocket.

~

At seventeen hundred hours, the men were called to make ready. They sat quietly together, their backs to the trench wall, each with his own thoughts. Some prayed, some bargained, all remained tense and quiet. Each man knew he had a one in four chance of coming through this night unscathed. Those were the odds for men on the frontline.

Three quarters of an hour later, the British bombardment of German lines began. German guns returned fire. It was obvious to Farrington that the bombardment was having insignificant effect in suppressing the fire from the enemy lines. He and Howell exchanged a steely look before he raised his whistle to his lips and blew hard and long. He was first up the ladder with Howell close behind, the men dutifully followed.

Suddenly the noise from the big guns ceased, there was an eerie few seconds of silence before the air was filled with the crack of machine gun fire and the whiz of bullets. Men hurtled forward, stumbling into thick smoke.

'Can't find a way through,' Ron shouted, hacking furiously at the twisted mess of wire.

'Argh.' Percy took a bullet.

Ron dragged him to a crater, a great yawning hole at least fifty feet deep. 'Let me look,' he said, examining Percy's shoulder. 'It's gone straight through.' He cleaned the wound and packed a dressing under Percy's tunic.

Dead bodies stretched in ghastly postures inside the crater. Along the lip, men tried to dig themselves in. Sergeant Howell slid in behind Ron and Percy.

'Sarg, help me.'

'I'm here, lad,' Howell turned to find Tanner. 'Are you hit, boy?'

'I dunno, Sarg. I can't feel nothing.'

Howell ran his hands over Tanner's legs and felt the warm slime of blood mingled with mud. Tanner's face was luminescent like a pearl shining on a muddy riverbank.

'It's alright, lad, we'll have you back in no time.'

Calls for help echoed around the crater while the barrage continued. 'Dig in, lads, keep low. Clune, Phillips, you got field dressings? See what you can do.'

The smell of cordite, stagnant mud and rotting flesh pervaded the crater. Percy gagged as he pushed past the dead to find the living and dress their wounds.

The firing from both sides stopped. Out of the stillness, a moan of despair swelled as men trapped on the barbed wire gasped out their last moments. Some tried to crawl away, but the wire held them in its cruel embrace. Men in the crater stuck their fingers into their ears but the cries cut like a drill until one by one, they faded.

One man's persistent cry continued. Howell dragged his periscope out of his pack, lunged onto his belly and peered through the scope to find the source. 'God save him, it's the captain.'

Farrington hung in a gruesome pose like a string-less puppet on a wire.

Ron squirmed closer to Howell. 'Sarg?'

'Stuck on the wire, ten yards, look,' Howell passed the periscope to Ron.

The two men climbed over the rim of the crater and crept towards Farrington. They slithered along the muddy surface as a volley of bullets flew past until they reached Farrington. They struggled to release him. For a moment, Farrington opened his eyes and looked at Howell. Then he was gone.

'We can't do anything for him now. Grab his ID and stars.'

Ron ripped the officers' stars from Farrington's uniform and took the small brown ID tag from his wrist.

Howell tore open the captain's pocket and grabbed his watch and papers. 'Stow those things safely, lad, as soon as we get a lull, we're going to get our men back to the trench.'

Apart from the odd crack of a sniper's rifle, the guns fell silent. 'Right, lads, we're going to make our way back to the trench. No point staying here, we can't move forward. Come daylight, we'll be like sitting ducks. Help the wounded wherever you can. Clune, you lead off with Phillips.'

'Right, Sarg. C'mon, Perc.' They each grabbed a man and staying low, they crawled back to the trench. The exertion opened Percy's wound; blood drenched his sleeve.

'Perc, you stay here. I'm going back to help the Sarg. Put the billy on, I won't be long.'

A slow stream of men followed Percy into the trench. They were quiet and beaten, some nursed minor injuries, others were not so lucky.

'Quick, take him, he's losing a lot of blood,' yelled Howell.

Percy and another man reached out and caught the bloodied body in their arms.

The maelstrom erupted again. *BOOM!* The trench vibrated with the impact of the explosion. Mud, blood, decaying body parts and shrapnel zoomed above and along the trench.

Percy shouted above the cacophony. 'Sarg, Ron's out there,' he grabbed a scaling ladder and climbed. Silhouetted against the backlight of flame, smoke and verey light was the figure of Ron, a man across his shoulders. *BOOM!* The blast threw Percy and Howell to the ground. They crawled to Ron, lying face down, a gaping hole in his back.

'He's gone.'

'NO.' Percy bawled, he grabbed Ron's arms and dragged him towards the trench. Bullets ripped into Percy's thigh and buttock. Mud and burning hot shrapnel tore the left side of his face. At first, there was no pain, but a stream of blood gushed like a fountain from his nostrils.

Howell dragged Percy, still clutching Ron's body, to the muddy trench. They landed with a thump onto the wet duckboards.

'Stretcher bearer,' yelled Howell. He gulped when he saw Percy's facial wounds. A long gash from his forehead, across the bridge of his nose and through his cheek gaped horrendously. Howell tore open his field dressing kit and bandaged Percy's head wound. He applied two pieces of shattered duckboard as a splint and bound his legs together. 'Alright, lad, we'll get you out of here soon.'

Howell grabbed a passing stretcher bearer by the shoulder. 'Take this man.'

The stretcher bearer shook his head. 'No point, Sergeant. That sort always dies.'

'Don't argue with me. Take him.'

Percy held Ron's hand in his.

'Let go now, we've got to move him on.'

'There's stuff in his pocket he'll want me to take. I

promised.'

Howell opened Ron's breast pocket and removed the contents: a crumpled card and Farrington's watch.

'Right, lad, here you go, now listen to me. You take this watch back to Captain Farrington's folks, understand? They live in Hereford, that's where you're from, isn't it? Right, you find them and tell them Farrington was a good man, a good officer, he did his duty. You got that?' Howell pushed the watch and papers into Percy's pocket. 'Good lad, you've earned your ticket to Blighty. Now, say goodbye to your chum.'

Percy turned to look at Ron, an enormous pain grew in his throat, and he began to sob.

'Get him out of here.'

All along the trench, the sobs and pleas for rescue were dreadful to hear. Sergeant Howell moved amongst them, attending to first aid dressings and ministering to the dying. His continued shout 'stretcher bearer' echoed up and down the length of the trench as Percy was carried away.

~

GRACE

Lace curtains quivered with the soft breeze drifting through the opened window. Cool air whispered across Grace's bare arm, causing goosebumps to rise on her pale skin. She stirred as the small town below awakened to the sounds of people going about their business.

If I keep my eyes closed and don't move a muscle, this moment might last forever. Grace lay on her side, framed by her lover. She felt the weight of his arm across her torso; the coarse hair of his thighs teased her softness; their legs intertwined; his lean ankle held hers captive. *If only it could always be like this. Here in our little hideaway, safe from the world and the horrors of war. Oh, how I love this haven, our place.* Without opening her eyes, Grace explored the little room above the Café Hérisson. In her mind, she had a clear picture of the yellowed sloping ceiling and bare floorboards. The double bed took up most of the space but just beneath the window stood a small chest of drawers, on it a lace doily, a mirror framed in ebony, two candlesticks and Freddie's pipe. Inside the drawers were bags of dried lavender, the perfume mingled with a trace of tobacco smoke. Their clothes were draped over the single armchair in the corner of the room.

Freddie woke, stretched, uncoupled his legs from hers, and cupped her breast again in his warm palm. He nestled his face into her neck, his bristly chin gently scraping her hairline.

'Freddie, can it really be July? It seems only yesterday when we first found this place …' she chuckled. 'Dear Monsieur Poquelin, whatever must he have thought when you asked for a room to rent? Do you remember how his round cheeks became very red and he puffed a little before pointing behind the bar to the door marked 'Prive – Aucune Entrée'?'

Freddie responded, 'Mmm.'

'Ah well, he seems happy to see us on the few occasions we have been able to get away from the hospital together. Madame Poquelin berated him at first, I am sure. Do you see how she simply averts her eyes as we slip through the little door to climb the narrow stairs? Freddie, are you sleeping?' She continued her thoughts: *Here we can escape the nightmare of Wimereux, even for just a few hours. How hard Freddie works. I still wonder at the huge logistical problems, the supplies, the sanitation, but he manages, God bless him. And the men, the poor dear souls. No, I must not think of them right now. We made a promise that whenever we snatch time to spend in this precious place, we will allow ourselves to temporarily forget.*

'Good morning, my love,' his warm breath on her neck instantly aroused her. She craved his touch and turned to draw him into her moist self.

~

It was a perfect morning, a light breeze, blue sky, and the promise of fine weather. They left behind the narrow winding streets of the village and gained the open road towards Wimereux, five miles distant. Their journey slowed as they reached the canal where ponderous convoys, loaded from barges, toiled along with their heavy loads. Grace laughed and held onto her hat as Freddie steered the ambulance half on and half off the road speeding past the wagons.

Their mood became more solemn as the familiar distant booming returned all too soon. Freddie leaned forward over the steering wheel. In the distance, he saw a man waving. He slowed the vehicle and turned off the road towards the ruin of a church where a small throng of soldiers sat amidst churned-up graves and lurching monuments.

A young corporal ran to Freddie. 'Oh, thank Gawd,' the young man peered through the window and, recognising Freddie's rank, stood to attention and saluted.

'At ease,' Freddie called as he and Grace climbed out of the ambulance.

'There's six men inside, sir, mortally wounded they are. We done our best; we bin carrying 'em half through the night. We had to stop for a rest as we weren't sure if we were goin' in the right direction. We was followin' the field ambulances, but we got separated and lost 'em.'

Grace grabbed her medical bag from the back seat and hurried past the church's outer walls, now just heaps of loose stones. Inside pillars supported the remains of a burnt roof. Fragments of glass and melted lead from the shattered windows littered the broken alter. Amongst the ruins, on bloodied stretchers, lay the bodies of six men. The quietness was eerie and unfamiliar; Grace was used to the frantic shouts and screams of the dying and injured, but in this instance, although one of the men raised his head to look at her, all lay still and quiet.

She quickly knelt by the nearest man. It was too late for him; he had bled to death. The next man was also dead, next, she reached the man who had raised his head. As she knelt beside him, he grasped her hand.

'Thank you, miss,' he wheezed through parched lips.

She found field bandages had been roughly applied but successfully stemmed the flow of blood from a stomach wound.

'Captain Morton,' she called. 'We must get these men in the ambulance.' Grace moved to the next man, dead, the next, dead. The last man moaned in pain and delirium. His head wrapped in blood-blackened field bandages, his left leg splinted with two pieces of board and his tunic covered in dried blood. She searched but could not find any abdominal wound. The man groaned again, gently she turned his head. Tracks of tears stained his muddied face. Grace drew a sharp breath. 'Percy! Oh my God, Percy, it's me, Grace.'

~

Doctor Lefreu was in the surgery when the ambulance pulled up. 'Vite, vite, bring them in.' He scrutinised both men's injuries. 'Sister, address that man's wounds, start with the head, please.'

'Yes, Doctor.' Grace fetched hot water and dressings.

'Percy, I'm here. We're changing the dressing now.' Very gently, she peeled away the blackened gauze. After the first layer, she found it was stuck to the wound. Conscious of not causing further tissue damage, she dampened the black fibres.

Percy groaned.

'It's alright, love, we'll soon have this sorted out.' Meticulously she peeled away at the layers. A commotion began behind her. The doctor called for more swabs and the man with the abdominal wound screamed, 'Oh, God.' His cries intensified, ending in a gurgling sound.

Grace reached the last layer of the dressing; she halted and bent to examine the wound. The sight jolted her. 'Doctor?' She stepped aside to allow him to see.

'Mon Dieu.' Shrapnel had severely gashed Percy's face from the forehead, across the bridge of his nose and through his cheek, it was a grizzly sight. Cloth fibres and dirt were embedded in the wound. 'This must be cleaned carefully, and you must keep him upright, do not allow him to lie flat. Take care now, the tissue is ragged.' He poked gently at the blackened flesh. 'I do not advise debridement, although this tissue here is severely burnt.' Lefreu wiped the back of his hand across his wrinkled forehead. 'I believe this injury is beyond my capability. All we can do is clean and dress to keep the infection away. Let us pray we can get some of these men to Rouen.'

'Doctor, please come?' Lily called.

'I'll manage, Doctor. Should I give him anaesthetic?'

'No, not yet. We'll need to operate on his leg wound, he'll need it then. For now, pray he faints.'

'Percy, I'm sorry, this is going to hurt like hell.' Grace

cleaned his wound with carbolic solution and gauze. She felt him strain and sweat against the pain, fists clenched, breath hissed between his gritted teeth until finally, he lost consciousness.

~

Letter from Grace. Wimereux 19th July 1918

Dearest Mother,

I have Percy in my care. He is safe. It is indeed a miracle that Captain Morton and I found him yesterday. It's a long story but let me tell you about Percy. He is sorely injured, his back and one side of his face and a part of his thigh are burnt, and he has bullet wounds to his leg and hip. But he is gathering strength, although Doctor Lefreau says his days as a soldier are over. He has been attended to very well here at our hospital. He is, however, very badly shaken. We have not been able to get him to speak yet, although I know he recognises me as he squeezes my hand tightly when he sees me. At times, his tears are almost unquenchable and when he is sleeping, he calls for his friend, Ron.

When Percy is well enough to travel, we shall take him to convalesce in our new hospital. Oh, this is such wonderful news, Mother! I had no idea Captain Morton was so well connected. He owns a large estate near the coast in Somerset. Under his instruction, a whole wing of the house is currently being refurbished as a repatriation hospital. We hope the place will be ready by the end of August, which is just one month away.

I must steal some sleep while I can. I will take this letter now to the captain, who assures me it will be placed in the correspondence sack to be collected first thing tomorrow.

Goodnight, my dearest, I worry so about you. How are your poor sore hands? I shall be home soon and will kiss them and rub away the pain for you, if only for a little while.

Please kiss Pa for me.

Your loving daughter, Grace.

~

In Hereford, a woman turned the corner from Barrs Court Road and was almost knocked off her feet by a scruffy red-headed youth running wildly. 'Impertinent boy!' she called after him as he ran to the station master's house.

Stanley would normally have been apologetic; his mother taught both her sons to be polite, especially to ladies, especially if they were running on the path, especially if they nearly bumped into someone. But today, it didn't matter, today he didn't care. He didn't care that he had nearly knocked the woman over; he didn't care when she shouted after him. He ran as though each jolt of foot on pavement would somehow drive away the pain inside. He sobbed. People turned to stare. He didn't care, nothing stopped the pain. By the time Stanley reached the station master's gate, he was struggling for breath, he clung to the gatepost, his face almost purple with exertion.

Sarah sat quietly in the parlour when she caught sight of the boy crumpled against the gate post. She hurried out. 'Whatever is the matter?' Young Stanley, is it? Are you hurt?' She took the sobbing boy into the kitchen and sat him down in a chair and found a rag for his running nose. 'Here you are, give a big blow now, and tell me what's troubling you.'

Stanley blew hard and wiped his red-raw eyes. 'Auntie

Maisie told me to come. To give you this, to let you know.' He pulled out a crumpled paper from his breast pocket and offered it to Sarah.

The note felt warm and damp in her hands. She sat beside him and gently laid her hand on the boy's shoulder. 'My husband will be home in a few minutes. Let's wait for him, shall we?'

The boy nodded. His red hair stained dark with sweat, his scalp hot, his pulse pounded. He looked at her through swollen lids and sobbed.

'What's to do here then?' Matthew looked at his wife's pale face and the boy with wet hair.

Sarah held the folded paper up to Matthew, he read:

> *'It is with the deepest regret that I have to inform you that your son, Private Ronald Clune, was killed in action on 19th July 1918.'* Matthew's voice quavered as he continued, *'His death was that of a soldier and a brave man. I shall miss him immensely. As his sergeant, I always found him to be a smart, thorough, and reliable soldier. Signed: Sgt. G Howell.'*

Matthew's hands shook, he stared in disbelief at the crumpled paper.

'Lord, poor dear Ronald, but what has become of our Percy?' Sarah's voice was just a whisper.

CHAPTER SIXTEEN

August 1918

GRACE

It was after ten by the time Grace and Lily ate their supper in the mess.

'I'm too tired to eat this,' said Lily, pushing the food around her plate with a fork. 'This past couple of weeks have been madness. Every ward is full and there were two lines of stretchers down the corridors this morning.'

'I know what you mean,' Grace replied. 'Just a constant stream of gravely wounded. Have you noticed how cheerful and bright some of the German prisoners are? It's odd. Almost as if they're pleased to be here.'

'They are just the same as our boys though, so young, some of them.'

'I need to get out and have some fresh air. It's a warm night, do you feel like taking a stroll?'

'Sorry, I want my bed. I can't stay awake any longer. Goodnight.'

Grace slipped out of the rear door. A small half-moon shed a pale light above the rooftops. She breathed in the sweet, salty smell of the seaside and closed her eyes, imagining that she was in some dreamy place, far away.

'Ah, there you are. I was looking for you in the mess.' Freddie kissed her cheek and sat next to her on the low stone wall. 'A penny for your thoughts.'

'Nothing much to report. I was just enjoying the cool, fresh air and imagining I was somewhere else,' she turned to face him.

'You must be exhausted, my love. But there is good news. The word is that the fighting at Amiens has proved to be the greatest defeat since the beginning of the war, although German counterattacks are evidence that the enemy is not giving up.'

'At a dreadful price, though. The wards are bursting at the seams.'

'Yes, we need to move some of the men on as soon as possible.'

'But move them where?'

'Evacuate them. And that's why I wanted to speak to you tonight. In a couple of days, we will be on the move again. Only this time the journey will be home, to England.'

'Freddie?'

'The plan is to move the injured and a team of nurses, including you, my love, by road, west, to Abbeville then we will be transported on the hospital train to Le Havre, where a ship will be waiting to take us to Southampton.'

'Us? You're coming too?'

'Yes, I'm coming with you,' he affectionately squeezed her wrist. 'We'll have to make do with my house as it is, preparations are still in progress. I've telegraphed my mother to inform her of the imminent arrival of the men and nurses. By now, Doctor Kirke will have met her. He has been overseeing the installations. He's a charming Scotsman, so I'm sure Mother will have been placated.'

Grace was speechless.

'Don't worry, all will be well. I'll stay for a while to make sure everything is in order.'

'And then what? Will you return to France and leave me behind?'

'One step at a time.'

'When is all this expected to happen?'

'On Wednesday.'

'That's only three days away.'

~

Early on Wednesday morning, the ambulances arrived to take the first group of injured to join the hospital train waiting at Abbeville. Three trips were planned, Grace and Freddie joining the final group travelling with the most seriously injured men.

Doctor Lefreu checked each man as they were carried into the ambulances. He shook hands with Freddie and kissed Grace on the cheek. 'Well, ma chérie, this is goodbye. I wish you all God speed.'

'You're not coming with us?'

'No, this is my home. I still have work to do. I shall remain here at Wimereux. Now go along, don't keep the others waiting.'

'Goodbye, dear Doctor.' She climbed into the back of the ambulance and blew him a kiss before the doors closed and they were on their way.

Freddie turned his attention to the journey as the ambulance lurched along the potholed road. 'Everything alright back there?' he called. 'We should be there in a couple of hours.'

Grace was relieved when the entourage finally arrived at

the railway station. Freddie opened the ambulance doors and helped her down. A team of orderlies waited to carry the men onto the train, she followed along behind and watched as they carefully lifted each man onto one of the three-teared bunks.

'What an efficient use of space,' she said, looking down the length of the carriage.

'Yes, they have improved greatly. This train can carry up to five hundred injured men. Each carriage has a small team of nurses and orderlies. There are even operating facilities in some of the carriages. We can take a break for a while. Let's find a comfortable place to rest. You look exhausted, my love.'

With a jolt, the train began its long haul; through the night, Grace lay on a pallet in the staff quarters and tried to sleep.

~

The next morning, on arrival at Le Havre, the men were stretchered from the ambulance train and placed under temporary shelters on the quay where a team of medical staff undertook hurried examinations and made notes on clipboards before attaching a label by string to the wrist of each of the men.

Grace and her nurses sought out the men who had been in their care from the hundreds now awaiting transportation by ship. Two had died en route, one of them the young man who had cried for his wife. She found Percy, flicked over the label on his wrist, and read WINCHESTER. 'Hello love, I'll be back in a minute.' She looked up and down the length of the quay, trying to locate Freddie; she saw him talking to two officers and hurried over to him.

'Sister Phillips, I was just advising these officers about the new facility at Broadleigh, it will take up to forty men. It is designed for recuperation; we have a resident doctor, and

Sister Phillips will oversee the facility.'

'The labels?' Grace enquired.

'Locations, the men have been assessed according to their injuries,' answered one of the officers.

'Some of these men must be taken to Broadleigh. They have been under our care.'

The second officer flicked over the pages on his clipboard. 'I can't see it listed here?'

'That's because it is a new facility. It isn't listed there yet. God sakes, man, aren't the hospitals already bursting at the seams?'

'True enough. Sister, please point out the men you want assigned to Broadleigh. Corporal Jackson, accompany her and record which men are to be reassigned.'

The task took a while, but she was satisfied that Percy and most of her patients were now confirmed for Broadleigh.

~

'Grace, we must talk to you.'

'I'll be with you in a minute, Lily.'

'Sister, if you wouldn't mind just signing here. Thank you,' Jackson attached the final label.

'What is it, Lily?'

'We're not coming with you,' gushed Mary.

Lily took Grace's hand in hers. 'We're taking a ride with the ambulance train. It's heading back to Abbeville and we're going with it.'

'What?'

'You don't need us now. The ship has nurses on board and when you get to Broadleigh, you'll have plenty of staff there.'

'We have to go now, c'mon Lily. Love you,' Mary threw her arms around Grace, followed by Pippa and finally, Lily, holding back her tears.

'Oh, goodness, I love you too. All of you. Stay safe.' With a final wave, the nurses hurried off to board the ambulance train.

'Sister Phillips? I'm Sister Crawley. I believe you will be accompanying us on board HS Baronia?'

Grace turned to catch one last glimpse of her friends, but they had gone from sight. 'Yes, Sister.'

'The men are being boarded now. Please follow me. Standard procedure, we'll have to take you through survival training before the ship gets on its way.' She led the way to a small room on the quay where four nurses waited. 'This is Sister Phillips; she'll be joining us on the journey to Portsmouth. I'll leave you to it.'

A young sailor gave the instruction. 'Firstly, we'll run through some survival tips for evacuating patients when abandoning ship.'

'Abandoning ship?' One of the nurses said. 'But we're only going across the English Channel.'

The sailor replied, 'Yes but we have to prepare in case the ship is bombed or torpedoed.'

'But the ship is painted white with red crosses. Surely the Germans wouldn't attack a hospital ship?'

'That hasn't stopped them so far, we've lost several hospital ships.'

'Please do go on,' said Grace.

'Let's look at the procedure for a patient with a wooden leg splint. First, remove the splint before evacuation.'

'Because?' asked the same nurse.

'His leg brace will float and cause his upper body and head to go under the water. He will probably drown.'

'I can see we have a lot to learn.' The nurses settled down to receive the instruction.

'Grace, there's someone here to see you.'

She found Freddie in the corridor, reading through a batch of papers. 'Is everything alright?'

Yes, all's well. How are you?' Freddie asked, looking at Grace's pale face.

'I'm alright, tired. And my friends, Pippa, Mary and Lily ... they've gone back to Abbeville. We've been together for so long. I didn't have time to say goodbye properly.'

'What marvellous young women. You should be proud of them.'

'Yes, I am, of course. I'll be alright, don't worry about me. It's so stuffy down there and I'm worried about our boys. I must go and see them settled.'

'It's going to be a long night, I'm afraid. I'll see you later. Try not to worry.'

'Must you go?'

He kissed her cheek. 'I'll be back, try to get a bit of rest while you can.'

Feathery tendrils of silky fog hung in the air giving the impression that the ship was hanging between sea and sky. The passageway smelt of diesel as Grace made her way to check on her charges. All was quiet.

She fell into an abyss of exhaustion as she collapsed onto a bunk bed. From the open porthole, the smell of salt water breezed through and briefly disguised the dank that pervaded the ship. She breathed out slowly, listening to the dense stillness around her. 'Thank you, God, for getting us this far,' she whispered as the ocean's gentle swell lulled her into sleep.

~

The ship arrived at Southampton at break of day. The passage was smooth and uneventful. Before the men were disembarked, Grace made sure to say farewell to all those who had been in her care and were assigned to different hospitals and reassured the men travelling to Broadleigh that she and Freddie would be going with them. She sat with Percy for a while as the disembarkation began. 'Not long now, Percy.'

At eleven o'clock, the last man for Broadleigh was safely on the train. As the morning light illuminated the wide expanse of Salisbury Plain, Grace thought of her brave friends who opted to stay in France. Lily, who she had first met on the transport ship that took her to France in January 1915. Mary and Pippa, who had nursed with her for the previous two years. *Dear God, please keep them safe.*

She thought of the future and what was in store. *What will Broadleigh be like? Will it be ready to house these men in need of care? Everything has happened so quickly. Only a few nights ago, Freddie announced the evacuation; there was no time to think. And here we are, on a train in England.*

Grace winced as she remembered Percy's terrible injuries. She knew broken bones and bullet holes could be mended but what about his face?

She thought of Freddie.

Yes, he was coming with her now but how long would he stay? Would he really go back to France without her? They had been together, or never far away from each other for three and a half years ... how would she bear their separation?

From her window, Grace looked down on the dark rows of leafless poplars that marked the boundaries along ancient lines of flat green meadows, where cattle grazed serenely.

The rolling motion of the train coaxed her to doze, soothing her troubled mind.

CHAPTER SEVENTEEN

The Broadleigh Auxiliary Hospital was a wonderful surprise for Grace. The estate included the country house, sculptured formal gardens and beyond, a small wood. The formal rooms downstairs had been transformed into an auxiliary hospital, a treatment centre, fully equipped for the care of repatriated soldiers. She and Freddie were accommodated in his past housekeeper's apartment, consisting of a parlour, converted to office space, a large bedroom and a small bathroom. Their rooms looked out across lovely formal gardens, surrounded by tall oaks.

'How on earth did you manage to organise all of this?' asked Grace.

'Aha, the Mortons have some influence, you know.' Freddie tapped his nose.

'Morton, old chap.'

'Doctor Kirke, how wonderful to see you.' The two men shook hands. 'Allow me to introduce you to Sister Phillips.'

Kirke's eyes sparkled as he looked from Freddie to Grace. 'Charming to meet you, my dear.'

'Doctor Kirke was Senior Surgeon at St Bart's Hospital.'

'Until this mess kicked up,' said Kirke. 'Put the kybosh on retirement, somewhat.'

Freddie laughed and slapped Kirke on the shoulder. 'He's a great surgeon and plays a mean game of tennis. He'll never retire.'

'Look, the ambulances are arriving. Better get on.'

As the first troupe of men were stretchered in, Kirke and Grace discussed each patient's condition before they were assigned to a suitable ward. Finally, Percy arrived, and Grace explained the nature of his injuries. She explained that the bullets were removed from his hip and leg, but his face had not been touched. Later that day, Grace peeled back the dressings so the doctor could take a good look at the extent of the injury.

'Mmm, good, no sign of infection.' Kirke examined Percy's notes. 'Now, young man, let's take a look at the leg. I see, so the bullet caused a compound fracture of the femur. The second bullet has gone clean through the hip.' He looked over the top of his glasses at Percy. 'The field surgeon has done a tidy job here, son. We're going to get a cast put on this leg and that will stabilise the femur to help it heal.'

When the rounds were over, they discussed the proposed treatments.

'Finally, these two men with severe facial injuries. The disfigurements are quite profound.' Kirke removed his spectacles and rubbed his tired eyes. 'I fear there is little we can do for them here. While they are in our care, we must remain vigilant and ensure they do not see their reflection in a mirror or whatever. The psychological impact of seeing their injuries may do irreparable harm.'

'I will see to that, Doctor.'

'There is some revolutionary work being done at Sidcup Hospital, specialising on facial reconstruction surgery, brought on by the increasing number of men stricken with these terrible injuries. I will investigate the possibilities first thing tomorrow morning. With luck, we will be able to organise something for the two young soldiers with severe facial injuries.'

'Thank you, Doctor. I should mention, one of those two young men is my brother, Percy Phillips.'

'Oh, dear girl. Thank you for letting me know.' He checked his watch. 'Now I must away, we'll talk more tomorrow. Goodnight, Sister.'

~

By the first week of September, twenty-eight men were hospitalised at Broadleigh; a further twelve beds were on order and the last ward was finally ready. The staff settled into a good routine. Grace had four trained and two trainee nurses and four orderlies under her charge. They found a marvellous cook who had her own team of cleaners and assistants all working efficiently.

A few days later, as Grace finished her round of the wards, she found Freddie and Kirke in conversation in the office. 'Oh, excuse me, I didn't know you were here,' she said, turning to leave.

'No, no, don't apologise, I was just leaving anyway,' said Kirke.

'I'll see you out.' Freddie opened the door for Kirke and winked at Grace as he stepped past. Outside, the men continued the conversation.

'Everything alright, Freddie?'

'Yes. Let's eat, I'm starved.'

The cook served them soup and bread in the kitchen. They sat next to each other at the scrub-topped table, eating in silence.

Freddie reached for Grace's hand. 'I have to go to London tomorrow morning.'

'Really?'

'Yes, my love. I won't be long, hopefully, I'll be back tomorrow evening,' he squeezed her hand. 'Tell you what, let's take Saturday off. We can go for a lovely long walk. What do you think?'

Grace nodded, smiling weakly. She feared the time for him to leave would soon come.

~

'Percy, dear, are you awake?'

'Hello, Grace,' Percy rasped.

'Doctor Kirke will be here soon. He'll want to talk to you before your transport arrives.'

'Give us a hand, Grace. I need a pee before the boss gets here.'

Grace handed Percy his crutches and supported his elbow as he pushed himself off the bed. He winced in pain with the first few steps.

'I'll come with you. I don't want you to fall and damage that cast,' she said, walking by his side.

'I'll manage from here,' he said, outside the toilet door.

'Percy, I'm a nurse, there's not much I haven't seen.'

No response.

'Alright, I'll wait here, call if you need me.'

Limping back to his bed, Percy said, 'I wish this darned dressing could come off. It's really hard to see where you're going with only one eye working. I nearly came a cropper in the toilet.' He sat on the bed and handed Grace his crutches.

For weeks she had worried about how he would react when finally confronted with the severity of his facial injury. 'Corporal Timms is going with you today, did you know that?'

'Good. Two eyes between us will be better than one.'

'Here comes the doctor now.'

'Good morning, my boy. How is the leg coming along? Managing with the crutches?'

'Yes, Doctor, thank you.'

'And the pain?'

'I'm so doped up most of the time. Doc, why have I still got all this bandage on my head?'

Kirke hesitated for a moment before answering and Grace intuitively took Percy's hand in hers.

'The wounds to your leg and hip are under management and healing nicely. Your facial wounds, on the other hand, will need specialist treatment. That is why we are sending you to Sidcup Hospital. There is a specialist there, Doctor Giles, he's going to take a good look at you and see what can be done.'

'I see. When will I be coming back here?'

Kirke looked at Grace. 'I don't know, son. Doctor Giles will make that decision. You'll be in excellent hands; I can assure you of that.'

'Grace, is it that bad? I want to see my face.'

'Percy, love, as Doctor Kirke says, you are going to the best place to receive the finest treatment available.'

'It is bad then.'

'I'll get a nurse to pack your things.'

'No. I don't need anything. There's just the watch,' he pointed to the bedside drawer. 'I promised to return it to Captain Farrington's family. Oh, and a card I have to take to a pal's ma.'

Grace opened the drawer and found the card and a watch wrapped in a piece of cloth. 'Don't worry, dear, I'll make sure they are kept safe.'

Corporal Timms was waiting for Percy by the ambulance. 'What took you so long, cock?' he jibed. 'Bloody 'ell, you're ugly.'

'Hahaha, not looking too good yourself, chum,' Percy replied.

As Grace waved them off, she could not help but wonder what lay ahead for them. Both young men, unmarried. Could any woman come near without repugnance? Would children run from them in fear of their monstrous features? How will they react when they first see the extent of their injuries?

~

On a balmy Saturday morning, Freddie fetched the bicycles while Grace collected a packed lunch from Cook.

'Good mornin'. Well, aren't you lucky with this weather? Lovely day for a picnic. I made you some sandwiches, there's a slice of pie and a couple of apples. Oh, and tea in the flask.'

'You are a dear, thank you, Cook,' said Grace.

Off they peddled to Potter's Wood. They strolled for hours amongst the woods and heaths, where trees and bracken, withered heath and reddening berries burned and sparkled beneath the late summer sun. At the edge of the wood, the vista opened to the glistening sea.

'C'mon,' Freddie laughed as he grabbed her hand and they ran down to the beach, shedding their clothes as they neared the frothing waves. He scooped Grace up in his arms and ran into the water.

'Put me down, Freddie, you know I can't swim.'

'Hold on, darling,' he said, gently lowering her into the water, her arms clinging tightly around his neck. 'Close your eyes, hold your breath, come swim with me.' Grace relaxed and allowed Freddie to support her in the buoyant seawater.

Remembrance of Love and War

Soon the breeze picked up and the waves gained momentum. They returned to the beach and gathered up their clothes. Beneath a sheltering rock, hung with fern, they rested, gazing out at the water. Seabirds whirled beneath scudding clouds. The air had chilled but the nearness of the man she loved, his arm around her and his life beating as if it were in pulse with hers, intoxicated her.

'It's beautiful, Freddie. And the sea is so blue.'

'Only as blue as your eyes,' Freddie whispered, his cheek nuzzled into Grace's neck. She leaned back into his embrace, ran her fingers through his hair, still wet from the swim. His lips traced the line of her jaw, tantalisingly near her mouth. His hands slid beneath her shirt, seeking the mounds of her breasts. She felt him harden against her as he squeezed and rolled his fingers and thumbs around her nipples. The sun was warm on her upturned face but warmer still was Freddie's breath on her cheek. She opened her mouth, craving his salt kiss. His hand moved down her belly. Trembling, she opened her legs.

'Yes?' he whispered.

~

A few days later, as the setting sun sent shafts of rose-coloured light across the walls of their bedroom, Grace watched Freddie pack his kit bag. She absorbed his every feature; the way his biceps contracted as he rolled his clothes; the curl of his eyelashes; the little scratch on his neck where he had cut himself shaving that morning. His hands ... how she loved his hands; the mere touch of them awakened her every nerve.

'Freddie, don't forget this.' Grace handed him a woollen scarf. 'The nights will be chilly.'

'Thank you, my love.'

Grace knew it was pointless protesting. They had talked about his return to France so many times. She forced back the pleading words, but her heart ached to say, 'Please, please don't go.' Instead, a passion rose within her, and she cried, 'I'm coming with you.' She jumped off the bed, pulled out her suitcase and began throwing garments, toiletries, and papers into it.

'No, Grace. I want you to stay here. I want you safe.'

'Don't you see there is nothing here for me without you? I want to be with you, no matter what the consequences.'

'I forbid it. You will stay here.'

Grace slapped Freddie's cheek so hard it made her palm sting. 'Oh God, I didn't mean that. I love you. I can't live without you.' She fell to her knees.

'My darling, I'm just trying to protect you. You've been so brave. Please hear me. Please say you will stay.' He scooped her into his arms and kissed her wet face.

~

Red, gold and burnished bronze oak leaves rustled in the light morning breeze. Grace opened the window and breathed in the fresh, crisp air. *How I love the autumn. I could let my eyes bathe in these brilliant hues. It's like the trees are rejoicing, dressed in carnival clothes ... if only they knew.*

'Darling. I have a small gift for you,' Freddie said, handing Grace a package.'

'What is it?' she fumbled with the paper. 'Oh, how lovely, Emily Bronte's poetry. Thank you, I shall treasure it.'

'I must go now. Please don't come outside. Just let me hold you for a minute.'

Grace trembled, her jaw was tight, she fought back tears and dared not look into his face, she turned away. 'I love you, but I cannot watch you go.'

'I love you,' he replied. Closing the door as he left.

Through the window, she saw him walk beneath the oaks. He turned and blew a kiss.

~

The day was a blur for Grace. She performed her duties, as usual, attending to patients, maintaining records, conversing with staff. Privately, she could not wait for the day to end. Later that night, in her darkened bedroom, she walked wearily to the window. The moon cast an eerie light. Her heart felt dry with longing and grief. Briefly, she experienced a strange numb moment when she felt nothing and could hardly remember why she was here in the hospital until anguish cut through the numbness like a blade. 'Freddie,' she whispered. 'Oh God, please keep him safe.'

~

During the following weeks, the steady flow of new patients coming into the hospital increased. Every day Grace kept herself busy to the point of exhaustion. However, tell-tale signs of pregnancy now became evident. Morning sickness, darkness and soreness of her nipples, a bump above her pelvis. This was her secret, no one else need know.

One morning, she found Kirke waiting for her, earlier than expected. 'Good morning, Doctor, Everything alright?'

'Yes, I am just a little concerned. Although Lady Morton has been generous in providing extra beds, linen, and surgical supplies, once again, it appears we have reached capacity. No room in the inn, so to speak. The casualty rate has increased since this recent advance. One can only hope the end is perhaps in sight.'

'Yes, indeed. I will ask Cook to send in some tea and biscuits.'

'Thank you, the sustenance would be appreciated.' He settled into an armchair. 'Any word?'

'No, I'm afraid not. It's been more than a month since he's been gone, and I've heard nothing.'

'From all accounts, the situation over there is chaotic. The headline in this morning's newspaper was GERMANY FALLING TO PIECES.' He sipped his tea.

Grace could not bring herself to join in the conversation. She sat quietly, waiting for him to finish his tea and biscuit before asking, 'Are you ready for our rounds?'

With each step along the corridors, she felt the sharp pang of memory of shared times with Freddie. This was his home, his compassion and generosity reflected in every corner.

~

Late that night, Grace turned off her bedside light and sank down beneath the eiderdown. She was ready to relinquish the work of the day and open herself up like a chalice to receive the flood of bittersweet memories. The images returned, tumbling like a pack of cards, she tried to hold one or two, but they fell beyond reach. In her dream, she looked down on her image, standing in the doorway, she was calling, 'I won't watch you go out of sight. It's unlucky to watch ...' He turned and waved.

Softly at first, she felt the touch like silk against her cheek, of cool fingers gently wiping away her tears. She held her breath for a moment and tried to distinguish between the dream and yearning. She felt Freddie's body pressed against hers. She wished for the touch of his hands, the sound of his voice speaking softly into her ear, the words he had uttered on their last night together.

As she lay on her side willing these sensations and listening to every click and sigh of the sleeping house, a vision of his smiling face came to her so vividly that she reached out to touch his wraithlike skin. 'Oh, Freddie, I'm having your baby.' For seconds she grasped at the shadow of his beloved face. His lingering smile, the last vision before darkness prevailed. She closed her eyes and slept. In her dream, she stood at the window and watched until he turned and waved as he walked beneath the copper-coloured autumn oaks and then was gone.

~

Freddie had been posted to the casualty clearing station at Henin-Sur-Patois. Injured men crammed into the tents with more flowing in every hour. Carried on stretchers, stumbling figures, wrapped in blankets or remnants of khaki uniforms, bandaged or splinted, stiff with mud, caked with blood and dust. Freddie worked tirelessly from early morning until late into the night.

Enormous numbers of men and transport had silently moved up the road to Ramicourt to support the allied attack on the Hindenburg Line. On the night of thirteenth October, the attack began. Verey lights and exploding shells sent flashes of light through the darkness. Freddie and his fellow exhausted Medical Core officers watched with trepidation. Although the front was six miles away, the ground shook with the continuous roar of heavy guns.

'I need volunteers.' The Commanding Medical Officer called. 'We need a team for the front. Chalmers bought it and we've lost another two stretcher bearers.'

The men looked wearily at each other.

Corporal Cooper stood. 'I'll go, sir.'

Freddie stood up next to him.

'Thank you. Captain Morton, Corporal, follow me, I'll get you some supplies.'

Cooper and Freddie examined the map. 'We'll follow the road up to this point and then we turn near this spot and head south. You've had a stint in the forward line here, haven't you?'

'Yes, Captain. We should be able to see a line of trees, well, what's left of them. We'll have to keep down as there's not much distance between our line and Fritz. Let's hope our boys are keeping an eye out for us and they've got the kettle on,' he grinned.

Freddie was heartened by Cooper's endearing optimism but then he thought: *He thinks he's invincible, the reckless youth.* He recalled how the corporal had dealt with the worst cases and the dying, lighting cigarettes for them and exchanging jokes before they were taken away. He had all the patience, tenderness, devotion, and gentle hands of a nurse.

'How old are you, corporal?'

'Nineteen, sir, twenty next month.'

Together they collected their packages and crept into the night.

~

'Where are those damned surgical kits?' Freddie swore as he banged his head on a beam. 'I can only find one box of dressings here.'

Cooper coughed the dust out of his lungs and dragged a wooden box from under the crumbling trench wall. 'Here, sir.' The last explosion shook the trench, sending frantic rats squeaking and scuttling past the men's feet. The timber beams leaned at a precarious angle against the ramshackle wall.

'Captain Morton,' a voice called.

Freddie made his way to the dugout entrance. 'Who wants him?'

'Beggin' your pardon, sir, you're wanted at HQ.'

'Corporal, can you manage? I'll send someone to help if I can find any of our men.' Freddie followed the young trooper along the rotting duckboards. Two stretcher bearers came hurrying along in the opposite direction. They recognised Freddie's insignia and saluted.

'Good men. Go and help in the aid post. Keep your heads down.' Freddie let them pass. This was his first opportunity to see the extent of the trench. They had arrived in the dark of night to an eerie silence until one big explosion rocked the trench. Since then, not a single gun had fired. The squeaking of bloated rats and hushed sobbing of men invaded the silence.

'Here we are, sir.' The trooper stepped aside to allow Freddie to pass him and enter the HQ dugout.

'Ah, Morton. Good to see you again. Bit of a tight squeeze we're in, I'm afraid.' Hargreaves pointed to a chart on the table. 'This is the key point in the line. We must hold. This trench is square in shape. On these three sides, we have German troops. It's gone bally quiet. One can assume they are bringing in fresh artillery. You've come through from the clearing station in the west tonight. Any sign of bother?'

'No, sir.'

'Medical equipment?'

'I've left my orderly digging out the dressing boxes and fixing up the dugout. We brought four cases with us; all the dressing station could spare.'

'Alright, chaps. It's now fourteen hundred hours. Break out the rum rations, those poor blighters will need it. Thank you, gentlemen.'

Freddie hurried back to the aid post and found Cooper and two young stretcher bearers had made an excellent job of clearing the dugout. The corporal had tallied up the supplies and handed Freddie the clipboard to check.

'Good God. Is that all the anaesthetic we have? Just six boxes of dressings?'

'Yes, sir. We're low on iodine as well.'

Freddie shook his head. 'They are handing out the rum rations; get some for yourself, take these men with you and see if you can purloin some extra for the aid post. We may need it. Get back as soon as you can.'

'Aye, sir. C'mon lads.'

~

Tension and a sense of dread were palpable in the German trench. Men lined the walls, silent and deep within themselves. Some overhauled their equipment, others played cards, a few muttered whispered prayers. As the soft light of early evening stretched across the grey landscape, Gefreiter Hans Kepler rubbed his tired eyes, ever watchful for any movement. A string of bare trees, stunted and ghostly, marked the boundary of the line and in between here and there, a leg or an arm protruded from the mud. Bodies piled against the sagging walls of the derelict pillbox. His eyes were dry. He had witnessed horrors he never thought possible; inhuman acts of cruelty, one man to another. Hans felt in his tunic for his pocketbook and pulled out the tattered photo of his wife and son. *Will I ever come home to you, my love?* He kissed the photo.

Hans squeezed shut his eyes and ducked beneath the sandbags as the barrage roared forth. His heart thumped so heavily he felt sure he could hear it. Cold perspiration trailed down his cheeks and his guts felt as though they would turn to liquid.

The earth shuddered and erupted as one shell after another exploded nearby. He checked his bayonet again. *Soon the shells will stop, the whistle will blow, and we will climb over the top. Once again, to thrust and rip and kill. Oh God, forgive us all.*

The bombardment ceased, rifle shots rang out and bombs exploded, the air crackled and sparkled. There were curses and groans from scrambling figures rising over the parapets and soon the screams of agony would come. Screams that cut like a drill into the heads of those waiting to take their place. Now Hans was up, running furiously, crouched, determined, into the fray.

~

Through the night, stretcher bearers brought an endless stream of broken men into the aid post.

'We've got no more room. Tell them I'll come outside and check them there.'

Freddie pushed his way out of the dugout. As he passed Cooper, he placed his hand on the young corporal's shoulder. 'We can only deal with the ones who have some chance of survival.' He looked at the long line of blood-soaked bundles. He moved along the line, examining the men. A shell exploded nearby, covering him in mud and hot ash.

'Captain,' Cooper helped him stand. 'You're bleeding, sir, let me help you.'

Freddie put his hand up to his ear, which felt hot. Even in

the dim light, he recognised the smell and sight of his own blood. Disoriented, he struggled to focus. He could see the corporal speaking to him, but all he could hear was a ringing in his head.

Cooper's eyes were wild, his red hair wet with sweat, he spat words that Freddie tried to understand. He put his arm around his waist and pulled him to the dugout but was stopped by a sergeant, shouting, 'Retreat back to the support line.'

'Sarg, we've got wounded in the dugout. Hold onto the captain.' George pushed Freddie into the sergeant's arms and ran back to the aid post.

'Don't be a bloody fool, son.' The sergeant shouted after him as he moved away, yelling and pointing men to a gap in the trench.

Freddie reached into his pocket. He wrapped a dressing securely around his hand and his journal, clutched firmly in his fist.

~

In the aftermath of battle, the silence was sinister. German troops, including Gefreiter Hans Kepler, were ordered to investigate the abandoned British trench. They stepped carefully, avoiding body parts and corpses, past remnants of machinery and twisted wire. Once they were sure there was no sign of life, one of the troopers signalled the all-clear.

Hans spotted a hand protruding from the mud with something clenched in the fist. He bent down and gently unbound the dressing. It was a journal. Opening the cover, he read: *If found, please send to Miss Grace Phillips, Broadleigh Repat, Somerset, England.* Hans pushed the wrinkled leather-bound journal into his tunic pocket.

'I'll do my best.'

Whatever led Hans to undertake this act of kindness, one will never know. A simple act of humanity from one soldier to another on the field of war.

CHAPTER EIGHTEEN

November

Huddled together for warmth, beneath rags, five men lay on a cold stone floor, oblivious to the sound of guttural voices calling to one another above the din of engines. They stirred as a rush of air passed over them when the cell door was pulled open.

'Für dich ist der Krieg vorbei.' *For you, the war is over.* The guard placed a bucket on the floor.

Tom instinctively pulled his arm over his head. He heard more shouts, doors slamming shut and engines fading away until it was quiet except for the shallow rasp of his breath. He felt the rag pulled from his chest and mechanically grabbed hold and pulled it back. He opened his eyes and saw a man crawling towards the bucket. He rolled to his knees and followed.

The guard had left water and bread. Not the hard black bread they had survived on; it was soft and white. The two men tore at the loaf, plunged pieces in the water, sucked and swallowed.

~

'Stront! Wat voor de donder?' *Shit! What the hell?*

An International Red Cross man entered the cell. 'Are they alive?' he asked, as another bent to examine the prisoners.

'These three are, those two have gone.'

'Get stretchers, let's get them out of here. Henk, call the others, check the rest of the cells.'

Tom and two companions were tenderly lifted onto stretchers, covered in warm blankets, and taken to an ambulance. A cry caught in Tom's throat as the vehicle drove away from the camp.

~

Dazzled by the bright lights in the hospital, Tom became aware of sounds and people moving around him.

A nurse wiped crusty discharge from his eyelids. She bathed his face and neck with a warm flannel. He slipped in and out of consciousness. Salve was rubbed into his wounds by tender hands. They spoke softly to him, dressed him in woollen shirt and trousers; his feet, too damaged to fit into boots, were clothed in woollen socks and pumps. A nurse placed a cloth beneath his chin and put a spoonful of broth to his lips.

He felt the warmth on his tongue, the velvet texture of the egg-broth. He swallowed.

~

Days later, Tom and a fellow POW were wheelchaired down a long corridor to a brightly lit office. Two men stood behind a desk, one dressed in khaki the other in a grey uniform.

'Bring them in, please. Can you tell us your names?'

'Hvad hedder du?'

Neither replied.

'Where are you from? What nationality?'

'Hvor er du fra? Hvilken nationalitet?'

No response. The two officers frowned.

'Look, we're trying to help you. You're being cared for by the International Red Cross. We need to know where you are from so we can repatriate you.'

Tom's companion pointed to himself and then to Tom. 'British.'

~

'It's over!' Nancy bolted into the kitchen, where Grace and several nurses were having lunch.

'It's really over,' she whooped and danced around the table.

'Nancy, settle down, what are you talking about?' Grace asked.

'The war. The radio said they had declared an armistice, whatever that is, the fighting stopped at eleven o'clock today.'

The nurses hugged each other, too shocked to speak, while Nancy continued to whoop from ward to ward, announcing the end of the war. Shouts of joy erupted in her wake.

~

After weeks of heavy rain and fierce winds, the weather changed in the first week of December. Grace woke early to an eerie quietness. Thick fog swathed the grounds of Broadleigh. From her office window, she watched the postman delivering mail. Her stomach turned anxiously as she prayed and waited for a knock on her office door.

'Sister, there's a package arrived for you.'

'Thank you, Sybil.' With trembling hands, she picked it up and read across the top: British Red Cross. She stood as an unfamiliar feeling in the pit of her stomach made her tremble. Grace steadied herself by holding onto the edge of her desk until the dizziness subsided.

'Sister, are you alright?'

'I'm fine, thank you.' She slipped the package into her apron pocket and smoothed her uniform; she would open it later. Grace carried the package with her until her shift was over. She took one more look into the ward and assured that all was well before returning to her room. From the moment it arrived, she yearned to open it but somehow managed to hold herself in check while she was on duty. Now in the quiet and privacy of her room, she peeled away the brown paper to reveal the contents. Grace removed the rubber bands which held the worn covers together. Tears blurred her eyes. She wiped them away and breathed deeply to quell the pain which rose in her throat.

Tucked inside the front cover was a message from the British Red Cross:

This journal was handed to International Red Cross on 14th November 1918 by Gefreuter Hans Kepler.

She turned the pages towards the final entries and read.

13th October: I have only Corporal Cooper left of my original crew of orderlies. We are using the wounded who are unable to fight to aid in stretcher bearing. We have a dugout as the dressing station. We're almost out of clean dressings and no supplies are getting through. Even the rum ration is getting low, and I have nothing left for anaesthetic.

15th October: Amputation after amputation. Again, we are running low on chloroform and ether. Men die before I can get to them. There is little time for consultation ...

Grace found a piece of paper pressed into the back pages. She unfolded it carefully and read the purplish-blue writing:

My dearest darling,

If you receive this letter, it means that death has caught me. I beseech you to remember only the love and laughter we shared. I love you now and shall do so for eternity.

You are the only thing that fills my mind now. I never believed I would meet a woman like you. Before I met you, I was satisfied with a single life. You changed my mind and my life, my dearest love.

Remember me. Pray for me. Speak of me to your grandchildren; tell them I was just a man who did the best for his country and his people. My soul will be with you until it is your time to join me. But that will be an awfully long time. I rejoice that you are safely home in England. Forgive me for returning here. I knew I was needed and could not refuse the call.

Goodbye, my dearest darling. I really want you to have a happy life. Forget these terrible times, they will pass. Live the life you want. Find love again.

Until we meet again in Heaven,
With all my love, always,
Freddie.

There was no word for the pain that drilled through her chest. She held in her trembling hands the story of her lover's last moments, captured between life and death.

Part Three

AFTERMATH

CHAPTER NINETEEN

March 1920

Huddled beneath a soiled blanket, Arthur Skaggs woke as light streamed through the cracks in the boarded window. He sat up, staring groggily about. With dirty nails, he scratched his head, clawed at the hairs on his chest and armpits. 'Filthy little buggers,' he spat. Fighting vertigo, he grabbed a rail and hauled himself up rickety stairs. The door to the old cellar had almost rotted away, he kicked it open. A blast of frigid air made him gasp. A sudden sharp pain beneath his ribs radiated down his groin. He retched and doubled over and vomited. He tasted acid in his mouth as if his guts were fermenting. 'I need a bloody drink,' he growled, fumbling in his pockets, he found a couple of pennies. Scooping water from an old tub, he cleaned himself and trudged down the dismal road to town.

~

Arthur peered through the grimy windows at the jumble of items displayed in the pawn shop. Teapots, worn saucepans stacked chaotically amongst watches, clocks, a painting of a water mill and a woman in crinoline. The bell tinkled as he pushed open the shop door.

A wizened pawnbroker appeared from behind a curtain near the counter. 'Not you again,' his sneering voice adenoidal. 'So, what've you got for me today then?'

'I've nowt to sell today.'

'Ah, I see. Buying, are we? Found some coin, did we?'

'Ow much for the box?'

'The box?' The pawnbroker was beginning to enjoy himself. 'You mean the box your good lady brought in.' His fleshy tongue flicked past thin lips like a snake sensing its prey. He reached into the window and retrieved the silver box, stroking it salaciously. 'Three pounds.'

Arthur's skin felt alive with creatures crawling, biting, sucking his blood. He scratched with one hand while the other searched his pocket for the pawn ticket. When he found it, he waved it at the pawnbroker. 'Yer a bloody thief. Three shillin's is all you gave 'er for the soddin' box.'

A smile danced around heavy-lidded eyes as the pawnbroker returned the box to its place atop the books. He treasured moments like this when his skill and cunning drew out the meanness and desperation in his fellow creatures. He prided himself on the fact that he never gave the true value of a pawned article. He argued to the very last farthing knowing that every time he would win. Why else would these people come to him if they were not already at the end of their tether?

'Wait,' Arthur pleaded. 'I can get my 'ands on some good gear. What'll it take to get the box back?'

The pawnbroker waved his hands in a contemptuous gesture. 'As you see, my shop is filled with the flotsam and jetsam of many households. An item of luxury or triviality may be of interest.' He turned his back, chuckling to himself and keen for the game to continue.

Arthur shook with rage. He hated this despicable profiteer. He wanted the box. He craved it. It was the only thing he had left in the world. He had lost everything. He wasn't going to lose that. *She took my box. The mad cow.* 'His hands shook as he remembered the sensation of squeezing her neck.

Possessed by fury, Arthur snatched up a rusty flatiron and

brought it down heavily against the pawnbroker's skull. The force sent the pawnbroker's spectacles flying off his face. He crumbled to his knees. His fingers reached for the back of his skull. A second blow smashed through the bony layers, blood and brain tissue spewed from the wound. He groaned, fell face to the floor, his legs jerked grotesquely.

Arthur felt a strange exhilaration. He dragged the bleeding corpse behind the counter and through the curtain to the gloomy parlour. The pawnbroker's blood left a dark sticky trail across the dusty floorboards. He dashed back to the counter to find the cash box. 'Only a few coins. That cunning old bastard. Where's 'e stashed it?' He climbed over the dead body and pushed through a narrow gap to a small dark room at the rear. 'Gotta be here,' he grunted as he thrashed through the drawers of an old tallboy. Ripping out the newspaper lining the bottom drawer, he found the timbers loose. He wrenched them out to find bundles of notes. Arthur ran back into the shop and grabbed an old suitcase. He stuffed the case with cash. His heart pounded in his chest. His hands shook as he ripped off his bloodstained clothes. He rummaged around the boxes until he found some garments, pulled on a shirt and grey flannel jacket and trousers. He shoved his bloodstained clothes into the cast iron heater, tossed coal splinters on top and waited to see the flames catch. Satisfied, he threw some more clothes over the cash and fastened the suitcase, pulled his collar up and his cap low across his brow. 'Can't leave you behind,' he said, reaching for the silver box. The bell sounded a muffled ring as he pulled the door closed behind him.

~

Arthur jumped on a train and rested his throbbing brow against the carriage window. He stared without really seeing the ribbons of colour, sultry greens, and browns. The sun and cloud drifted across the dappled quilt of fields, swaying grasses swept by the wind. Dark shadows appeared from leafless woodlands creeping up the flank of the hill. His breath left steamy circles on the carriage windows.

He felt for the keepsake in his pocket. His hands trembled; teeth chattered, flapping wings filled his guts. How long had it been since his last drink?

They won't find 'er in a hurry. Made a lovely noise when she hit the bottom. I can just see her now, bobbin' around, all bloated like. I should 'a dropped that miserable thieving pawnbroker down there as well. They'll 'ave found 'im by now.

He glanced at the suitcase in the luggage rack above his head. His world seemed to have shifted slightly. The things which bound him to that filthy town no longer applied. He could be anyone. Anything was possible. No one to ask questions. No one to recognise him. Arthur Skaggs was no more.

~

He woke with a snort as the train pulled into Hereford Station. At the edge of the town, he was drawn to a small brick house, the garden overgrown with weeds and the gate hanging by a single hinge. He looked nervously over his shoulder, pushed open the gate and strode through the nettles and thistles. Newspaper lined the windows, so he could not see in. He found the door unlocked, stepped inside, and waited while his eyes adjusted to the shadows. The narrow hallway was bare; shapes, where pictures had once hung, stood out like pale apparitions against the grubby wall. He climbed the stairs, the air heavy with forlorn memories. He felt like a trespasser, unwelcome. He pushed open a door and stepped into the front bedroom. The air was putrid, a familiar smell to him. *Dead rat*. Stained curtains dimmed the light. He heard voices in the street. A woman calling a greeting, a man responding jovially. Arthur stepped away from the window. Floorboards creaked and a voice called.

'Is there someone there? Can I be of assistance?'

Arthur looked down at a wide, well-dressed man.

'Are you perhaps interested in leasing the property?' the wide man asked.

'I was just lookin',' he replied, descending the stairs.

'I see,' the wide man smiled an antiseptic smile. 'It's offered for a very reasonable price. I'm Cadbrooke. Property sales,' he said, proffering a gloved hand to Arthur.

''ow much?'

Cadbrooke unbuttoned his jacket and reached for a shiny pen. 'Sixty guineas for a twenty-four-month lease. May I show you through?'

Arthur nodded and followed him, taking little notice of the coaxing monologue.

'I'll take it,' Arthur interrupted. 'Fifty. Cash.'

'Done.'

~

Alice Bellamy leaned against the red brick wall of Railway Hall, it felt damp and cool across her shoulder blades; she shivered and pushed herself upright. She pinched out the end of her cigarette, extinguished the red ember and popped the remaining half back into the green Woodbine box.

Women gathered in small groups outside the hall. Alice acknowledged a few acquaintances with a wave of her hand but decided not to join them. The doors opened and the light from the hall cast a golden glow across the old warn steps. Inside it smelt stale and mildewed. She sat towards the back in the hope that the doors would stay open and let in fresh air.

Three middle-aged women sat at a trestle table on the stage. Behind them, a large green and red banner featuring three hammers and sickles caught Alice's attention.

A woman at the end of the table stood up and spoke. 'Welcome, sisters,' her gaze swept the room. 'We have fought for and now won the right to vote, but only those of us aged thirty or more, who are householders, or married to householders, can vote. Still, they hold us in shackles. We who have kept this country going while our men fought and died.'

A rumble of discontent swept the room.

'We have our first woman in the Parliament, all praise to Nancy Astor and her success. But who is she? A lady aristocrat? What will she know about the struggles of working women?'

Another rumble from the crowd. 'Who will look out for the workers?'

The speaker continued. 'The shackles of family, housework and even prostitution lie heavily on working women. Not to mention the women raped and abused, left widowed with illegitimates on the way and little bastards filling up our orphanages.'

The crowd hummed their disproval.

A second woman spoke. 'This war has been a tragedy of inconceivable proportions. Do you realise just how many of our menfolk have perished or are no longer fit and able persons? We face a future of spinsterhood.'

Murmurs from the crowd.

'So few men returned. What chance do you think you have to marry? To hold your own baby in your hands. One in ten of you is the answer. Happy homes, happy families are a thing of the past. We face an enormous struggle and will have to make our own way in the world as best as we can. We must fight for an equal chance to find and keep work.'

Clapping and cheering erupted.

When the third woman stood to speak, the crowd fell silent. She was an older woman renowned for her bravery and determination as a suffragette. She joined forces with the Pankhursts in 1911 to fight for women's rights and had suffered imprisonment and hunger strikes. Her name was Maud D'Lauren.

This was the woman Alice had come to listen to. She sat forward in her seat.

'Women of Britain, unite! Words are not enough. We must act now.'

The crowd roared.

~

Drawn by curiosity to the lights from the hall, Arthur stood with his back against the door, listening to speeches. He spat in disgust, muttering under his breath. The sound of chair legs scraping indicated the meeting was over. He slipped around the side of the building out of sight of the emerging crowd. His eyes narrowed when he saw Alice. Her red curls, highlighted by the lamplight. He watched her collect her bicycle and walk towards Back Lane. 'Bugger me,' he hissed. 'That's the Bellamy girl.'

~

As she pedalled her bicycle, Alice thought about the issues raised during the meeting. Maud D'Lauren advocated women become more involved in politics, support each other and gain equality with men. *Sadly, I think equality is still a long way off,* she thought.

Arriving home, she pushed open the gate and walked her bicycle up the garden path. A fleeting shadow caught her off guard. She turned quickly. 'Is there someone there?' The light was still on in the kitchen, she wondered if Tom was up but found the housekeeper knitting by the kitchen stove.

'Here, you're out late.'

Alice closed the door and pulled the curtains closed. 'It's only nine o'clock, Mrs C, anyway, I've been to a meeting. Where's Tom?'

'He went up an hour ago. Would you like a cup of tea? Everything alright?'

'Yes, thank you,' Alice sat down and pulled out her Woodbines, then, thinking better of it, pushed the packet back into her pocket.

'So, where have you been tonight?'

'Just out; nothing important. Mrs Chadwick, who's our Member of Parliament?'

The housekeeper laughed, surprised by Alice's question. 'It's Claude Bradfoot. You know, he's got that big white house at the top of Ayelstone Hill. Why do you ask?'

'As our Member of Parliament, what does he do? How does he know what the people want him to do? Have you ever met him? Has he ever asked anyone you know what they need?'

'That's a lot of questions, but now that you ask, no, I've never met him, well not personally. Why are you asking?'

'I can't say,' she sipped her tea.

Later as she lay awake in her bed, she began to formulate the conversation she planned to have with Claude Bradfoot MP.

~

A chill wind swept along the lane, but it did not deter Arthur from his position. 'So that's where the bastard lives, is it?' He remained by the gate for a while, watching until all the lights in the house went out.

~

The next day, Alice walked nervously along the white quartz driveway, past neat lawns and colourful rhododendrons, their pink and purple candles standing proud above deep green leaves. She felt nervous, as though a flock of pigeons were flapping around inside her stomach. She had thought this was a promising idea, but now she wondered about her commitment to the cause. She took a deep breath and walked past two marble peacocks, up the tiled steps to the impressive double mahogany doors and rang the bell.

A woman dressed in a tweed jacket and skirt, her hair swept back in a neat bun, opened the door. 'You're early.'

'Early?'

'Please, come in.'

Alice entered the impressive hallway. A large sparkling chandelier hung from the white plastered ceiling. She admired the timber panelled walls, festooned with colourful paintings of landscapes and ships at sea. Alice was particularly impressed with the floor tiles, patterned in deepest blue and crisp white.

'Come this way,' the woman led Alice through a door off the entrance hall. 'Do take a seat, Miss ...?'

'Bellamy. Alice Bellamy.'

'May I call you Alice?' the woman enquired as she opened a journal and dipped her pen in the inkwell.

'Yes, please do.'

'My name is Margaret Dawkins; I am Mr Bradfoot's private

secretary,' she smiled. 'Alice, tell me a little bit about yourself.'

'What would you like to know?'

'Well, what experience do you have? Are you working at present? Can you type?'

'Type?'

'Can you use a typewriter?'

'No, I was a lady groom. You know, for the war effort.'

'No matter, the typewriter is easily learned. More important is when can you start here? Mr Bradfoot has instructed me to secure a new office assistant as soon as possible.'

Alice was speechless. She tried to think of a way to explain that she had come to speak to Claude Bradfoot about social issues, not apply for a job. 'I can start on Monday.'

~

On the following Saturday morning, Tom finished his breakfast in the kitchen. 'Is that tray for Mother?' he asked.

'Yes, I'm just going to pop it in her room.'

'Allow me,' he said, taking the tray. 'It's me, Mother. Is it alright to come in?'

'Yes, darling.'

Tom placed the tray on the bedside table and kissed his mother gently on the cheek. 'Shall I pull back the curtains? It promises to be a fine day.'

Ellen patted the eiderdown. 'Come and sit by me.'

'Let me pour you some tea first,' he replied.

He watched her sip the tea. Her thin, white fingers, the delicate sweep of her eyelashes against her pale cheeks and her soft, silver-grey hair, he thought she appeared almost diaphanous.

'Are you well rested? Is Mrs Chadwick looking after you?'

'Yes, of course.' Tom stood and looked out the window. 'I think I'll go for a walk today.'

'Well, be sure to wrap up, won't you?'

~

Tom arrived at the station master's house. The latch slipped neatly back into its cup as he pushed the wire gate closed behind him. A crazy-paved path, between two herbaceous borders, led to the front door. He knocked twice.

Matthew Phillips' inquisitive blue eyes appraised the visitor.

Tom removed his hat. 'Good morning, sir. I'm a friend of Percy's, Thomas Bellamy. Is this a convenient time?'

'Please come in, Mr Bellamy. Percy has stepped out; he'll be back any minute.'

Tom ducked his head as he entered and followed Matthew down the hallway.

'Take a seat in the parlour, if you please, I'll just see if Mrs Phillips has got the kettle on.'

A loud, 'Bugger it,' surprised Tom.

'You've got a visitor,' whispered Matthew, pointing to the parlour.

'Tom,' Percy grinned, setting his walking stick against the wall before taking Tom's hand in both of his. Grace stood smiling in the doorway; her cheeks flushed.

'What're you doing in here? Pa, is the kettle on? I could murder a cuppa tea,' Percy winked at Tom and led the way to the kitchen.

Sarah pulled a tea cosy over the big brown teapot and straightened her pinny. She had already set a tray with a teacup, saucer and two currant biscuits on a small plate.

'Do you remember my old school chum, Tom Bellamy?'

'How d'you do, Mr and Mrs Phillips,' Tom said, extending his hand.

'Of course, you know Gracie already.'

'How are you, Grace?'

'Well, thank you, and you?' She sat at the table, motioning for Tom to do the same.

'Where are my manners? Do sit down, Mr Bellamy,' said Sarah. 'Unless you'd be comfier in the parlour?'

'Ma ...' Percy and his mother exchanged glances. 'Got any more of those biscuits? After this morning's escapades, I've worked up an appetite.'

'What's happened?' asked Sarah.

'The usual display of total ignorance.' Percy loosened his collar. 'I can take their nasty looks and snide remarks about me, but when they start on Grace, well, it makes my blood boil.' He munched hard on a biscuit.

Grace sighed. 'It's just the way things are, Percy. Don't let it upset you so.'

'Grace, I wish you wouldn't go out shopping. I can manage it,' said Sarah.

'No, you can't, Ma. Standing in long queues for groceries will do you no good at all. Anyway, I'm sure Tom doesn't want to hear about this. He's come to see Percy, not listen to our grumbles.'

'No, that's fine. I am sorry to hear that you are experiencing such unpleasantness.' *Oh, that sounds awful,* he thought.

'Come on, Tom. I could do with blowing off a bit of steam. Fancy a pint?'

Tom rose to make his farewells. 'Mr and Mrs Phillips, thank you for your hospitality. Grace, it was lovely to see you again.'

'Yes, it was nice to see you, too,' she smiled. 'You are looking well.'

Tom remembered the same sad but lovely eyes of this woman who had nursed him during his stay at the repatriation hospital. 'Thank you, Grace. You are looking well too.' He realised that may have been insensitive and blushed.

'Let's go, Tom,' said Percy pulling himself off the chair. 'Blasted thing, gets stiff when I've sat too long; a walk will do me good.' He took his stick and cap from the hall stand, hesitated in front of the mirror for a moment, then pulled his cap low across his left cheek.

Tom watched and wondered how his friend had sustained such a terrible injury. They walked, silently at first, the regular tap of Percy's stick setting the rhythm to their step. The midday sun was warm, Tom took off his jacket and folded it into the crook of his arm; Percy took off his jacket too, hooked a finger through the loop and draped it over his shoulder. They stopped outside the Craven Arms. 'Shall we?' said Percy with a grin.'

Why not?' replied Tom. 'It's nearly one, apart from those few biscuits, I've had nothing since breakfast.'

Inside, a strong smell of hops and cigarette smoke was too much for Tom. 'I'm not so sure this is a clever idea, Percy,' he said as they waited at the bar.

'What'll it be, gents?' asked the landlord.

'Do you have any food?'

'I can do you a nice cheese and pickle sandwich and I got some pickled eggs?'

Tom nodded. 'No eggs for me, thank you.'

'Two sandwiches, one with eggs, half a Porters Ale for me. Tom? What about half a cider? And we'll sit out the back.'

'Right you are, one and eight pence, please.'

'I'll get it,' said Percy, placing the coins in the landlord's palm.

They found a small table in the back courtyard amongst large barrels and a wire bin full of old bottles.

Percy rolled a cigarette and offered it to Tom as the landlord set their drinks on the table.

'Lovely day for it,' he said, placing an ashtray in front of them.

'No, thank you. Not keen on cigarettes.'

The two men clinked glasses. 'To ...' Percy couldn't find words to finish the toast.

'Surviving,' added Tom.

Percy licked the creamy foam off his lip. 'Everything all right, Tom?'

'Yes, fine. I haven't had a drink for a long while.' He turned the glass around on the table, it left dark circles on the scarred wood. He raised the glass to look at the straw-yellow liquid, which was cloudy; sediment had gathered in the bottom of the glass. The aroma reminded him of the orchard near his house in winter, when as a child, he and Percy played fruit-fights with fallen apples, dotted with white mould. They made wonderful missiles and when one found its target, the apple burst into a spray of sticky syrup and brown flesh.

'That's a good drop of Old Dora's you've got there,' Percy smiled. 'Made right here in Cartwright's Cider Mill. I can vouch for it myself.'

Tom sipped the cider. It was delicious; the flavour of sweet apples and tangy citrus and after he swallowed the first sip, the aftertaste was mellow, bittersweet.

'You're working back at the cider mill?'

'Yes, Old Mr Cartwright's a saint. He'd left a message for me to come and see him once I got home. Gave me a job in the office. Accounts, can you imagine it?' he shrugged. 'Well, I'm grateful for it. With a face like this and a bung leg, I couldn't expect much more. I would have loved to get back to engineering, though. I learned a lot about motor mechanics over the last year and would have liked to put that into practice.'

'At least it's a job. I have no prospects at all unless you consider what my father has in mind for me.'

Percy subconsciously rubbed the purple puckered flesh which ran from the lower lid of his left eye down across his cheek to the corner of his mouth.

Tom wanted to ask him how that had happened but just as he was searching for the words, the landlord arrived with two plates of sandwiches and Percy's pickled eggs.

'Anything else I can get you, gents?'

'No thank you, we're fine,' said Percy, picking up one of the sandwiches and biting into it.

Tom approached his sandwich carefully. 'Still a bit sensitive,' he said, patting his stomach. The meal over, he sat back in his chair and wiped his forehead where little beads of sweat gathered. He felt warm and relaxed. 'Very nice, but I'm not sure I shall manage to walk home if I drink anymore,' he said, draining his glass. 'What happened this morning? Do you want to talk about it?'

'It's these damn busybodies with nothing better to do than

make spiteful comments and cause grief. Honestly, if only they knew what Grace went through. That's what makes me so mad. The fools call her rude names and this morning, one of them deliberately bumped Grace and knocked her basket clean out of her hands. That's when I saw red!'

'There is a lot of ignorance, I'm afraid,' Tom sipped his drink.

'D'you know she was one of the first nurses to go to France? She left before me, in fact. She spent three and a half years there, dodging bullets, working day and night in terrible conditions and always her first concern was for the men dying and injured all around her. I know, I saw it for myself when I was found, by some miracle, by Grace and Freddie, after …' Percy shifted awkwardly on his seat.

'I hadn't realised Grace was in France. Who is Freddie? Was that her husband?'

'Not her husband, but the father of her child. He was a good man. Grace says he didn't know she was pregnant when he returned to the front for what turned out to be the last time.'

'Dear God,' Tom whispered.

'Missing, presumed dead. He'd taken her back to England with a bunch of patients in August '18; he knew it was going to get bad. He transformed his country house into the repatriation hospital. Well, you know all about that, you saw it yourself. Anyway, he could have stayed with her but when the big push was on at Artois last October, he returned to the front.'

'Missing? What about his papers, was nothing found?'

'You'd have to see it to know what it was like out there. The quagmire, the mud just sucked men down. There will be thousands upon thousands who'll never be found.' Percy took a long drag on his cigarette. 'You'd be on watch and there, not three yards in front of you, the wet surface would start to sort of bubble, and next, a corpse or bits of it would suddenly appear.' Percy shook his head. 'It wasn't killing like I ever thought it would be. Not war. It was a pointless bloody massacre. You can't imagine what it was like.'

'You're quite right, I can't imagine.'

'Sorry, old friend, I didn't mean ... As it turned out, they did find something of Freddie's, his journal. Even more peculiar is that it was a German soldier who found it. He handed it to the Red Cross, and they sent it to Grace.'

'How remarkable.'

'D'you see what I mean. It's been really hard on her and yet she keeps going. That's why it's so bloody unfair that she has to put up with this shit.'

'This will sound awkward; I'm having trouble finding the words. I think what I'm trying to say is that you and Grace have experienced a far different war than I. It seems so long ago since I was at Sandhurst. In some ways, I imagine I was turning into one of Crabbe's tin soldiers. There was so much pomp and ceremony. Thorough training, of course, as well. We learned to fight with a sword and rifle. In hindsight, that was wasted; it was a different show when we got there. The cavalry conducted reconnaissance, guarded the flanks, defended the rear, charged approaching enemy formations. But it soon became clear that we were not the most effective force against a static enemy line. In October, I rode out, the battle ground was at La Bassee. We faced an unbroken German line of rifle, machine gun, and artillery fire. My mount saved my life. She reared up when a shell exploded in front of us. I was thrown to the ground, covered in her blood, presumed dead, left by my companions and taken prisoner.'

He wiped sweat off his brow. 'You see, I only spent three months fighting in battle; I know nothing of the horrors you and Grace experienced. In my mind, I feel I didn't fulfil my duty; that I still have a job to finish.'

'Don't say that. You left out the bit about how you then spent the remaining years fighting to survive. You don't owe anybody anything.'

'Well, that may be the case, who knows? I'm tired.' Tom sighed.

'D'you want to talk about the camps?'

'No, not yet. It's hard to find the words. I need to get home, I think. Let's meet again soon.'

They shook hands outside the pub. 'Would you like me to walk you home?'

'No, I'm fine.'

'Alright. See you soon then,' said Percy turning, leaning heavily on his stick.

As Tom watched Percy walk away, he wondered what had happened to him, where he had sustained his injuries. Would they ever find the resolve to be able to speak about their experiences? There was so much he did not know, so much that was unclear. Four years of war passed while he was in the prison camp; they received little news. Some men received packages and letters. New prisoners were the only source of information, and they came in regularly enough. Arthur had a way of getting what news there was thanks to his work in the kitchen and mess hall. Usually, the men were so distraught they could only tell of the fear and loss in battle. They rarely communicated any strategic intelligence.

My God! A thought suddenly occurred to Tom. *Arthur said he'd given my details to the Red Cross doctor after I'd been beaten.*

If he'd really given my name and corps details, how come I didn't hear from my family? Surely someone would have been in touch with them. Is that why I never received any mail or any packages? Did he have anything to do with me being sent on to that hell hole in Hochfenitz?

Walking along familiar streets, the nightmare of his incarceration seemed a lifetime away. Although his hometown appeared untouched and unchanged, there was something about the disposition of the people. Did each passer-by look at him with sideways glances? Was it suspicion? Surely not fear. He thought again about Percy's exasperation towards the women who had taunted Grace. *How can I help them? There must be something I can do.*

CHAPTER TWENTY

Tom took his time walking home and was still deep in thought when he arrived at the front gate of the house and was surprised to see an unfamiliar motor car parked there. This was no ordinary car; certainly not the black Bentley his father travelled in. Deep blue side panels, red wheels, highly polished brass round-topped radiator. *What a beauty,* Tom thought as he walked around the side of the house to the kitchen, where he found a jubilant Mrs Chadwick setting a tray with freshly baked scones.

'You've got a visitor,' she beamed, picking up the tray. 'In the dining room.'

'Major Crabbe!'

'My dear boy,' the two men embraced. 'I've been chatting to your mother.'

'Are you sure you're warm enough sitting in front of that open window, Ma'am?'

'Yes, Maisie, thank you,' replied Ellen.

'I'll get you a wrap, just in case,' she said, placing a tray of warm scones, jam, and cream on the table.

'Mmm, they do smell good, thank you, Mrs Chadwick,' said Crabbe. 'Well, my boy, it is good to see you. I waited for a few days to give you a chance to settle back home again.' Crabbe appraised Tom's emaciated features.

'I say, that's a pretty nifty looking motor car you have parked out the front.'

'It is. Goes like the clappers. Oh, pardon my language, dear Mrs Bellamy. She's a Morris Oxford Bullnose, 1018 cc four-cylinder side-valve engine. Not that means a great deal to an old equestrian like me, of course. I slip her into gear, put the foot on the accelerator and off she flies.' Crabbe laughed. 'Fancy a little jaunt to Llancillow, Tom? After these delicious scones, of course.'

'I'll say.'

~

Either side of the road, hedgerows grew tall enough to touch the lower boughs of the trees. Dappled light reflected off the shiny car bonnet.

'It's like driving through a tunnel,' said Tom, pulling his cap down and tying his scarf tighter around his neck.

Crabbe slowed the car as they approached the property. 'D'you mind getting the gate?'

Tom jumped out of the car and held the gate open as Crabbe drove through. He noticed the old sign had been replaced with a simple board which read: 'Crabbe's Farm – Fresh Produce Available.'

'The crops are coming along nicely, oats in the left field and barley in the right. The house garden is now devoted to cabbages, potatoes, and carrots. We have the ladies from the land army to thank for the vegetables.'

'What about the horses?'

'I still keep a paddock for those that remain. You'll remember old Punch and one of the pit ponies, Elvira, of course. In 1915 the two lower fields were set to crops. By the middle of that year, the country experienced severe shortages. Not only food, two of my poor old hacks were commandeered for war service, they'd have taken Elvira, but she put up a rather good show of temperament so was deemed unsuitable.'

The house, with its glorious castellated roof and crown of ivy, came into view. It was just as Tom remembered it. The tyres crunched along the gravel drive coming to a stop at the front porch. The dogs gave a token bark, wagging their tails to greet their master and sniffing at Tom's trousers. The male cocked his leg and peed over the rear wheel of the car as a dour looking woman appeared in the doorway.

'Gerroff, Shep,' grumbled Crabbe. 'Ah, Mrs Foggerty.'

'I'll get the kettle on.'

'We'll stretch our legs first, thank you, we'll be in shortly.'

The men walked towards the paddock to the east of the house, where a long lane of pens stood empty. Crabbe pointed with his stick. 'These were all erected for the Army Remount Service in fifteen. Well, you'd know all about that as your sister was stationed here.'

'Yes, Alice mentioned that briefly, although we've had hardly any time to talk in the last couple of days.'

'Fine troop of young women they were,' said Crabbe, gazing at the lengthy line of pens. 'We had more than a thousand horses here over the years.'

They walked for a while until Crabbe said, 'Well, we best get in. I don't want Mrs Foggerty chasing me.'

~

Crabbe stood with his back to the fire, poking his pipe with a matchstick, then sucking on the mouthpiece as he waved the lighted match over the bowl. He let out a puff of smoke, an aromatic spice, hung in the air.

The housekeeper brought in a tea tray. 'What time would you like supper? And will young sir be staying?'

'You're very welcome to stay. Plenty of room. I'm sure Mrs Foggerty won't mind making up a bed.'

'Already done, sir.'

'There you are, won't you stay? You can telephone home and let them know where you are.'

'Well, if you're sure it's no trouble, I'd love to.'

~

As evening set in. Crabbe pulled the curtains closed and stoked up the fire. 'Well, I'm going to have a whisky. What about you, my boy?'

'Perhaps a small one, with water, please.'

Tom settled back into the comfortable armchair. The gaslights shed a mellow light; he thought how little the room had changed since his last visit all those years ago. Leather-bound tomes still adorned the bookshelves, the farrier's axe remained in its place on the wall. Something was missing, though, *what was it?* Tin soldiers. 'I was just thinking how comforting it is to see that some things never change but I remembered the tin soldiers you had on the table next to the bookshelf.'

'Yes, put away.' Crabbe set his pipe aside. 'And you, my boy, how are you adjusting to being home again?'

'Everything seems so untouched and yet there is something I can't quite put my finger on. It's in the faces of the people I meet, a look in their eyes.'

'This war has been like nothing we've ever experienced before, and the consequences are far reaching.' Crabbe paused to take a sip from his glass. 'The flower of our nation's youth sent to their graves, while, some say, generals remained safely behind lines. Young men slaughtered in stupid battles led by stupid generals.'

Tom was surprised by Crabbe's words and leaned forward in his seat, anxious to engage in a meaningful conversation about the war.

'Everyone was full verve when it all started, spoiling for the fight. We thought it would be all over by Christmas, how wrong we all were. There is hardly a family in Britain not touched by this experience. Even in our little village here, everywhere you went, you would see it, haggard women bent from weeping. One simply stopped asking after their sons or husbands, dreading the response. And now the figures are coming out. It's staggering and beggars belief.' Crabbe reached for the newspaper. 'Here it is ... over one million soldiers of the British Empire dead; forty-one thousand returned, maimed for life with one or more limbs amputated, and this figure is astounding, more than one hundred and sixty thousand are missing, presumed dead.' Crabbe shook his head. 'Ten thousand blinded and eleven thousand who will never work again as their lungs were ravaged by gas. Gas, I ask you, what kind of evil fiend decided gas was a rational weapon to implement in the rules of war? And now there's this new damn thing. This insidious ailment that affects so many of the returned men. They're calling it shell shock. Not bloody surprising! I've heard stupid generals referred to it as malingering. D'you know they even shot them. Executed their own men. Can you believe it? Shot them because they were shell shocked!'

Crabbe noticed that Tom was pale and quiet. 'I'm sorry, my boy. Forgive the ravings of an old soldier.'

'Not at all, most people I meet avoid the subject or skirt around it. I can see in their eyes that they want to ask me questions, but they don't. Perhaps they are trying to save my feelings. It's damn frustrating. I appreciate this opportunity, please don't let me interrupt you.'

'I can't imagine what you've been through. Would you like to talk about it?'

'I would but it's finding the words ...'

'Take your time, my boy. Here, let me refresh your glass.'

Perhaps it was the drink, or the old familiar surroundings, or just the simple fact that he was in the company of a man he deeply respected. The words Tom had struggled to find began to flow. He spoke of the battles in early the months of the war. The exhilarating cavalry charges, the camaraderie of the men, the devastating losses. He explained how his own horse reared up when a shell had exploded in front of him, ripping apart the horse's gut. Shrapnel embedded in his neck and shoulder, he fell to the ground unconscious and was left for dead by his retreating corps members.

Crabbe listened intently. Now came the difficult part. He had not spoken about his incarceration with anyone except the army officials after recovering in the repatriation hospital. They were not interested in detail. Simply where, when, and how he got out. Tom suddenly thought about Grace. He had a vision of her face, gently smiling encouragement.

'I was taken prisoner at La Bassee.' He looked at Crabbe, who nodded reassurance. 'In a camp hospital to begin with. They cleaned me up, fixed up wounds and dug out shrapnel. It was there that I discovered my identity tag and papers were missing.'

'Ah, that explains why your parents received the letter advising you were missing, presumed dead.'

'Poor Mother. I wasn't there long, maybe a week. Next stop was the camp. It was basic; they put us to work building huts, erecting fences. It seems ironic when you look back that we were building our own prison.'

'I don't think the Germans had any idea how the war would turn. They certainly had not planned to take prisoners; they simply did not have the facilities. I read that the Germans held over 2 million prisoners by 1918,' Crabbe swirled the liquid in his glass. 'Please go on.'

'It was bitterly cold that first winter. We were all glad when finally, the huts were waterproof, and we could sleep in the dry. By spring, I began to plan my escape. I'd been selected to work with a blacksmith on a nearby farm. I owe the smith a great deal. I often wonder what happened to him. He helped us escape, me and another prisoner. Anyway, we got out easily enough. Ran for our lives. Reached the river but they were onto us. We could hear their shouts, dogs barking and whistles blowing. It was the river that defeated us in the end. The current was too strong; Skaggs, the other prisoner, wasn't much of a swimmer.'

'Next thing I remember, I was being treated by a Swiss doctor from Red Cross. I owe him my life. Once I could walk again, I was put on shit-cart duty,' Tom instinctively screwed up his nose in memory of the disgusting stench associated with this work. 'I can't remember how long, but out of the blue one day, a cluster of lorries turned up and about eighty of us were herded onto them. The camp was overcrowded, you see,' Tom felt the panic rise. 'Eighty men walked into the camp at Hochfenitz but only a handful of us came out.'

Crabbe made a sharp sound a bit like stifling a hiccup; his face was hot and red; he pulled out a handkerchief from his trouser pocket and blew his nose hard as a tear slid from his eye.

'The match case you gave me. I managed to keep it safe for so long, I buried it deep in my straw mattress. Right up until I was taken away to Hochfenitz.'

The fire slowly diminished in the hearth as they talked long into the night. They spoke of the age of innocence, before the war, where people went about their lives with humdrum joys and customary despairs, completely unaware of what was about to befall them. They talked of the wave upon wave of young men, who sang hearty songs as they marched off to battle, and how that changed towards the end, where scepticism crept in, and the singing ended. They discussed the savagery of the war, unlike any experienced before. How it had left a deep scar on the nation and left a shadow of death on almost every family. The shock of so many lives cut short echoed through social and political platforms. They debated whether anything positive had evolved through the catastrophe. The advances in technology and medical science were worthy of acknowledgement. They considered the opportunities that might be gained through social change as both men and women protested for justice and moral rights.

Although Tom felt the conversation cathartic, he and Crabbe finally succumbed to the hour. As grey ash settled on the grate, they bid each other goodnight and went to their beds.

~

The next morning Tom awoke to birdsong, surprised to find that it was already eight o'clock. He washed and dressed then made his way downstairs to the aroma of bacon cooking.

'Good morning, Mrs Foggerty.'

'There's tea in the pot on the dresser. Will you 'ave an egg with your breakfast?' she called without turning from the stove.

'Yes, thank you.'

'I'll bring it in. Major Crabbe's down to the horses already.'

By the time Crabbe came in, Tom had finished his breakfast and was mopping up the plate with a piece of bread and butter.

'Good breakfast?'

'Excellent, thank you. I hadn't realised how hungry I was. I think I'm getting my appetite back.'

The housekeeper came in to collect the dishes and Tom thanked her. 'Will there be anythin' else?'

'No, thank you, Mrs Foggerty, we'll be off soon. Ready, Tom?'

Crabbe opened the garage door to reveal the Morris parked next to another familiar car.

'You still have the Crossley,' said Tom, running his hand along the bonnet.

'Yes, she's ready to be put out to paddock, I think.'

'What's wrong with her?'

'Darned if I know. Can't find a decent mechanic.'

'I could ask Percy. I'm sure he would be happy to look.'

'Splendid idea, my boy,' he said, tossing Tom the keys for the Morris. 'You drive, don't you?'

'I'm not sure.'

'Never a better time to find out.'

After crunching the gears several times, Tom got the hang of things and found great delight in driving the car.

'Whoa, watch your speed, my boy.' Crabbe cautioned as they approached a narrow bend. 'That's it, ease off the pedal a bit. You say Percy has mechanical knowledge?'

'Yes, he took instruction in motor mechanics and was

hoping to be able to work in the field. As it happens, he is working at the cider mill in the accounts department. He's not happy about it, thinks it's due to his scarred face and dodgy leg.'

'Oh, my word.'

'I caught up with him yesterday. We had a drink together. Would you believe his sister was the nurse who cared for me when I was first repatriated? We didn't recognise each other back then; of course, at that stage, I wasn't communicating fully.'

'Well, I never. Watch out for that puddle; sometimes, they're deeper than you think. The road is pretty rough at this point.'

Tom concentrated on driving.

'Are you pressed for time this morning?'

'No. I am going to look for work but apart from that, I don't have any commitments this morning.'

'Jolly good, I think we should pop into the Council Office and secure a driver's licence for you. If you get Percy to come and look at the Crossley and if he can get it going, you could use it for a while. Do you have five shillings for the licence?'

'Not on me, I'm afraid.'

'No matter, let's go and get the licence, you can pay me back next time.'

~

A few days later, Tom telephoned Major Crabbe to let him know that Percy could look at the car on Saturday morning.

'That would be ideal, thank you, Tom.'

'I hope you won't think I'm being impertinent if I asked your permission to invite Percy's sister to come along, I believe she could do with a trip to the countryside.'

'Please do invite them. Will you manage the train to Pontrilas? I will get Bert Wallace to bring you to Llancillow in his new taxicab.'

'Perfect, thank you.'

~

On Saturday morning, Crabbe waited in the courtyard.

Percy and Tom helped Grace down from the car.

'Good morning, Major. May I introduce Miss Grace Phillips and you remember Percy?'

'Indeed,' said Crabbe, shaking Percy's hand before turning his attention to Grace. 'My dear, a pleasure to meet you,' said Crabbe, his eyes searching hers yet his voice compassionate and courteous.

'Well, dear boy, Tom tells me you have come to liberate my troubled Lady Crossley.'

'I'll certainly give it a try,' Percy laughed.

'But where are my manners? Can I offer you tea? I'm afraid Mrs Foggerty has been called away but I'm sure I can find the kettle and then I will introduce the gentlemen to the challenge.'

'I'll make the tea,' said Grace.

'Splendid. Come this way, gentlemen.'

~

'Can you try that one more time, Major?' Percy leaned over the Crossley's engine.

'Still no spark.'

'Can you manage without me for a few minutes?' asked Tom.

'Yes, of course,' said Percy as he deftly removed a spark

plug. 'Let's see what this little blighter has got to say for itself.'

Tom found Grace in the kitchen.

'Hello, the kettle's boiled. Are you ready for tea yet?' She asked.

'I think they'll be a while. Percy's in his element back there and the Major seems delighted with the prospect of his pride and joy being resurrected.'

'It is so lovely here,' she said, gazing out towards the hills. 'What a splendid place to live.'

'Yes, this house has been in the Crabbe family for generations, I believe. When Percy and I first came here, it was a refuge for old horses.'

'That's right, I remember Percy telling me how you and he had come out to visit an old dray. Didn't you come out on your bicycles?'

'We did. We had some adventures in those days. I returned regularly after that first visit. The Major taught me to ride in exchange for helping out, you know mucking out the stables and wot-not,' he smiled as Grace wrinkled her nose. 'The horse I learned to ride on is still here. Come to think of it, old Punch, the dray, is also still around and one of the pit ponies. Would you like to see them?'

'Yes, please.'

Tom offered his arm to Grace, and together, they walked to the paddock, stopping to pick up a handful of twisted carrots from the sack near the stable on the way. 'You're not frightened of horses, are you?'

'Not if you are with me,' Grace replied.

As soon as they entered the paddock, Elvira trotted up to them, snorting and nodding her head. Tom held out a carrot on his flat palm and she took it, munching and snickering at the same time. He patted her neck and spoke to her tenderly in a low voice.

'May I try?' Grace held out her hand. The horse shook her head and stepped backwards.

Tom spoke softly close to Elvira's neck. 'It's alright, old girl. Grace is a friend. Try again; hold your hand out flat, that's it.'

'Here come the others.' With legs like tree trunks, Punch plodded towards them. In contrast, the little pit pony trotted lightly at his side.

'Goodness, he's huge.'

'Don't worry, he's very gentle. Aren't you, old boy?' Tom allowed the enormous head to nuzzle his neck, the coarse hair of his grey mane falling like a shawl. He scratched and rubbed the dray's massive shoulder while the little pony nudged Tom's pocket. 'Hello, I know what you're looking for,' he said, pulling out a carrot. He shared the last of the carrots between the three horses. With a final pat for each of them. 'Shall we go?'

As they walked back to the house, Grace said, 'There is something special about this place. I haven't been here long but already I feel safe. Does that sound strange?'

'I believe it has a lot to do with the Major. He is kind and generous in so many ways.'

'You seem very fond of him.'

'I am. I suppose you could call him my mentor and benefactor. He taught me to ride, shared his knowledge and passion for horses. He's an old cavalryman, you know. More than anything, he is a great moral support to me, both when I was growing up and since my return.'

'How lucky you are, Tom, to find someone both wise and compassionate.'

He turned to look at her and noticed that her cheeks had coloured a little, just like the blush on a peach. They sat quietly watching the white clouds scudding above purple hills beyond.

'I can't tell you how much I appreciate you bringing us out here today,' her eyes were soft and sad.

Tom looked away to the hills as the clouds cast their shadows, the deep mauves and greys intensified on the landscape. He tried to imagine her light-hearted, laughing, in love. He reached for her hand, surprising her.

Grace snatched her hand away and hurried back towards the house with Tom trailing after her.

'Oh, there you are, just in time for tea,' Percy's laughter fell away. 'Grace, love, what is it?'

She fell against Percy's shoulder, her tears soaking his shirt.

'I'll leave you in peace,' Crabbe said, adding, 'Oh, my dear girl.' He found Tom in the garden. 'Ah, there you are, my boy. Grace is in the kitchen with Percy. Let's give them a bit of privacy.'

'Of course.' Tom looked forlorn. 'I didn't mean to upset her.'

Crabbe shook his head. 'I think life has treated her very poorly and I imagine she has a great more suffering to go through yet.'

'She nursed me back to health; she was so kind to me in the hospital.'

'It's astonishing how life can catch you unawares sometimes.'

'Whatever will become of her? How will she manage a child with no father?'

'Her family seem nice; I'm sure they will support her.'

'Yes, they're good people. But that's not what I mean. I watched her today when I met them at the train station. She looked nervously up and down the platform as though she was expecting taunts. She's too good for the spiteful treatment being meted out to her,'

'Take the car and drive back to Hereford. I had no idea Grace was met with such awful behaviour. It will be much more comfortable for her in the car. And you can keep it for a few days, now you have the licence.'

'Hello?' called Percy.

'We're out here,' Tom replied. 'How is Grace?'

'She's asked me to apologise to you both.' Percy grinned sheepishly.

'Oh, Perc, she mustn't apologise.'

'Agreed,' said Crabbe. 'She's a fine young woman. C'mon, I'm more than ready for my tea now.' Crabbe stood and rubbed his arthritic knees.

~

'Is that you, Tom?' Ellen called as she heard the front door open.

'Yes, Mother.'

'Come in, dear. I want to hear all about your day.'

Tom found Ellen sitting on a sofa by the window. She patted the cushioned seat and he sat next to her. 'You look troubled. Is everything alright?'

'Yes, it's been a long day.'

'I can see something is vexing you.'

'I'm just very tired. I need to take a nap. Please excuse me, Mother.' He kissed her cheek, closed the door softly and went upstairs to his room. He pulled the heavy drapes across the window and sat at the end of his bed. In the dim light, he surveyed the room. *Where are all my things? The dresser is full of new underclothes, socks and woollen sweaters. New shirts and trousers in the wardrobe, new leather slippers. All new. Where are my greatcoat and grey woollen shirt and trousers the nurses gave me? Where are my old books and pictures and paintings that used to hang on this wall?*

Only one book remained on the bookshelf, his old school dictionary. *How did that survive?* He lay back on the bed and stared at the ceiling. In no time, he was asleep.

~

Next morning, Tom went down for breakfast and just caught Alice before she left.

'Good morning,' she said, kissing him on the cheek. 'I'm off to work, see you this evening.' She picked up an apple and left through the kitchen door.

'Work? What?'

'She's got herself a job. You're looking very smart. Going somewhere special?'

Tom knew better than to try and hoodwink the wily housekeeper. 'I'm going into town, actually.'

'Righto,' she said, continuing to shell peas. 'Will you be back for supper?'

'I'm not sure.'

'I'll leave you something in the pantry, just in case,' she continued shelling while Tom pulled out a chair.

'Mrs C, I've been meaning to ask you. Do you know where my greatcoat is?'

'Yes, I've put it in the cedar box in the cupboard under the stairs.'

'I've got to hand it back. They'll give me a pound when I do. Oh, there haven't been any letters for me, have there?'

'No, not as I've seen. Are you expecting something?'

'My war service gratuity payment, the second one must be due about now.'

She put away the peas, wiped her hands and sat opposite him. 'Is something troubling you?'

'I'm a bit short of money. I went for a job interview at the flour mill the other day, but I don't think I'm what they're looking for.'

'I see. Have you thought about asking your father?'

'No. I don't want to ask him.'

'Well, let me see ...'

'Goodness, no, Mrs C, I don't want you to give me any money.' Tom scraped the chair as he quickly rose. 'I'm off out now.' *How embarrassing. I'll get a job somehow. Although the truth is I have no skills apart from those learned for war. A fat lot of good that will do me now.*

~

Tom walked into town. Up ahead, he saw a line of men outside the Shire Hall.

'Excuse me. What's this queue for?'

A gruff man, with a deep scar across his forehead, pointed to a sign above the entrance to the building:

THE COUNTY SURVEYOR OF HEREFORDSHIRE
LABOURERS WANTED
PRIORITY GIVEN TO RETURNED SOLDIERS

MUST BE FIT
STEAMROLLER DRIVERS: 36s 6d per week
TRACTOR DRIVERS: 29s 6d per week
GENERAL LABOURERS: 25s 6d per week
NO EXPERIENCE NECESSARY
TOOLS SUPPLIED
APPLY WITHIN

Tom joined the back of the queue. *Well, I can drive. Maybe I can get a job driving a steamroller.*

The gruff man turned to Tom. 'Got a light?'

'Yes,' Tom struck a match and held it under the man's cigarette. He noticed how the skin around the scar was grotesquely furrowed. 'Where d'you get that?'

'Mons.'

'I was at Mons.'

'Yer?' The man turned back to his companion.

Twenty minutes passed before the queue started to move towards the open door. The street was in full sunlight, he felt sweat gather in his armpits and dampen his back. Finally, he was through the door, and it was his turn to speak to two men sitting behind a desk in the foyer.

'Name?'

'Thomas Bellamy.'

'Bellamy?' the man writing notes looked up at Tom.

'Yes.'

'What position are you applying for?' the second man asked.

'Steam roller driver.'

'There's only labourer positions left.'

'Alright, I'll apply for that.'

'Are you fit?' asked the first man.

'Yes,' Tom replied.

The two men conferred quietly.

The second man shook his head and called, 'Next.'

'Sorry,' said the first man.

'What do you mean? Sorry? I can do the job. I need the work.'

'You and the rest. Some are more in need than you, I think.'

'What a bloody waste of time,' Tom said.

'Here, watch your language.'

As he left the building, he looked at the faces in the line of men that now stretched some fifty feet down St Owen's Street … eager, hopeful, beaten. He walked towards High Town, determined that he would build up his fitness. He spent the rest of the afternoon walking around, looking for job opportunities, all to no avail. He was exhausted when he arrived home and went directly to his room to sleep.

Tom woke to the sound of soft tapping on his door. White clouds were tinged with pink. *It must be eight o'clock at least.* 'Mrs C?'

'I wondered if you wanted some supper. Haven't seen you all day. I've made some vegetable and barley soup,' she whispered.

'I'll come down right away,' he said, following her to the kitchen.

'Ah, you're here, Thomas. When you've finished that, come into my study.'

'Delicious, thank you, I'd better go and see what Father

wants.'

Tom knocked on the door.

'Enter,' Edward sat at his desk. 'Good, Thomas, we have important business to discuss.' He tapped a black leather folder. 'Something you might be interested in and it's not criminal investigation.' He removed papers from the folder and waved them at Tom. 'We are moving forward into the age of technological progress and the new machine culture,' he said with a wry smile. 'This is the Constabulary's new policy on traffic control. Road signs will control the speed and traffic constables will enforce it. We'll put a stop to those menacing reprobates in their machines racing through our defenceless English countryside, ravaging the road surfaces, polluting the air, and endangering the lives of its innocent inhabitants.'

'That does sound ... impressive.'

Edward continued. 'Here is an opportunity for you to join this new traffic control force. What do you think?'

'I'm unsure, Father. My interests lie in other prospects.'

'Such as?' Edward waited for a response.

'I've been looking for work today.'

'And?'

'I haven't found anything suitable.'

'*Tut*. With one million unemployed, that does not surprise me. Despite the fine skills you learned at Sandhurst, none, I believe, will set you in good stead for available employment. For instance, what technical skills do you have that might be required by industry?'

'You are correct, Father, but I'm determined to find something.'

'Don't you see, Thomas? The Constabulary is the perfect

opportunity.'

Tom cast his eyes down. *Perhaps Father is right. Joining the Constabulary may be my only hope for employment.*

~

That same evening, Grace scrubbed at her coat, trying to remove stains received when a spiteful woman threw an egg at her. She was ready to sit down and have a good cry when she heard her mother call.

'Grace, come quickly, Pa has fallen.'

She found him lying on the floor, sweating and trembling. She felt his pulse. 'His heart rate is elevated. Pa, can you hear me? We need to get you up off the floor.'

Matthew groaned and opened his eyes. 'Oh dear, what happened?' he said, sitting up.

'Oh, Matthew,' cried Sarah. 'You frightened me so.'

He patted his wife's hand.

'Can you stand, Pa? Carefully now.' The two women steadied him as he walked to an armchair in the parlour.

'You've been out all day and it's been warm. Have you eaten? I'll fetch you some water,' said Grace hurrying off to the kitchen. 'Here, sip this.' She felt his pulse again. 'It's settling down now. How are you feeling?'

'I'm alright. Don't fuss.'

She looked directly into Matthew's eyes. 'Something is troubling you, what is it?'

'Nothing.'

'Pa?'

Matthew sighed. 'Oh ...' he fidgeted. 'Well, I will have to tell you anyway,' he sighed. 'I've been to Worcester. I had a call to visit the railway office at my earliest convenience. I'll come straight to the point. The rail lines are to be expanded. They will take back this house and it will be demolished.'

Sarah gasped. 'But this is our home, whatever shall we do?'

Matthew continued. 'They have offered us a one-bedroom flat for reduced rent in the John Venn Building in Bath Street. It's up on the third floor.'

'That's no good at all. Ma will never be able to climb three flights of stairs. And how will you get to work each day? The station master's job incurs long hours.'

'Well, that's the worst part of the news. I am to be retired from the role of station master.'

'What? I don't believe it. After all the years of service,' Grace said, her face reddening with anger.

'They have offered me a job in the parcel's office.'

'How humiliating. Pa, how much time have we got? There must be something we can do.'

'They said it will be several months before the work starts but they want us out of the house by the end of June.'

~

All three fell silent but Grace's mind was racing. *There may be an obvious solution to this dark situation, but do I have the courage to pursue it?*

CHAPTER TWENTY-ONE

Arthur pulled a package out from behind the loose brick in his cellar wall and started to count. 'Eighteen pounds. That'll keep me goin' for a while, but I need to get some regular cash.' He had been lying low for weeks, not wanting to draw attention to himself. He left the house early in the morning or late in the afternoon to avoid commuters. He used the same route each time, through the back garden gate, turn right into the narrow laneway shielded on both sides by overgrown brambles. A second right turn led down a gravel track behind an old railway siding and then onto the path alongside the railway, where a stone bridge led to the rail station. He preferred not to cross the bridge into town. He walked a further thirty yards to a small grocery store which catered for his requirements.

Arthur masked himself in anonymity, refusing to acknowledge anyone who greeted him. After initial curiosity, the shopkeeper and locals' interest in him waned. Most thought of him as just another returned soldier, drab and uncommunicative. Occasionally he noticed the curtains sway as the neighbours tried to get a glimpse of him, but he kept his head down and his collar up.

He exercised daily, doing push-ups to rebuild his strength. Best of all, he had not taken a drink for over a month. *I've beaten it, bloody oath! No news from Birmingham. Not that I expect to hear anything in this backwater*. Still, a sudden noise or neighbours passing made the hairs rise on the back of his neck and he was ever watchful.

He stashed cash back in the linen bag and pushed it into the hiding place. As Arthur bent to light the stove, he heard the squeak of his gate and footsteps on the path. He pushed himself flat against the wall and held a pan ready in his hand. His breathing strained, he listened anxiously for a knock on the door.

The letterbox creaked, and a voice called, 'Hullo? Anyone home? Walter Cadbrooke here.'

'What does that silly prick want?' Arthur mumbled under his breath.

'I have something you might be interested in.' Cadbrooke waited a few minutes before pushing a folded pamphlet through the letterbox.

Arthur heard Cadbrooke's footsteps on the path and the creak of the gate close before he moved to pick up the pamphlet and read:

Middleton Stakes – Group One Flat Course –
Open to two-year-old colts

Wot's this? Gambling on horses? That's a game for mugs, he thought. Arthur's stomach growled. He was hungry. it was getting late, he needed to shop today. He turned off the gas, put the pamphlet on the kitchen table, grabbed his hat and jacket and left the house by his usual route.

~

Tom pulled into Wright's Garage at the end of Whitecross Road and topped up the car with six shillings' worth of petrol, just short of two gallons but sufficient to get back to Llancillow and enough to leave the tank at least a quarter full. He felt glum about returning the car but was sure the Major would understand. *I just need a damn job,* he thought as he drove along the dusty road past black and white cottages with thatched roofs. Sheep and cattle grazed in lush paddocks. *How serene it all seems,* he thought.

He parked the car outside the garage, the two dogs came bounding up to him, woofing and wagging their tails. They followed at his heels as he went in search of Crabbe. Tom knocked on the front door, then the kitchen door, he peered through the kitchen window, called out, 'Hello,' but no one replied. He walked round the side of the house to the stables and shouted, 'Anyone home?' *Where is he?* 'I don't suppose you know where they are?' Tom said, patting the dogs.

One of the dogs whimpered in response before they both ran off. Tom followed them past the chicken coup to the rear of the stable. There he saw Crabbe, he waved and walked down the path to meet him.

'Hello, Tom. Just give me a minute and I'll get the kettle on.'

'What? No Mrs Foggerty?'

'Ah, no. I'll tell you all about it in a minute. Let me get cleaned up.'

Tom was surprised to find the kitchen in disarray, it looked as if no one had washed up for days. He filled the kettle and placed it on the stove, ran hot water into the sink and put plates to soak.

Crabbe came in. 'What a to-do,' he sighed.

Tom brought the teapot and cups to the table. He found a jug of milk and sniffed it. 'I think that's gone sour. Black tea, alright?'

'Yes, with plenty of sugar.'

'I've just buried the little pony, he took poorly a couple of days ago, I think he had a seizure.' Crabbe sipped his tea. 'I dragged him down through the paddock with the tractor and buried him in the bottom of the garden. Poor old Punch has taken it badly. He hasn't left the gate yet, still waiting for his little mate to come back.'

'I wish I'd been here to help.'

'So do I. That was a damn big hole.' He pushed himself up awkwardly. 'Argh. I'll pay for it for the next few days. Wretched arthritis.'

Tom started on the washing up.

'Here, come out of that sink. I don't want you cleaning up after me.'

'Nearly finished. Where's Mrs Foggerty?'

Crabbe sighed. 'That's another story. In short, we've lost Mrs Foggerty. Her sister got that ghastly Spanish flu, nearly saw her off but she rallied and asked Mrs Foggerty to stay while she recovered. They're both widows and only have each other, so she has decided to stay *permanently*. Bad timing, I could have done with her help in the house. I've bought twenty Herefords, magnificent beasts. They'll be delivered on Saturday. I must get the fences finished by then. I must see if I can get Cyril up here to help. I've fallen behind a bit these last few days.'

'I can give you a hand with the fences.'

'Oh, could you? That would be splendid. If I can get Cyril as well, we could have it done in no time. Anyway, as you can see, I'm not much of a dab hand in the kitchen either, so I'll have to advertise for another housekeeper. They're a bit thin on the ground around these parts. Ah, it's nearly eleven o'clock. Let's get a bite to eat and then we'll go find Cyril. He should be home for his lunch around one. I would like to show you where I need the fences. Are you up for a walk?'

'Yes, I'd like that. Thank you for allowing me to use the car but I'd like to return it to you,' Tom slid the keys across the table.

'No need; I said you could use it until you got on your feet.'

Crabbe rubbed his chin. He looked in the pantry for something to eat and came out with some crusty bread and cheese. 'It's a bit dry, I'm afraid. I better pick up some stores from the village shop.' He made a couple of sandwiches. 'Let's take them with us and eat while we walk.'

They took a shortcut along the old footpath through the wheatfield, talking as they walked. Crabbed looked pleased as he appraised knee high green stalks. 'Good, exceptionally good,' he said. 'Looks like this will produce a higher yield than last year. We sowed seed last autumn; I think that's made quite a difference, allowed the wheat to grow through the winter. Much better than planting in spring.'

The two dogs ran on ahead, finding sport in disrupting yellow wagtails from their nests amongst the wheat.

'It certainly looks lush, considering all the dry weather we've had.'

'Ah, that's because of the water meadow my father created back in 1890,' Crabbe said, pointing to the rise across the field. 'Do you see the terraces?'

Tom looked where Crabb pointed.

'Stream water is channelled from the top of the meadow. The terraces were formed, so the water trickles down in a zig-zag fashion through the field. Marvellous for crops and pasture alike. See, the system continues into the next meadow.'

'What have you got growing in there?'

'Turnips, an excellent forage crop, the cattle will love them. They can eat the tops and roots right through the summer and winter. Beyond that, where the new fence will go is a large field of clover. One half of that field will be fenced for the cattle and the other half will be ploughed under for next year's hay.'

'This is probably a silly question but why can't you put the cattle in the same field as the horses? I mean, there are only two of them and there seems to be plenty of room.'

'Ah, my boy. It's the adage: horses will kill cattle; sheep will kill horses.'

Tom was surprised.

'Horses nibble the grass so low that there is nothing left for the cattle to feed on and sheep crop the grass even lower, so there is nothing left for the horse,' Crabbe explained.

'I had no idea, it's all very technical.'

'It is indeed.' Crabbe was quiet for a few minutes before continuing, 'I believe my father was disappointed with me. He loved this land and operated a productive farm. Of course, he wanted his only son to take over but along came the Boar War and then the Second Boar War. He died while I was in Africa and when I came home after witnessing the colossal sacrifice of horses in that debacle, well, I decided to devote my time to making amends as it were.'

They walked on silently for a while.

'He would have been pleased to see I eventually found my farming feet,' laughed Crabbe. 'Although it's all thanks to the land army ladies and of course Cyril and his boy. They worked on all this over the last few years.'

A thought began to hatch in Tom's mind. 'Major. I'm not sure if this is appropriate, but with Mrs Foggerty leaving and considering Grace's situation …'

Crabbe stopped walking. 'Oh, what a splendid idea. Do you think she would be interested?'

Tom laughed. 'It wouldn't hurt to ask.'

Soon they arrived at the lane to the village.

'That's Cyril's house just over there,' Crabbe pointed to a tiny red brick house. 'Heel,' Crabbe called to the dogs. They came bounding up and he attached leashes to their collars.

They pushed through the gate and walked along the garden path past rows of neatly tied green wigwams bearing slender runner beans.

A woman opened a window and called out, 'Afternoon, Squire.'

'Good afternoon, Mrs Tapley. Is Cyril home?'

'No, he's not due for another hour at least. Was there something you wanted?'

'I just called by to see if he would come and help Thomas and I with a fencing job.'

The woman squinted at Tom, sizing him up. 'He won't be able to do that til the weekend. Got himself a job on the road, driving one of them bigguns. Fairly makes the ground rumble when he comes along.'

'Oh, I see. Can't wait til the weekend, I'm afraid. What about your Harold? Would he be interested d'you think?'

'Sorry, Squire. He's working with his dad today, labouring. I can send him over tomorrow and the next day.'

'Jolly good, thank you, Mrs Tapley,' Crabbe turned to leave.

'Just a minute,' she called. 'You can take the post auger if you like. That might lighten the load a bit. It's just round the back, by the shed.'

'That's truly kind. Thank you, Mrs Tapley.'

'Thank you,' echoed Tom.

'Perhaps we should have brought the car after all,' said Crabbe, examining the device.

'It looks like a giant corkscrew,' laughed Tom. 'We'll manage it between us.'

Mrs Tapley waved and pulled the window closed as they carried off the auger.

'I must just pop into the shop quickly, then we'll get this contraption back home. Are you able to stay for a couple of nights? We could start on the fencing.'

'Yes, happy to.'

'In which case, let's get an early start this afternoon. Oh, and of course, I'm going to pay you for this work.'

Embarrassed, Tom replied, 'No, sir. I couldn't.'

'I need the help and you want the work, don't you?'

'I do, yes.'

'Then that's sorted.'

Later that afternoon, Crabbe fetched the tractor and asked Tom to meet him at the back of the stables. A cold shiver went down Tom's spine when he found the huge roll of barbed wire rolled on the back of the trailer. It evoked horrible memories of years of imprisonment. Crabbe backed the tractor and Tom helped to hitch it up.

'When are you expecting the cattle to arrive? I would be happy to come and help. I'm not having any success with finding work in town.'

'Oh, I say, that would be splendid. I believe the cattle will be here on Saturday, I'll call Farmer Ablett and check.' Crabbe gave a sigh. 'I rattle around in this big old house … it's very lonely sometimes. I did love it when the young lady grooms were here. Despite the challenging work, we had a jolly time. I enjoyed their company and seeing the house come to life again.'

'When we've finished the fences, I'll pop home and pick up some clothes. While I'm there, I could go and see Grace and ask her if she would be interested in coming to Llancillow.'

'Jolly good idea.'

~

Driving to Hereford, a couple of days later, Tom thought about the prospect of Grace moving to Llancillow. *It would solve so many problems, it would get her away from the taunts of ignorant and spiteful people and secondly, she would be a great companion for the Major. I wonder how she will feel about leaving her parents. The baby will be due soon, would she manage on her own? I'll find out soon enough.*

Tom decided to go to the back door when he arrived home and was greeted by the housekeeper.

'Hello, what have you been up to?' she asked, looking at the dirty state of his clothes.

'I've got a job helping Major Crabbe. We've been fixing fences and the cattle will arrive on Saturday, so I've come home to get some spare clothes and my boots.'

'And time for a nice bath too, I hope.'

'Yes, haha. I'll head back tomorrow morning. Is Mother here?'

'She's resting now.'

'I'll clean up and pop out for a bit. Please tell Mother I'll be back for supper.'

Tom took a shortcut to the station by walking down Back

Lane. He marvelled at the number of speckled butterflies feeding on the long grasses in the dappled shade of the orchard canopy. Beneath the apple trees, the ground was rich with late spring flowers; red campions and oxeye-daisies nodded in the breeze to the sound of buzzing bees. He breathed in the warmth and fragrance. Feeling refreshed and in good spirits, he arrived at the station master's house and knocked on the door.

'Tom, hello. Percy is still at work, I'm afraid,' said Grace.

'Actually, Grace, it was you I came to see,' Tom replied, feeling suddenly tense.

'Oh, goodness. Well, please come in.'

He followed her down the hallway.

'You don't mind if we sit in the kitchen, do you? Would you like some tea?'

'Lovely, thank you.'

'Ma, Tom has come to visit.'

Sarah quickly pinned up a stray lock of hair and gathered up papers from the table.

'Hello, Mrs Phillips, my apologies for intruding, unannounced.'

'That's alright, dear. I'm afraid you'll have to take us as you find us today,' she said, putting the papers on the sideboard.

Tom sensed a tension in the air.

'So, Tom, to what do we owe this pleasure?' Grace asked.

He was lost for words. The mood in the Phillips kitchen had thrown his confidence. 'Ah ... I've just returned from visiting Major Crabbe. Uh, may I ask, is everything alright?'

'Yes, of course. Please go on.'

'Very well, umm, Major Crabbe was wondering ... that is

we were discussing ...' Tom felt completely out of his depth, not aided by the fact that Grace stood with her arms folded with a frown upon her face. He took a deep breath and continued, 'Wondering if you might consider a position of companion and housekeeper for the Major?'

'You do realise that I am expecting a child in July.'

'Yes, fully understood.' Tom fumbled for words. 'The difficulties you spoke about, you know, the treatment from ignorant ... I just thought it might be a solution ... for both of you. He is a dear man, but Mrs Foggerty has left Llancillow to care for her sister in Birmingham. She won't be coming back. And, quite frankly, he is lonely, so I thought ...'

Grace turned away and cupped her face in her hands.

'Oh dear, Grace, I didn't mean to upset you. Please forgive my clumsiness.'

She sat next to her mother and held her hand. Moments passed before she spoke. 'You haven't upset me, Tom. We are in the middle of a family crisis and, frankly, your news has offered a glimmer of hope.'

Sarah squeezed her daughter's hand. 'Don't you worry about your father and me. I think you should take Tom's kind offer. Perhaps the Major will permit me to come and stay with you when the baby is due?'

'Please don't think I'm prying. I can sense there is something worrying. Is there anything I can do to help?'

'Mother, do you mind if I tell him?'

Sarah nodded approval.

'Tom, please keep this to yourself. My father is terribly upset and embarrassed. In short, he is to be retired as station master and we will lose our home. The railway has offered my parents a flat to rent but it only has one bedroom, no garden and is situated on the third floor.'

'But that doesn't matter, dear, if you take the position at Llancillow, then we will only have Percy to worry about and he has already said he can find a room near the cider factory,' said Sarah.

'The flats are awful. I have seen the building. I stepped inside the main entrance, and it looked so dreary and unkempt. You will never be able to get up and down those stone steps to the third floor, Ma.'

'Do pour some tea, dear.' Sarah pleaded.

'I'm sorry to hear that. How awful,' Tom said while his mind began to plan a conversation with Crabbe. *All the unused rooms at Llancillow. He said himself how he "rattled around the big old house." I wonder ...*

'Do you take sugar, Tom?'

'Two, please.' *I think I should talk to Percy before I say anything else.* 'Thank you.' He sipped his tea. 'I must get going shortly. Grace, I urge you to consider the offer. I've got to go back to Llancillow tomorrow morning but here, let me write down the telephone number for Major Crabbe. Give him a call when you've had a chance to discuss it with the family.'

'I will, thank you. I'll see you out.'

Tom followed Grace to the front door. Before leaving, he took her hand in his. 'Try not to worry,' he said. 'I'm sure things will work out.' He stood looking at her pale face and wistful smile. 'My heart goes out to you and your family.' He hurried away before she could answer.

~

Twenty minutes later, he arrived at the cider factory. Unsure where he would catch Percy leaving, he decided to go inside and look for his office. 'Ah, there you are,' he said, finding his friend seated at a small desk, surrounded by filing cabinets. 'Fancy a quick drink on your way home?'

'Good idea. I'll meet you in the Market Tavern in about ten minutes.'

Tom found a seat in a quiet corner, away from the bar. He waved as Percy entered.

'I bought you a half of cider, hope that's what you like.'

'Cheers, it will do nicely. Anything to wash the dust of that stuffy old office away.' He skulled his drink. 'Ahh, that's better. What brings you by?'

'Actually, I went to your house to visit Grace.'

'Oh, yes?'

'In hindsight, I wish I had waited to talk to you first, or at least had the common sense to let them know I was coming.'

'I see. Things are a bit unsettled at the moment. What did you want to talk to Grace about?'

'I've been working at Llancillow ... look, I was probably poking my nose in where it wasn't needed, but after speaking to the Major, I approached Grace to see if she would be interested in moving to Llancillow as a companion and housekeeper for him. I suggested she talk the idea over with the family, so I expect she'll want to chat to you about it when you get home. Of course, I had no idea about the dilemma regarding your father and the house.'

'She told you?'

'Yes, about having to leave the house and that he had been offered a one-bedroom flat. It all sounds horribly unfair.'

'Bloody unfair is right. Did she tell you about the job they've offered him? Working in the parcels' office. Bloody hellfire ... he's been with the railways for more than thirty-five years ... worked his way up the hard way, starting off at fourteen, as an underman, packing ballast under and between railway sleepers. By the time he was eighteen, he progressed to shunter, hooking on the locomotives and carriages. From there, he became a leading man, directing and organising rail freight and conducting safety checks. After an injury at work, he landed a cushy job in the railways' office for a while but didn't like being stuck in a box, as he used to say ... I know what he means. Eventually, he got the job of station master. Can you imagine how he feels being offered a job in the parcels office?'

'No, I can't imagine.' While he finished his drink, he wondered how to tackle this conversation.

'Another one?' Percy asked.

'Not for me.' *I must be careful what I say now. I don't want to upset Percy as well.*

'There's a lot of dust in that office.' Percy grinned and raised his glass.

'Look, Percy, I don't want to tread on anyone's toes and certainly do not want to offend Grace or your father, as I know he is an enormously proud man. Can I ask, what do you think of the idea of Grace and perhaps even your parents moving to Llancillow?'

'Whoa. I appreciate that it would be a smart move for Grace, although I don't know how she would manage work and baby, but my parents? Where did that idea come from?'

Tom rubbed his temples. 'I don't know; it's just something that popped into my head when I was at your house. I'm going back to Llancillow tomorrow morning. Let me sound out the Major first, then we can talk some more.'

~

Arriving at Llancillow, Tom spotted Crabbe, leaning on a fence post, talking to a tall, wiry man. He parked the car and walked over to the pair.

'Tom. Come and meet Joe Ablett.'

'How d'you do?' Tom shook hands. 'My, the cattle are here already.'

'Yes, handsome beasts, aren't they?' Crabbe beamed.

'Indeed, they are. I was hoping to be here in time to help.'

'They were no trouble,' said Ablett. 'Took one look at that lovely green meadow and through the gate they went. Herefords are docile animals, good temperament and all. You'll get some good calves off that lot, especially with Henry over there.' He nodded towards the next field where a huge red beast was grazing. 'Home bred he is. Three years old and sweet as a baby. You'll get a good nine years out of him.' They walked along the fence to the adjoining field. He put two fingers in his mouth and blew a loud, shrill whistle. Henry raised his head and ambled over to the fence; with his white face and thick down-curving horns, he portrayed an imposing figure. The bull shook his head from side to side. Ablett reached over the fence and scratched Henry's tufted crown. 'Here you go, boy. This is your new home. Now you be good, eh?'

Tom was amazed. 'He's huge. What does he weigh, I wonder?'

'Near on sixteen hundredweight, maybe just over.'

'Good gracious,' said Tom as he reached over and patted the bull's head.

'Well, Crabbe, I must get on. All the best then. Call if you need me. I'm sure they'll settle in, though.'

'Excellent, thank you.' The men shook hands.

Back at Llancillow, Tom waited for the Major to look at the information folder Ablett had left him.

'Well,' said Crabbe, flicking through the paperwork. 'Let the adventure begin.' He read on: 'Grain supplements ... ah for winter. Hay must be nutritious. Hmm, pasture and forage ...' Crabbe scratched his head. 'I fear we'll need to find some extra hands.' He read again. 'Here's the list of jobs: feeding and herding, checking they are all getting adequate food and staying on the lookout for sick animals ... special dietary requirements, calving, distributing fertiliser, seeds for hay and forage. We'll need someone to operate and maintain the equipment, not to mention repairing tools. Then there will be administration: sales, employees pay, and tax records. I do hope I haven't bitten off more than I can chew.'

This is the right time, I must let him know about the Phillips, Tom thought. *Gently does it ...* 'I may have a solution, although it is just an idea at this stage.'

'Do tell, my boy.'

Tom took a deep breath to calm his nerves and gather his thoughts. 'As you know, I visited Grace yesterday. I walked into a rather awkward moment, although now, it seems like it may serve as a solution.'

'I don't follow. I thought you were going to talk to Grace to see if she might agree to come here.'

'I did, it's complicated. I'll just try to explain what happened as briefly as I can.' Tom tried to clearly outline the situation he had discussed with Grace and Percy.

'Well, that's just a dreadful thing to happen. That poor family.' Crabbe reached for his pipe. 'So, what you are suggesting is that we see if Mr and Mrs Phillips would be willing to move here as well as Grace? Can the man work, do you think?'

'Put it this way, I can handle most of the manual labour, but I have no idea how to manage administration. Mr Phillips has been managing the administration of Hereford Railway Station for years. I don't know exactly what that entails however, I should think the need for accuracy and accountability would be very high. I also know that he hates the idea of being shut in a small office, well that wouldn't be the case here. Mrs Phillips could help Grace immensely by minding the baby while Grace performs housekeeping duties, for instance.'

'Mmm, interesting.'

'Let's not forget Percy. I can't think of anyone better equipped to look after farm machinery.'

'Slow down, my boy. I agree but I'm not sure how to tackle this.'

'It is of prime importance that you consider yourself and your needs, Major. How would you feel about having all these people staying here, in your own home? If they agreed to take on the jobs, that is.'

'It would be important for me to maintain my privacy,' he relit his pipe. 'However, I do see some great advantages in having the family here. We could open the east wing for them. It has been closed since my father died and there is no furniture in there, although I assume they have their own. There is a kitchen and bathroom, two bedrooms and a large living room that looks out on the orchard. It will need some work and a touch of paint. Grace could have Mrs Foggerty's old apartment.'

Tom felt elated. 'That sounds perfect. I can prepare the

rooms with Percy's help.'

'Let's not jump the gun. What do you suggest we do about approaching the Phillips?'

'I gave Grace your telephone number. Hopefully, she will call. If not, I could drive back to town and set up an appointment for us to meet the family.'

'Very well. That sounds like a good plan. In the meantime, shall we go and look at the east wing and decide what needs to be done?'

'Wonderful,' said Tom. *Grace, please call,* he thought as they walked to look at the potential new home for the Phillips family.

~

At three o'clock the next afternoon, the telephone rang. Tom answered, 'Pontrilas 349, Major Crabbe's telephone.'

'Hello, Tom, Grace here. May I speak to the Major, please?'

'Yes, of course, I'll fetch him. Uh, have you had time to think about the idea I suggested?'

'Yes, Tom, that's why I'm calling.'

He was anxious to hear her response and momentarily lost for words.

'Are you there?'

'Yes, sorry, my mind was busy ... I wanted to let you know ...'

'Is that Grace?' Crabbe asked.

Tom nodded and handed the telephone to him.

'Hello my dear, Crabbe here.'

Tom stood nearby, hoping to catch the conversation.

'Yes, that's correct ... Tom mentioned that ... most

distressing, yes ... I completely understand ... oh, well that is very encouraging ... Look, *erum*, there is something I would like to discuss with you and in fact your parents as well. It's rather involved, much easier to meet and talk through a few ideas, if the family will permit, of course ... tonight? Let me put Tom on ... talk to you soon, my dear.'

Crabbe put his hand over the mouthpiece and whispered to Tom. 'What do you think about driving over to the Phillips tonight? We could be there by five o'clock.'

'Yes. What did she say about coming here as a housekeeper?'

'Not averse to the idea, just concerned about her pregnancy. I'll tell you later, here, quick, try to arrange a time.'

'Hello Grace, it's Tom. Would it be convenient for the Major and I to visit tonight? Perhaps five o'clock?'

'What's this about, Tom?'

'I'll tell you more when I see you. Will your parents be there? What time does Percy get home?'

'Yes, they should all be here by five. I'll warn Ma, otherwise, she will go into a flap. What is the mystery about?'

'Nothing to worry about. We'll see you shortly. Bye for now.'

~

During the drive into Hereford, they discussed the pros and cons of their plan.

'Of course, we could go through all of this just to find out they aren't remotely interested,' said Crabbe.

'Indeed,' Tom agreed. 'Although I think the biggest hurdle will be Mr Phillips' pride. Anyway, we'll soon find out, here we are.'

Percy opened the door. 'Tom, Major, please come in. My parents and Grace are in the parlour, come this way.'

Matthew Phillips stood by the fireplace, looking stern. Grace sat next to her mother on the couch.

'Good evening, Mr Phillips, Mrs Phillips, Grace. You all know Major Crabbe, I believe.'

'Good evening,' said Crabbe, reaching to shake hands with Matthew. 'Mrs Phillips, I don't believe we've met. Grace, dear, you are looking very well.'

'Please, do sit down,' said Percy, indicating to the armchairs. 'It's a warm evening. Can I offer you a cool drink?'

They declined. An awkward silence followed until Grace spoke.

'Thank you for coming, I have to say, we are a little overwhelmed and ... intrigued.'

'I apologise for that,' said Crabbe. 'Where to start?' He cleared his throat. 'I won't mince my words. We have all come to a crossroad in our lives. With your permission, I will begin by telling you about my dilemma as an opening point for consideration.'

'Please do,' said Matthew, his face softening a little.

'Thank you. My situation is totally self-imposed and for that, I accept that I am now bound to search for a solution. I have emerged from what was an assumed normality as my home was once a successful farm, albeit run by my father, whose skills and knowledge, sadly I admit I have not inherited ... and now things have suddenly overturned. In short, I have taken on more than I can cope with in the form of purchasing livestock. Hereford cattle, to be precise. Tom has been an immense help so far; however, we both believe important aspects of current essential requirements are way beyond our capabilities. These are the skills and knowledge we lack; administration tops the list. I need someone who has strong organisational skills and can communicate with various suppliers and future customers. Someone who will demonstrate excellent customer service, values collaboration and administer the farm records,' he paused to gather his thoughts. 'Secondly, someone to run and maintain the farm equipment and machinery, including repairing tools when required. And thirdly, but by no means least, someone who will manage the household and I have already spoken briefly with Grace regarding this position.' He wiped his brow. 'There you have my predicament.'

'May I speak?' Grace said. 'I have to say, I was quite taken aback when Tom first mentioned your offer, but I have given it a lot of thought and I would accept at the drop of a hat if I were not in this condition,' she blushed.

'I would give anything to be working with machines and tools again. I was grateful to old Mr Cartwright for giving me a job; not many would employ an ugly sod like me. I would like to accept the position, but I have no way of getting to Llancillow from here every day.' Percy looked glum.

Matthew spoke next. 'Major Crabbe, I want to thank you for coming here this evening and for telling us about your dilemma. It pains me to say that we have an unfortunate situation ourselves to deal with, so I'm unsure if we are in a position to assist you.'

'Making big decisions can be daunting.' Tom broke the silence that followed Matthew's speech. 'I think it is quite natural for us to feel overwhelmed by our choices, and we worry about taking the wrong path in whatever decisions we make.'

'Yes, Tom, you're quite right. Pa, please let's be open to

what the Major is saying. If there was a way I could manage my condition and my baby, I would certainly take your kind offer, Major.'

'There is more to say about this,' said Tom, looking at Crabbe.

'Quite right, Tom. I hope you will hear what I have to say and understand that it is something I have thought through thoroughly. I have accommodation to offer. It is a small wing of my home, completely private, with two bedrooms. There is a kitchen, bathroom and a large sitting room, all on the ground floor. Now, this wing has been empty for some thirty years, so it will need work to prepare it. Oh, and it is not furnished.'

The family looked from one to another.

He continued, 'Grace, there is an apartment on the ground floor which has traditionally been made available for the housekeeper. This would be yours, should you accept the position.'

'Yes,' Tom added. 'So, it solves the transport problem, Percy and, if you are willing, it means Mrs Phillips would be on hand to help mind Grace's baby.'

'I make this offer for the mutual benefit of both my needs and your family's,' Crabbe said directly to Matthew. 'I completely understand that you must take time to consider. Perhaps you would care to come out to Llancillow in the next couple of days and we can discuss this further. I'm sure Tom will drive you.'

'Yes, of course,' said Tom.

'Thank you, Major Crabbe.' Matthew said.

After a short silence, Crabbe said, 'Well, we must be getting off.'

'I'll see you out,' said Percy. At the front door, he whispered, 'Thank you so much, I'm sure my father will come around. He just needs a little time.'

'Talking of which, Percy, will you have time to come out and give me a hand to prepare the accommodation? Thirty years of cobwebs will take some cleaning.'

CHAPTER TWENTY-TWO

Arthur had watched and waited for this opportunity. Now was his chance. He saw the housekeeper leave the house with shopping bags on her arm. A police car had driven the fat copper off earlier. Tom had left the house a couple of mornings ago and the pretty redhead was off on her bicycle.

Arthur slipped in through the gate off Back Lane and ran to the kitchen door. He found the key under the mat. 'Stupid,' he muttered to himself as he opened the door and peered in. He cackled. *snooty bastards,* he thought. 'Ever so neat and tidy, a place for everything and everything in its place,' he scoffed. He closed the kitchen door quietly behind him and stood for a moment, gathering his wits and courage. He breathed deeply the spicy aroma of baked fruit loaf, cooling on a tray. His stomach rumbled, and he felt tempted to cut a thick slice. He imagined golden butter melting on the warm bread. 'Stop it,' he cursed. He walked across the kitchen's red quarry tiles into the hallway and looked in both directions. *You can never be too careful.* The thought made him chuckle. *Now, where do you think they stash the cash? Funny – stealing from a copper, especially a big-wig copper, eh?*

As he approached the study door, a creaking floorboard startled him. He paused, sweat gathered in his arm pits. He held his breath.

'Maisie?'

Arthur pushed himself back against the wall knocking into a collection of umbrellas in the hall stand.

'Maisie, are you back already?'

Arthur froze.

Seconds passed until the woman's voice called again. 'Maisie?' Ellen climbed out of her bed and reached for her dressing gown.

Arthur retreated backwards down the hallway, fumbling his way towards the kitchen.

Ellen appeared from her room, surprised to find the interloper, she gasped, 'Who are you? What do you want?'

'Who the hell are you, is more like it?'

He saw how frail she seemed, almost ghostly, framed by the light from the hall windows, she stood completely still.

'Er, I'm here to see Bellamy. Tom Bellamy. He's not here, eh? Not to worry, I'll see meself out.'

'Wait,' Ellen reached to support herself on the polished dado. 'I demand to know who you are and how you got into my house.'

'I told you. I came to see Tom Bellamy. He owes me. And your housekeeper let me in.'

'What do you mean? *Argh*.' Ellen fell to her knees, clutching her chest.

He reached for her as she fell and caught her frail arm. Her skin felt cold in his hot, sweaty hand.

'Tom? My Tom, he's ...' Ellen struggled to breathe and the pain in her chest overwhelmed her. 'Don't hurt him. Please, don't hurt him.'

He looked down on Ellen's frail form and gulped. 'Oh fuck, no, this wasn't supposed to happen.'

'Please ...' Ellen whispered.

Arthur tried to calm himself. He knew he had to get away

as fast as he could. He tried to think about all the situations that had recently occurred. Was there anything that could link him to this? *No, nothing came to mind. Can't waste this time,* he thought. *I may never get another chance. Must find something.*

'Stupid bitch. I told you, I just came to get what's mine.' His anger erupted and he yelled, 'Didn't I help him? Yes, I bloody did. Now isn't it my turn to get pay-back?'

He ran into the study and ransacked Edward's desk searching for money but found none. He scraped books off the shelves, still searching. He heard a moan from Ellen lying on the cold floorboards. *Shit.* He grabbed a coat hanging on the study door and threw it over her. He ran back to the kitchen, empty handed, reached the door, then turned back and grabbed the fruit loaf before making his escape.

~

Maisie Chadwick set down the two heavy shopping baskets and reached under the mat for the key. 'Where's that darn key?' she huffed while poking her hand in her pockets before moving the pot plants around. She tutted, reached into the basket for her purse but the key was not there. *That's queer.* She gingerly turned the knob and was surprised to find the door opened easily. 'Hello,' she called but there was no response. In trepidation, she tip-toed into the kitchen. The first thing she noticed was a trail of crumbs leading to the kitchen table, where she had left the fruit loaf to cool on a rack. 'Where's ...' she whispered and stood in the silence, thinking what to do next. *Oh, Mrs Bellamy,* the thought gave her the courage to move. In the hallway, she found Ellen lying face down on the floorboards underneath Mr Bellamy's winter coat. Maisie ran to her mistress's side and fell to her knees. 'Mrs Bellamy, wake up, it's me, Maisie,' she cried but Ellen didn't stir. She put her hand on Ellen's forehead, her skin was chilled. She reached for her wrist and felt a weak pulse. 'Don't worry, I'll get help,' she said. Scrambling up off her knees, she reached for the telephone.

'Hereford Constabulary. Sergeant Turley speaking.'

'Sergeant, this is Maisie Chadwick, there's been a … well I don't know what, please help. Mrs Bellamy. She's unconscious, lying on the hall floor.'

'Alright, Mrs Chadwick. Now, have you tried to wake her?'

'Sergeant, I can't, she won't, I don't know …'

'I'll inform the Chief Inspector and drive him home right away. You call the doctor. I will call for an ambulance. Stay with her and try to keep her warm.'

Maisie dialled again.

'Doctor Farrington's Surgery, can I help.'

'Please ask the doctor to come right away. It's Mrs Bellamy; she's unconscious on the floor.' Maisie broke down and sobbed.

'Mrs Chadwick, can you hear me?'

'Yes, yes, I'm sorry.'

'Don't be sorry, dear. The doctor is on his way.'

Maisie returned to Ellen's side, took her cold hand in hers and prayed while hot tears ran down her round cheeks.

Minutes later, Edward Bellamy erupted through the front door, Sergeant Turley on his heels. He dropped to her side. 'Ellen, my love, what has happened here?' His voice had a ragged edge to it.

Turley turned to see the doctor hurry down the pathway. 'Here's the doctor now, sir.' Turley held his hand out to help Maisie up and said, 'C'mon dear, let's leave the doctor some room.'

Turley led Maisie to the kitchen and pulled out a chair for her.

She sat down heavily, pulled out a hanky and blew her nose hard.

Turley brought in the shopping baskets, closed the back door, and put the kettle on the hearth.

Maisie stared at the rack on the table, her mind a blur.

A sound of despair came from the hallway.

'Just a minute,' Turley excused himself.

He found the doctor and Edward carrying Ellen into her room. 'Can I help, sir?'

'Ask Mrs Chadwick to fill as many hot water bottles as she can find.'

'Yes, doctor. I called for an ambulance. It should be here any minute.'

'Good man.'

Turley hurried back to the kitchen. 'Doctor wants as many hot water bottles as you can find.'

'I heard that,' she said, unscrewing the metal tops from a line of bottles. 'How is she? Will she be alright?'

'There's an ambulance on its way and she's in good hands.'

They filled the bottles and wrapped them in towels, then hurried them along to Ellen's room.

'Ah good, bring those bottles here, lay them either side of her, like this,' instructed the doctor.

Ellen lay on her bed, motionless, silent, pale. The sight of her caused Maisie to sob again. She spun on her heels in response to a loud knock on the door.

'Ambulance service.'

'Come in, please.' She pointed to Ellen's bed and stepped out of the way.

'Sergeant Turley,' Edward called. 'I will accompany my wife and the doctor to the hospital. Find out what happened here.' He rubbed his heavy brows. 'Get one of the constables here, we can't leave Mrs Chadwick on her own. Oh, and my son and daughter, I'm not sure their whereabouts at the moment, but they must be told.'

'Yes, of course, sir, right away. Pardon me, but I do hope Mrs Bellamy will be alright, sir.'

'Thank you, Turley.'

Maisie started unpacking the groceries while Turley made his call.

'Now, Mrs Chadwick,' Turley said, unbuttoning his tunic pocket to retrieve a notepad and pencil. 'Tell me what has happened here.'

'I went shopping. I always shop on Thursday mornings. I left the key for the kitchen door in its usual place, but it wasn't there when I got back.'

'Its usual place being?'

'Why, under the mat, of course.'

'Under the mat, hmm. And where is the key now?'

'I told you, it wasn't there, and the back door wasn't locked either.'

Turley opened the back door, wriggled the knob, searched under the mat and around the pot plants. 'I see,' he said furtively, making notes. 'Where was Mrs Bellamy when you went out shopping?'

'Why, she was in her room, like always. I took her a cup of tea and a biscuit before I left.'

'The coat she was covered with, that was obviously a man's coat. The Chief Inspector's, I assume?'

'Yes.'

'How did it come to be placed over her like that? Did you put it there?'

'No. That's how I found her.' Maisie gasped and put her hand over her mouth.

'Well, we may have an intruder in the house. Have you noticed anything missing?'

'The fruit loaf,' Maisie said, pointing to the empty rack. 'I made it before I went out and left it to cool.'

The door knocker sounded loudly.

'Ah, I'll get the door. Mrs Chadwick, this is Constable Bolland. He'll be staying with you for a while until we sort this out. First, though, let's get that kettle boiling for a cup of tea. You stay here please while the constable and I look around.'

'Sergeant, in here.' The young constable stood outside the study while Turley stepped inside.

Maisie could not stand the tension any longer, so she went to see what was going on. 'Oh goodness,' she exclaimed as she saw the mess.

'Don't touch anything, please,' instructed Turley. 'We'll wait til the Chief Inspector gets back and he will know if anything is missing. How about we have that cup of tea now and then I'll get back to the station and Constable Bolland will stay on guard.'

~

The fading light of the early evening brought a sharp chill to the air as the Crabbe and Tom returned to Llancillow.

'Thank you, my boy,' Crabbe said as he eased the tractor

through the gate and continued round the side of the house. 'Good day's work, I couldn't have managed without you,' he said, patting Tom on the shoulder. 'Quick wash and then let's see what we can find for supper.'

'The telephone is ringing; shall I get it?' Tom asked.

'Major Crabbe, please, this is Pontrilas Exchange.'

'It's the exchange,' Tom handed the telephone to Crabbe.

'Hello, Myrtle.'

'I've been trying to get hold of you. You've missed lots of calls. Please ask Mr Thomas Bellamy to call home.'

Crabbe handed the phone to Tom. 'Call home, my boy.'

'Yes, hello. Please connect me with Hereford 221.' Tom listened to the clicks and whirring noises in the background until he heard Mrs Chadwick's voice.

'The Bellamy residence.'

'Hello Mrs C. Is everything all right?'

'Oh, thank the Lord. I've been trying to call you all day.'

'I've been helping Major Crabbe.'

'You need to come home straight away.'

'What's wrong?'

'It's your mother. She's been taken to the hospital. Doctor says it may be a heart attack.'

'Oh my God. I'll leave at once.'

'Go straight to the Hereford County Hospital.' He heard the phone click.

'What is it, my boy?'

'Sir, may I take the car? It's my mother, she's in hospital.' He spun around, looking for his jacket and wallet.

'Of course, you must take the car. What dreadful news.

Would you like me to drive you?'

'No, sir, thank you. I'll be fine. I must go.'

'Drive safely,' Crabbe called as Tom ran out of the door.

~

The hospital receptionist gave Tom a disapproving look as he approached her desk. He was still wearing work clothes and wellington boots and smelled of sweat.

'I've come to see my mother,' he spoke urgently.

'Name?'

'Bellamy. Mrs Ellen Bellamy.'

The receptionist checked her register. 'She's in Ward Eight. That way.' She pointed to a corridor on the right.

'Thank you.' Tom pushed open the heavy swing door to the ward.

'Thomas,' the doctor said, taking Tom's arm and leading him to a quiet corner. 'Sit here for a minute.'

'How's Mother?'

'She's had a heart attack. Your sister and father are with her now. She needs absolute rest. You may go in to see her, but very quietly, please. She is sedated, so she will not be able to respond to you.'

He crept into the ward. Edward and Alice sat either side of Ellen. They turned to acknowledge his presence. After a few minutes, Farrington came in and signalled for them to come outside.

'There's absolutely nothing you can achieve by sitting here, I'm afraid. I encourage you to go home and get some rest yourselves. I assure you Mrs Bellamy is well cared for. If there is any change to her situation, we will telephone you immediately.'

'Thank you, Doctor. Thomas, please take your sister home. I will stay for a while longer.'

Alice hugged her father.

~

Later that night, Tom sat in the kitchen with Alice while Mrs Chadwick outlined the day's strange events.

'Good Lord, who would do a thing like that?' exclaimed Tom.

'It's scary,' said Alice. 'Thank goodness Father has put a police guard on the house.'

'I'm really torn about what to do now,' said Tom, rubbing his temples.

'What do you mean?'

'I promised the Major I would help out, but I can't leave Mother like this.'

'Don't be silly. I will visit her every day, and we'll call you if there is any need for you to hurry back.'

'Are you sure?'

'There's nothing you can do. Doctor Farrington says she must be kept still and resting. I promise we'll call you if anything changes.'

'I don't like leaving you on your own.'

'Father is here in the evening, and a constable will be here during the day.'

'Alright, I need to wash. I'll stay tonight and head back to Llancillow tomorrow.'

~

Two days later. 'Half-past one already,' said Margaret Dawkins, glancing at the clock. 'Alice dear, how would you like to leave early today? I'm sure you will want to visit your mother and then I wonder if you would mind picking up a package for Mr Bradfoot on your way home. It will be arriving at the station on the four o'clock train and I'm afraid I still have rather a lot to do here. You can bring it into the office with you tomorrow morning, nothing urgent.'

'Yes, that's fine, thank you.'

'Run along now, dear, no need to wait here until four.'

~

Arthur walked briskly along the path, occasionally glancing at people going about their business on the other side of the track. He bought his groceries and began his journey home. He felt comfortable in his isolation, but this afternoon was different. He wanted noise, bustle, and people. This time he stopped and sat on a stone wall that ran alongside the track. His skin prickled and he shivered, not knowing why, for although the day was overcast with a threat of rain, it was warm. He watched people coming and going as the feeling grew.

The smell of baking drew him to the Copper Kettle Café. The bell tinkled as he pushed open the door and looked around for a place to sit. A woman and child vacated a table near the window. He took their place and looked across to the low stone wall and the line of sycamore trees which defined the path beyond.

'Can I help you?' asked the matronly waitress.

'Tea, with sugar.'

'Anything else with that?' She held her pencil poised above the notepad.

'Yes, bacon sandwich.' Arthur didn't see the scathing expression on the waitress's face.

The patrons' chatter buzzed. He began to wish he had gone

straight home. But today was different; today he needed to test himself.

The waitress returned with his tea and sandwich. Tea had slopped into the saucer and wet the spoon. He found the sugar basin and dolloped three large teaspoons into the cup. He frowned at the plate, picked up a corner of the neatly quartered sandwich and looked under the bread. It was not what he imagined ... he had expected two thick pieces of bread with oily, crisp bacon inside and grease dribbling down his chin. Instead, he had two thin slices of bread with cold gammon ham finely sliced as a filling. He found it difficult to get his fingers through the handle of the fine china cup and the tea was warm but weak. *Tastes like gnat piss!* Arthur felt rage growing in the pit of his stomach.

The doorbell tinkled and the chatter quieted. Alice glanced around the room. She had visited her mother but, finding her deeply asleep, decided not to stay too long. She took a few steps further into the cafe looking for somewhere to sit.

As she walked past Arthur's table, he smelled her perfume; it was sweet, *like flowers,* he thought. He could not take his eyes off her. *It's her, the Bellamy girl.* He noted how her bobbed hair finished in curls at the nape of her neck. Her slim waist, accentuated by a tight belt drawn around her skirt, drew his eyes to her svelte hips and long legs. He felt his sex stiffen. How long had it been since he had felt like this? Not since before the war. *That slag, Hilda, tricked me into marrying her, she did. I was just gettin' on me feet. Out of Brum and in the army. Didn't know the bloody war was going to start, did I?*

'Can I help you, miss?' the waitress enquired.

'I would like some tea please while I wait for the train.' Alice saw Arthur staring at her. 'Never mind, here it comes.'

The waitress peered out the window. 'Bit early for the next

train,' she said but Alice had already turned to leave.

Toffee-nosed bitch. I saw the way she looked at me. All the bloody same these women. He followed Alice with his eyes as she left the cafe and walked away. He pulled his tobacco and match case out of his pocket and rolled himself a cigarette.

The waitress took away his plate and cup and left the bill beneath the ashtray. She looked curiously at the silver match case before she walked away.

Arthur lit his cigarette, ran his fingers over the fine engraving on the silver box. The meaning of the Latin words escaped him, although he remembered Tom had told him once. That seemed long ago. He rubbed the box on his sleeve to bring back a shine and then tucked it safely in his pocket. He counted out coins to pay his bill. Picked up his shopping and left the cafe. He was anxious to get back to the house. *It was a mistake,* he thought. *Too risky. Never know who might be travellin' down from Birmingham. There must have been something in the newspapers by now.* Arthur's eyes narrowed; he watched Alice peddle towards the railway station.

She placed the package in the basket behind her saddle and cycled towards Back Lane.

Silly girl, Arthur thought. Licking his lips, he followed, hurrying to keep up with her and trying to stay in the shadows.

Halfway down the lane, the ground became potholed. Alice dismounted, pushed the package further down into the basket. *All that bumping, just as well it didn't drop out,* she thought. She looked behind and saw the shape of a man in the shadows. Her heart began to pound. She broke into a sweat as she struggled to push the bicycle over uneven ground.

Arthur was catching up to his prey. His mouth filled with

saliva, he spat it out, increased the speed of his walk and broke into a run.

She tripped. The bicycle fell into a ditch along with the parcel. 'Help,' she cried.

Arthur fell upon her, trying to pin her down and pulling at her clothes.

'Get off me! Help!' She fought back with all her might. Aiming for his eyes, she scratched him, her nails gouging his skin.

'Argh! You bitch,' he yelled and slapped her face hard, causing her nose to bleed.

She grabbed his wrist before he could hit her again. She tried desperately to throw him off, but she was pinned down. She managed to free one leg and kneed him in the groin.

He shrieked, his mouth frothing and cursing.

She grabbed a stick and stabbed at him. 'Help!' Alice shouted as loud as she could.

Dogs barked. A man called, 'Who's there? What's going on?'

With a final punch to Alice's jaw, Arthur struggled to his feet and left her semi-conscious and bleeding on the ground. He tore a piece of her shirt to hold against his bloodied cheek and ran down the lane.

'Miss Bellamy, isn't it? Good Lord, what's happened to you?' The man helped her up off the ground. 'C'mon, let's get you home.'

'Oh my,' said Mrs Chadwick, helping Alice into a chair.

'I heard a commotion and found her lying in the lane,' said the man.

'Thank goodness you found her.' The housekeeper dabbed gently at the wounds on Alice's face with a warm flannel. 'Sit there, I must call your father.'

'I better get back. Left my back door wide open. You never know who's around these days. I'm Hadleigh, from number twenty-one if Mr Bellamy needs to speak to me.'

~

At Llancillow, Crabbe picked up the telephone. 'Pontrilas 439.'

'Putting you through.' *Click.*

'Major, it's Maisie Chadwick. Is Thomas there?'

'Yes, Mrs Chadwick. Not bad news I hope.'

'Yes, it's Miss Alice ...'

'I'll fetch him. Please wait.'

'Tom, here, what's happened?'

'I've just rung your father, can you come home straight away? Alice has been attacked.'

'Oh God, I knew I shouldn't have left.'

'Here, my boy, take the keys and please drive carefully.'

~

'Alice, darling, what happened?' Tom said, kneeling by her side.

'Oh, Tom. I thought he was going to rape me. Horrible, it was horrible,' she sobbed. 'Oh no, my bicycle and the package ... they're still in the lane.'

'Don't worry about that, I'll fetch them. Has Doctor Farrington been called?'

'No, I don't want to see him. I don't want to see anybody.' Alice sobbed.

'Thomas, in here please,' Edward called.

'You go,' said the housekeeper. 'I'll stay with Miss Alice.'

'Sergeant Turley will be here any moment. We are

launching a full-scale investigation. We must find the perpetrator. God knows we can't let your mother worry about this.'

'I understand, Father. I'll go and collect Alice's bicycle and a package she is worrying about.'

'Take a torch with you. Have a good look around, see if you can find anything that might help us identify this fiend.'

He picked up the bicycle and the package and pushed them through the gate before returning with the torch. Carefully scanning the area in wide sweeps, he was ready to give up when a glint on metal caught his eye. Nestled in weeds at the edge of the dirt lane was a small metal object. He picked it up and examined it in the torchlight. 'How the hell?' He hurried back to the house.

Sergeant Turley and the Inspector were in deep conversation when Tom rushed through the door to his father's study. 'I found this in the lane,' he said breathlessly. 'Father, this is the match case that Major Crabbe gave me when I graduated in 1914.'

'What?'

'Look at the inscription. It's my match case.' Tom began to pace. 'Now it's starting to make sense.' He stared at it and gripped it in his fist. 'The Red Cross. No identity. He knew that. He could have given them information, but he did not. What was it? Jealousy? Spite? Then that last day when I was in the lorry. I saw him standing on the steps. I thought he was waving goodbye. Something sparkled in his hand. I'd hidden the match case in my mattress. No time to retrieve it. He found it, the bastard. He was waving it at me.'

'Thomas, who are you talking about?'

Tom spat the words, 'His name is Skaggs. Arthur Skaggs.'

~

Arthur sat at the kitchen table, battling the craving for liquor. This was the first time for weeks he had felt like this. It was a hunger that gnawed at his stomach. He stretched out his hands and watched them tremble. He sweated even though it was cool in his kitchen. He clawed at the skin on the back of his hands, drew a deep breath to calm himself, banged his fists on the table and ran upstairs to grab his suitcase. 'Fuck it, time to go. That bitch. Ruined everything she has. They're all the same. Bitches.'

He tore the brick out of the cellar wall to retrieve his cash, wrapped it in newspaper and pushed it in his suitcase beneath a pile of clothes. Under cover of shadow, he ran to Cadbrooke's house. *Good, there's a light on.* He clambered through weeds to the back door and knocked.

The second round of knocking woke Cadbrooke. Nervously, he picked up the poker from the fireplace and called, 'Who's there?'

'Open the door, you prick,' the voice growled.

He let him in. 'What happened to your face?'

'Fight,' Arthur said, pushing past. 'Get me some grub and something to drink. I'm moving in for a bit.'

'You can't do that. What's wrong with your house?'

Arthur swung his fist into Cadbrooke's stomach, knocking the breath from him. 'I've got to get away from here. If the police catch me, I'll spill the beans on you. Got it?'

He gasped for breath. 'Yes. Alright. You can stay here tonight.'

~

Next morning, Arthur snarled as he dabbed a wet cloth over the bloodied scratch on his face. He chuckled as he remembered the condition his host was in when he found him this morning. He had crept downstairs, stealthily approached the sleeping man in his chair and shouted, 'Wake up, you fat bastard.'

After a night of over-indulging, Cadbrooke was almost comatose. When Arthur shouted, he had leapt up from the chair and hugged his chest as pain and shock registered. When he recovered, he pointed to his watch and said, 'Look at the time. I must open my office. You better keep out of the way just in case any clients come in.'

Still chuckling, Arthur looked in the pantry for something to eat. He found bottles of brandy and port, a tin of cracker biscuits and a pot of jam. The remaining shelves held boxes of papers marked 'Archived'. The brandy was tempting, he imagined he could taste the fine silky liquor and feel the heat as it travelled over his tongue and down his throat. He overcame the temptation and took the cracker biscuits and jam.

~

At eight o'clock, Inspector Bellamy gathered his men in the staff room. 'Thank you for coming in so early. By now, you will all have been briefed about the events of yesterday evening. Another vicious attack, this time my daughter,' Edward paused. 'The assault occurred in Back Lane. She had earlier visited the railway station and Copper Kettle Café. We suspect the perpetrator is a man by the name of Arthur Skaggs. I have brought my son, Thomas, into the investigation as he may have already encountered this villain. We don't have an address for the man but considering that last night's attack occurred in Back Lane, we believe he must be located within these parameters.' He spread a map on the table and tapped it with his pencil. 'From here to the Copper Kettle Café. What d'you think, Sergeant? A fifteen-minute walk? And here is Back Lane.' Edward traced the thin line with his finger. 'See how it comes out close to the railway station. These houses all back onto the lane. Over to you, Sergeant.'

'A murmur surged around the room. Turley coughed.

'We are interested to talk to a man fitting this description.' Turley opened his notebook. 'Short stature, stocky build, untidy dresser, possibly not from these parts, may have an accent.'

'I believe Birmingham was his hometown,' said Tom.

Turley acknowledged with a nod. 'Right men, we need to progress this investigation with all haste. Constables Greenaway and Clarke, house to house along Westwell Street. Constable Bolland and I will investigate these shops and the café. On your way. We'll meet back here at two o'clock sharp.'

'Sergeant, Percy Phillips knows this area like the back of his hand. He and I will see what we can find in the lane.' Tom hurried to find Percy.

~

Shortly after two, Turley and Inspector Bellamy met to discuss the witness statements and events of the search.

'Can it be a coincidence?' the Inspector tapped papers with his pencil.

'What, sir?'

Edward shuffled through the papers and pulled out the waitress's statement; he read: *"Rude. Nasty little bloke looked like he needed a good wash. No manners. Kept his cap on. Not from around these parts. Sat near the window. Silver box."*

'Yes sir, interesting,' Turley said, flipping open his notebook, 'she also said: *"He sat there having a fag. Left ash all over the table."* Then I asked her about the silver box, and she replied: "*I thought it was odd d'you see? A scruffy little bloke like that and he's got a fancy box for lighting his fag.*"' Turley continued. 'There was one house we got no response in Westwell Street. Greenaway reported: The lady opposite number 19 said: "*A man on his own lives there. He keeps himself to himself. I hardly ever see him, except a couple of times, down at the shop. The house was empty for ages before he moved in.*"'

Edward rubbed his chin. 'Sergeant, where is the nearest grocery shop to the cafe?'

Turley tapped the street map. 'That'll be Browne's the Grocers. Here on the corner of Howell Street. Bolland interviewed the grocer.' He pulled out Bolland's report. 'Here we are, Mrs Browne said: "*I think I know who you mean. Scruffy person. Yes, been in here regular, once a week. Not much of a talker, he never says much at all. Comes from round Birmingham way.*"'

Constable Clarke knocked on the Inspector's door.

'Come.'

'Sir, your son is on the telephone.'

'Thomas.'

'Father, we've found something in the laneway, towards the end, near the railway. It's a bit of cloth with blood on it; it was stuck on a branch near a gap in the hedge. Brambles have recently been cut and pulled back into the hedge to disguise the way through. I pushed and it gave way easily. We could see the back of a house. Percy's there now. I'll go back and keep an eye out with him.'

'Be careful. We're on the way,' Edward slammed the phone on its cradle. 'Sergeant, take two men with you to Back Lane,' he said, barking instructions as he hurried out the door. 'Constable Clark and you two men with me. Clark, you'll drive.

Remembrance of Love and War

Constable Bolland, take the remaining men and form a cordon at the junction of Pitt and Westwell Streets.'

Hidden by tall brambles with brick walls on either side, dull light stole into the unkempt back yard. Old newspapers, yellowed with age and glued together from dampness piled in one corner. A path to the back door had been cleared through nettles and weeds. Percy took a deep breath and crept towards the house. He listened against the door before squinting through the bottled glass window. He jumped at the snap of a stick behind him.

Tom appeared through the gap in the hedge. 'They're on their way. See anything?'

Minutes later, Turley pushed through the hedge, leaving two constables to keep watch. His lip curled as he peered through the bottled glass into the gloomy interior.

Meanwhile, Constable Clark parked the Inspector's car in front of 19 Westwell Street. Curtains drew back as neighbours inquisitively watched the Chief Inspector push open the gate.

Edward knocked heavily on the door. He waited for a moment before calling out, 'Police. Open up.' He knocked again and repeated the call. Still, no answer came. 'Constable, the crowbar, if you please.'

Clark retrieved a crowbar from the vehicle and forced it into the door latch. He manipulated it backwards and forwards until the wood cracked and gave way and the lock sprang out of its socket.

The inspector and his men followed Clark as he pushed through into the dark, musty smelling hallway. They pulled truncheons out of their belts. Edward indicated for two men to keep watch downstairs while he and Clark went up. Clark winced as the boards creaked beneath his boots. Holding his truncheon at shoulder height, pushed open the bedroom door. Both recoiled at the stale air, heavy with the aroma of dirty bedding and stale sweat. Nothing of interest, they returned downstairs. The hall door was ajar. Edward pushed it open with the end of his truncheon. The lounge room was bare no furniture and nowhere for anyone to hide. They continued cautiously to the door at the end of the passage.

Turley saw the interior door opening slowly and gripped his truncheon.

'What's happening?' whispered Tom.

'Shh,' Turley replied, pressing against the window. 'It's alright, it's Constable Clark.' Turley, Tom, and Percy joined the other men in the kitchen.

'Anything, Inspector?' Turley asked.

Edward shook his head. The men searched cupboards and drawers, looking for clues.

'Sir, look,' said Greenaway. 'It's a note 'Cadbrooke Property & Estates'.'

'Where does that go?' Tom pointed to the trapdoor underneath the kitchen table. Turley's eyebrows arched high. He put his finger to his lips and drew everyone's attention to the floor. Four men lifted the table out of the way. Turley bent on one knee over the trapdoor and lowered his head to listen for any sound. It opened easily, bringing the dank aroma of stale air and dampness. They peered down into the darkness.

Tom found a candle on the dresser. He lit it and passed it to the sergeant.

Turley cautiously descended the steps, Clark followed closely. The steps creaked under the weight of the two men. The light from the candle flickered and grew steadily as they reached the floor of the cellar.

The other men waited anxiously, peering into the dim light.

'Nothing here,' reported Turley.

'Damn. Sergeant, get over to Cadbrooke's. See what you can find out.'

~

Cadbrooke belched loudly as he shuffled through papers littering his desk. 'Where are those peppermints?' he growled. His head throbbed with a monotonous rhythm. It felt like the Salvation Army was using the inside of his head for band practice. His hands shook as he struggled to remove the lid. In frustration, he banged the side of the tin on the desktop, and the mints tumbled out in every direction. 'Damn and blast,' he spluttered.

A wave of nausea overcame him as he bent to retrieve the mints. He groaned as a sharp cramp gripped his stomach before a long, foul fart erupted from his anus. 'Oh God,' he begged. 'Have mercy.' He fetched a glass of water and dropped in a large spoonful of Andrews Liver Salts. The effervescent spray coated his glasses and stuck to his nose hairs as he gulped the brew and closed his swollen eyelids, relishing the relief of the cooling liquid as it worked its way to his stomach. Without warning, he burped again, bringing up sour liquor which burned his tongue and throat. 'Never again,' he muttered.

'Anyone here?'

'I'll be with you in a moment,' answered Cadbrooke, wiping his face with a damp tea towel and straightening his cravat. 'Good morning, Sergeant. To what do I owe this pleasure?'

Turley's lip curled as he watched the estate agent gather up papers and peppermints. He pulled out his notebook and pencil and flicked through the pages. 'I'm calling regarding the property at 19 Westwell Street,' he paused and looked at the man's flushed features and red raw eyes. 'Feeling alright, sir?'

'Uh, yes, thank you,' he felt the bile rise in his gullet and swallowed hard.

Turley continued. 'I believe the property was let in February of this year?' he paused for a response.

Cadbrooke nodded and attempted a weak smile.

'I understand that you are the estate agent managing the property?'

'That is correct, Sergeant.'

'And the tenant, sir? Can you give me the name, please?'

'Excuse me a moment, Sergeant,' he rushed through the back door to the toilet.

Turley made notes to the accompaniment of groans, expulsions of air and finally, the flush. 'Feeling better, sir?' he asked.

Cadbrooke opened the top drawer of a large oak cabinet and began to sort through the contents. '19 Westwell Street, February ...' His hands shook and sweat beaded on his temple. 'Ah, here we are. Smith. Mr A Smith is the tenant,' he pushed the papers back inside and closed the drawer.

'Smith, you say, may I see the tenancy agreement?'

'I'm afraid not, Sergeant. Confidential, you see.' He dabbed his forehead with a handkerchief.

The sergeant puffed out his chest and thrust his shoulders back. 'Now, sir, otherwise, I will ask you to accompany me to the station.'

Cadbrooke's mind raced. He cursed the day he had met

Smith. The old widow at number nineteen had died with no living relatives, well, not to his knowledge anyway. It was a dirty house and needed a lot of work ... work he did not have time to organise ... but he received a fee for management of the property and did not want to lose it. Then along came Smith, obviously a shady character. The perfect patsy, he even had cash. Too good an opportunity to miss. How would he know about the intricacies of leasing a property? He was a peasant; he would not know the tenancy agreement had to be registered.

'Well, sir?'

'Here it is, Sergeant,' he said, clearing a space on the desk and spreading out the document.

Turley bent over the document and opened his notebook. 'Smith, Arthur. Of ... does this mean his previous address? There's nothing written here,' he tapped his pencil on the paper.

'Ah, well, you see, he was away, overseas, in the war, that's it. No address required.'

The sergeant examined the estate agent's face before returning to the document and reading. 'Fifty guineas for that little house?'

He nodded and dabbed his forehead.

'Leaseholder: Mrs Alma Stock.' Turley straightened and tapped his chin with his pencil. 'That's old Bert Stock's widow, isn't it? Thought she'd died more than a year ago?' he peered closer at the document. 'How come she's signed this document as the leaseholder then?'

Cadbrooke's guts were churning. 'Ah,' he said, fumbling for words. 'Mrs Stock signed the document before her death when she appointed me to manage the property on her behalf.'

Bent closely over the paper, Turley exclaimed, 'Well blow me down. Mrs Stock's signature is dated the same as the tenant's. Mr Cadbrooke, I'd appreciate it if you'd accompany me to the police station.'

Arthur overheard the conversation from his hiding place,

Once they were in the street, Cadbrooke broke down. 'Sergeant, thank God. You have saved my life.' Tears ran down his face.

'Walk on.' Turley gripped Cadbrooke's arm and marched him down the street. 'What's all this about?'

'It's him. The man you're looking for. He's in my house.'

~

'We've got him, sir,' Sergeant Turley stood to attention, his cheeks puffed and red, eyes raised to the portrait of the King on the wall above the Inspector's desk.

Inspector Bellamy turned slowly in his chair. 'Excellent, well done, Turley. Call my son, tell him to come to the station without delay. He will need to verify the identity of this degenerate.'

'Sir,' Turley turned on his heels and opened the Inspector's office door as Constable Bolland called out, 'Telephone, sir, the hospital, Dr Farrington for you.'

Bellamy's jaw tightened.

'Edward, you'd better come, quickly.'

'Sergeant Turley arrest the felon. Constable Bolland, fetch the car. Constable Greenaway, call Thomas, tell him to go immediately to the hospital. The identification can wait.'

~

Arthur lay on a wooden bench in a grey prison cell. The air felt thin, and the light was dim. He whispered to himself. 'This is a well and I'm drowning. This is my tomb.' He sniffed and wiped his nose on his grubby shirt sleeve. He drew his knees up to his chest, wrapped his arms about himself and chuckled.

~

The doctor was waiting for the inspector's arrival.

'Edward, old friend. I'm so sorry.'

Inspector Bellamy stood rigid, staring at the doctor. He found it difficult to breathe. He felt cold and disoriented, dizzy, light-headed. He reached out a hand to balance himself.

'Edward,' Farrington took the Inspector's arm to steady him. 'Come to my office. We can talk there. Nurse, bring hot tea, please.'

Tom pushed through the hospital door. 'My father, Dr Farrington?'

'Yes, this way,' said the nurse at reception, leading Tom down the corridor. She knocked on the doctor's door.

'Come in, Tom. Sit down.'

Tom remained standing, he placed a hand on his father's shoulder and felt Edward flinch.

'I'm afraid there was nothing more we could do. Her heart ...'

'Where is she? I want to see her now.'

'Of course, Edward. Follow me.'

The three men walked stoically down the corridor. Farrington pushed open the door to a small private room.

'Father,' Alice cried. She threw her arms around his neck; he gently pushed her away.

Tom wrapped his arms around Alice and peered over her shoulder at his mother. Ellen's skin seemed as pale as milk.

Her silver hair draped along the pillow.

'Please leave me.' Edward's words were laboured as he attempted to contain himself.

Doctor Farrington signalled to Tom and Alice to leave with him, closing the door behind them.

The silent corridor suddenly resounded with a dreadful cry and terrible sobbing as Edward fell to his knees beside his wife.

~

Arthur uncoiled himself, stretched and paced, muttering. As his pacing became faster, his muttering grew louder. He stopped suddenly when the inspection hatch in the door opened and Turley shouted, 'Hey, you, what's going on in there?'

Arthur pressed his back against the wall and thought for a second before answering. 'It's bloody freezin' in 'ere.'

'Bugger.' Turley fetched a blanket from the store. 'Stand away from the door,' he commanded and threw in the grey woollen cover.

Arthur wrapped himself in the blanket and curled up on the bench, feigning sleep, until Turley closed the viewing hatch.

The blanket was old and thin, it took Arthur no time at all to tear three long strips, which he meticulously plaited. He'd seen enough of death by hanging in the camp. The sudden drop, the desperate kicking and jerking and then the snap of a broken neck. He'd also seen men who did not wait for the noose. With a good slip knot and their own weight, they did not need to hang from a height. He just needed enough pressure to get it to tighten. Arthur looked around the cell and decided on the bench post.

Kneeling, he secured the ligature around the post, slipped the noose around his neck, and lunged forward. 'Fuck the lot of you,' were his final words.

CHAPTER TWENTY-THREE

The family sat silently in the dining room while the housekeeper set crockery. Maisie had been up since four o'clock that morning baking and making sandwiches in preparation for the wake. She glanced at the kitchen clock. *Oh my, quarter past nine already, the cars will be here soon,* she thought, *such a sad day.* She pulled out her handkerchief and wiped away a tear.

'Mrs C?' said Tom.

'Oh, you startled me. Can I get you something? Cuppa tea?'

'No thank you, I just needed to stretch my legs for a minute. This waiting is tedious.' He stepped quietly along the hall and opened the door to his mother's room. Everything was just as it had been. The bed neatly made, her books on the bedside table, fresh flowers in a vase on the windowsill and the familiar fragrance of lavender wafting in the air. Oddly, the scene agitated him. He felt bile rise in his gullet as anger and sorrow collided within him.

'Hard to believe, isn't it?' The housekeeper stood in the doorway, dabbing at a tear. The doorbell rang and she turned to answer it.

'My boy,' said Major Crabbe, holding out his hand to Tom.

'Dear Mrs Chadwick, do come with me. I have Grace and Percy in the car.' Crabbe offered his arm and escorted the housekeeper out of the house, glancing back at Tom with a look of encouragement.

'The car is here, let's get this over with,' Edward said, his voice cracking.

~

The Reverend Snell stood at the wrought iron gates at the end of the gravel driveway. Nearby a group of five police officers, in dress uniform, stood to attention as the hearse, followed by a Bentley, carrying Tom, Alice and Edward, drew to a halt. The driver signalled to the policemen as the family members climbed out of the car.

Tom acknowledged Percy and Grace standing at the edge of the crowd. Percy bowed his head, but Grace held Tom's gaze and he felt, in that brief moment a notion to be still, to settle and soften the harsh voice of grief that raged within, as though he could make the choice to refrain from charging forward and take the time to stop, to breathe and walk slowly into the befalling event.

'Right, gentlemen,' said Sergeant Turley. 'Fall in pallbearers.' Tom joined them. Gently and reverently, they lifted Ellen's coffin to their shoulders. Reverend Snell led the procession with Carstairs, the funeral director. Behind followed the six pallbearers with Edward supporting Alice and behind them a lengthy line of mourners. The cortege slowly made its way through the great timber doors of Holy Trinity Church to the celestial and soothing pipe organ playing *Dominus Regit Me*.

Seated in the front pew alongside Alice and Edward, Tom shivered as he watched the Reverend Snell climb the steps of the pulpit. Everything today seemed as grey and foggy as his emotions. He felt cold in the waiting silence. Ellen's coffin, adorned with white lilies, drew his attention. *Lilies signify that the soul of the deceased has returned to a peaceful state of innocence. Where did that come from?* he thought.

Snell began, his words echoing along the stone walls.

Mother. The knot in Tom's stomach tightened.

Alice reached for his hand and laid her head on his shoulder.

Briefly, the sun shone brilliantly, lighting up the stained-glass, sending shards of rainbow light across the floor to Ellen's coffin. Tom squeezed Alice's hand. His tears began to flow. He was not ashamed. He loved his mother and would forever remember the soft glow of her smile and the feel of her tender touch.

> *... May the souls of the departed, through the mercy of God, rest in peace and rise in glory. Amen ...*

~

At the end of the service, Bellamy family members, accompanied by Reverend Snell, climbed back into the Bentley and followed the hearse to accompany Ellen to the final part of her earthly journey. Soon the low wall of the ancient cemetery came into view and beyond, weary gravestones could be seen leaning torturously amidst a tangle of weeds. Looming yews overshadowed the wall leading to the entry gates. The vehicles paused before the iron structures while the driver opened the gate. Nearby, Sergeant Turley and his constables waited.

Under instruction from Carstairs, the pallbearers lifted Ellen's coffin to their shoulders, and the cortege began past a labyrinth of sepulchres and Gothic tombs. Past rows of silent stone angels, witnesses to pomp and ceremony of days long gone.

'Here we are now,' said Carstairs, indicating a turn off the path to reach Ellen's family mausoleum, encompassed by elaborate black wrought iron picket and chain fence.

Tom stared at the sarcophagus supported by eight griffins.

Angels, both beautiful and terrible, adorned each corner and along the sides, circular tablets carried inscriptions, separated by inverted torches.

Alice sobbed as her mother's coffin was interred into a prepared cavity in the mausoleum. Tom wrapped his arms around her and whispered, 'Don't worry, Mother's light can never be extinguished. We'll hold her safely in our hearts.'

~

Later that evening, after the mourners had been provided for and copious words of condolence offered and received, Edward retreated to his study and Maisie disappeared to her room.

Tom poured two glasses of whisky for him and Alice, and they sat in the dining room.

'What now?' asked Alice.

'I really don't know the answer to that,' replied Tom. For now, the quiet moment they shared was more than adequate for his needs. Although already an idea began to dawn in his weary mind, but it would take him a while to find the words to articulate his thoughts.

CHAPTER TWENTY-FOUR

Tom waited at home for three days until he was sure he could leave his family and return to Llancillow. He had not spoken to anyone and wondered if any progress had occurred regarding Grace's move. He decided to telephone.

'Pontrilas 439. Crabbe speaking.'

'Major, it's Tom here.'

'Hello, my boy, good to hear your voice. How are you coping?'

'As to be expected, sir. I'm sure you understand. Actually, I was calling to see if anything transpired about the Phillips situation.'

'Yes, in fact, Matthew Phillips came out to see me yesterday. We had an excellent chat. I showed him around and we discussed the administrative requirements. You'll be pleased to know that it's all organised. That is, Grace will take the apartment this weekend and Mr and Mrs Phillips will plan to move in at the end of the month.'

'Marvellous, that doesn't give us a lot of time to prepare the rooms. What about Percy?'

'Yes, he is keen too, I'm relieved to say. I believe his skills will prove invaluable. I understand he is giving notice to Cartwright's."

'Alright, I'll find out when he'll be free to come and help.'

'Righto. I have Harold, Cyril's boy, helping me now. He's keen to stay on but needs some direction. It will be wonderful to have you back. That's if you're still willing, of course.'

'Absolutely. I don't believe I'm needed here; I will be at Llancillow tomorrow morning.'

'Would you stop in at Lennard's and pick up some paint, brushes and so on. I have an account there. I'll telephone them and tell them to expect you. See you tomorrow.'

~

On Saturday afternoon, Percy and Tom dragged Grace's trunk into her sitting room.

'Good Lord, Gracie, what've you got in there?' Percy arched his back.

'Is it alright here?' asked Tom, straightening the trunk against the wall.

'Yes, thank you both,' Grace smiled.

'I could use a cuppa after that.'

'You two go on ahead; I'll follow you shortly.'

The two men found the Major in the kitchen with a fresh pot of tea set on the table.

'Job well done, gentlemen. Is Grace joining us for tea?'

'She said she'd follow soon. She's probably getting used to her new surroundings,' Percy said. 'I can't tell you how grateful we are, sir. She's been putting on a brave face, but it's been absolute misery for her every time she stepped out the door. Our poor old mother has been beside herself wondering what to do.'

'It's a pleasure, my dear boy. Grace is most welcome, and I am delighted to have her company, not to mention her help around the house, only light duties, of course. Which reminds me, when is her baby due?'

'I think she's got about a month to go.'

'It's disgraceful. I don't understand it.'

'Eh, what?'

'The way Grace has been treated,' Tom replied. 'It's exasperating. Don't these people know how brave she is? They have no idea what she endured.'

'All wars divide, my boy. The emotional pain and negative experiences suffered by so many cause people to act in unnatural ways. Spitefulness, anger, ignorance. These are the effects portrayed by people who have suffered through war.' Crabbe closed the kitchen door.

'I apologise for the outburst; this really is not the time ... It just makes me so angry.'

'I agree, Tom. It is insidious. I saw it every day at work. People looking sideways at me, pretending not to notice that I limp and have a face that would make you vomit. They don't know what to say.'

'None of us really know the hell you went through. Both of you.'

'Was it all worth it?' Percy continued, 'I've seen things no man should see. I've seen bodies blown apart. A pal shot at dawn because he just couldn't go over the top one more time and they called him a coward. As long as I live, I'll remember the hundreds I knew who didn't make it back, my own dear friend, Ron. Lucky Ron, that's what they called him. He was like a brother to me.'

Tom stood beside his friend. 'Percy, I wasn't there, but I share your pain; you survived against all odds.'

'Hah. Any courage and nerve I had were stolen from me. That bloody war shattered my nerves. And now back in this civilised world, well, they might as well have taken my body too, they did a bloody good job at breaking it.'

'Gentlemen, please, let us spare a thought for Grace. This is not the way to welcome her arrival.' Crabbe pleaded.

She stood in the open doorway. 'I couldn't help but overhear you, Percy, love.'

'Sorry, Grace.'

'Don't say that. We've all paid a price.' She looked over Percy's shoulder and her eyes met Tom's. 'You don't need to stop talking just because I have come into the room; nothing you can say will frighten me.'

'War is hideous. If this war is the last and the world becomes the better for it, well and good. If not, God help the world!' Crabbe's voice rumbled.

'I hear those words ringing in my ears like the daily din of shellfire in the trenches. But what if those who died could come back and see what they fought for? I wonder what their thoughts would be.'

'Percy,' Grace chided.

'I cannot forget the endless years of privation and wretchedness and yet, I hunger to understand what I missed. Yes, I hear and read about the horror of trench warfare, but it is beyond my understanding. Worst of all, I feel ashamed that I was inactive all that long time.'

Crabbe responded passionately, 'Good heavens, Tom. What are you saying? You were one of the first ...'

Grace reached for Tom's hand. 'I nursed you. I saw the horrendous injuries you sustained.'

'Well, I have to do something about it. I just can't go on until I find out how to make sense of all of this. Major, do you have the Times?'

'Yes, I'll fetch it for you.'

He flicked through the pages. 'Ah, here it is, this article about War Graves. Work of the Imperial Commission. They are looking for volunteers to search for the bodies of our soldiers, to exhume them, identify them and re-bury them in organised cemeteries.'

Grace's eyes welled with tears. 'Dear Lord,' she whispered.

'Tom, for God's sake, you're not thinking of going there? My God, you've got no idea what's it's like. This is madness,' said Percy.

'Be that as it may, I am going to enquire.'

An awkward silence followed until Crabbe spoke. 'You must do whatever you think is best.'

'I hope you understand how grateful I am to you, Major. I don't want to let you down after all you have done for me. In any event, I won't leave until the household is settled and you have all the help you need here at hand.'

'Besides,' added Percy. 'We've got a whole lot of cleaning and decorating to get on with. So, we better get started without further delay.'

The tension in the room broke. They each settled down to discuss the jobs at hand. All the while, though, Tom thought: *It will all work out. I hope I'm right.* But his mind filled with 'what ifs.'

~

There was a great feeling of anticipation at Llancillow on the following Friday morning. Tom and Percy undertook a final inspection of their work on the east wing.

Crabbe came in and exclaimed, 'Marvellous job, gentlemen.'

The dogs started barking. 'Ah, that might be the lorry now.'

Remembrance of Love and War

'I'll get the gate, said Tom.

'Reeves of Hereford & Ross' furniture lorry rumbled into the courtyard, followed by the Crossley, driven by Cyril and carrying Matthew and Sarah Phillips.

'Welcome, welcome,' called Crabbe.

Cyril touched his forelock in greeting. 'Mornin' Squire. Picked up a letter for you.'

Crabbe thanked him and tucked the letter in his back pocket.

Grace took her mother into her apartment while the men began emptying the lorry and carrying furniture and belongings into the Phillips' new home.

~

Work finished, Crabbe remembered the letter and reached into his pocket to retrieve it. He felt a pang of sadness when he saw that it was addressed to Tom. 'Letter for you, dear boy,' he said, handing it to him.

Tom looked at the envelope, turned it over and hesitated for a moment before saying, 'It's from the War Graves Commission.'

Later that evening, Tom and Crabbe talked in private.

'The time has arrived, it seems. What will you do now?' Crabbe asked.

'They have sent me a ticket. I'm to leave via ship for L'Havre on the third.'

'That's next Thursday.'

'Yes, not a lot of time.'

Crabbe lit his pipe, 'You must not worry about us here at Llancillow,' he said. 'Thanks to you, everything is in order. I have good help and company.' He took another puff.

'Although, I shall miss you terribly, of course.'

'I shall miss you too, sir. I don't know how long I'll be away, or whether indeed, I will cope with the work ...'

'But you will, my boy. I have no doubt of that. Do keep in touch, please, let us know how you are and whether you need anything. And, most of all, come home safely when your work is finished.'

When Tom looked at his mentor again, there was a distance there and he had turned his eyes away.

~

The following Thursday morning Tom was packed and ready to go; he dialled 439.

'Major Crabbe's residence.'

'Hello, Grace, Tom here. I thought I'd give you a quick call before I leave.'

'Are you off so soon?' She paused. 'I wanted to tell you how much I admire what you are doing and to say how grateful I am.'

Tom could not speak.

'Tom, are you there?'

'Yes, I was distracted.'

'I'll fetch the Major.'

Words caught in his throat, but she was gone.

'Tom, dear boy. Off already?'

'Yes, sir, eleven o'clock train to Southampton, then a steamer overnight to L'Havre.'

'Good man. Well, take care now. Proud of you, my boy. Call if you need anything.'

'Thank you, sir.' He heard a click on the telephone.

~

The trip began smoothly until Tom changed trains in Reading to find it was standing room only. He was relieved to step off at Southampton Station, released from the unpleasantly claustrophobic journey.

'Can you tell me how I get to the docks?'

'It'll 'ave to be Shanks's Pony, pal.'

'Is it far?'

'A mile or so that way,' the porter said, pointing.

Tom set off through the crowded town. He turned a corner to find a raucous mob of men hurtling in his direction. Ahead of the mob, a handful of black men ran in terror, their eyes wide and chests pumped as they raced into side streets. Tom walked past brawling men spilling out of public bars, beggars, and suspicious looking scoundrels. In the distance, he spotted the funnels of steamships. He walked along the bustling dock to the SS Kardinya.

'Ahoy there, mate.' A sailor called.

'Good evening,' Tom replied. 'I have a ticket for Le Havre.'

'Crikey, mate, you're cutting it fine, aren't ya?'

'I thought the departure was nine o'clock.'

'S'orright mate, just kiddin'. Come aboard.'

Tom climbed the gangway. 'You're Australian?'

'Got that right. This old girl's an Australian ship. She's been used as a hospital for the last four years. Now she's going home.'

'Via Le Havre?'

'Still have some of our boys there, volunteered on the recovery at Villers Bretonneux. Once we pick them up, we're heading home. Follow me,' he said, leading along the deck.

'They've dismantled the medical stuff, except for the beds. Take your pick.'

Tom appraised the long rows of narrow metal beds, selecting one by a porthole, and dropped his rucksack on the stripy mattress.

'I'm goin' to miss them pretty nurses,' the sailor winked, handing Tom a blanket and pillow. 'Come down to the lower deck when you're ready and we'll find you some tucker. O'right? Gotta keep an eye out,' he said, tapping the manifest. 'Couple more to look out for, then we can get going.'

Tom descended to the lower deck, drawn by the aroma of food and the buzz of conversation, laughter and clattering of cooking pots.

'Room over here.' Men waved in welcome.

'I'm Tom,' he said, reaching across the table to shake hands.

'Hello, my name's Jimmy and this is my da.' The boy's cheeks were flushed with booze while Da bore a solemn expression.

'Right, you lot, come and get it. Tuckers up. Line up, you buggers,' yelled the cook. 'Ain't you learned no manners?'

'Meat and tatties. Tuck in, Da.'

Tom savoured every mouthful of the rich beef stew.

After the meal, men brought out packs of playing cards and dice; the air thickened with cigarette smoke.

'Hey! Ain't no room for two-up in 'ere, you take that up-top, you buggers,' shouted the cook. 'And don't start without me.'

'Ever played two-up?' Asked a man sitting next to Da.

'What's that?' asked Jimmy.

'Starts off with the ringer, see? He puts two pennies, tail-side up on the kip. The punters gather around, in a circle, like this.' He drew the shape with his finger on the table. 'Then they all yell out their bets. *Two bob,* that sort' a thing.' The man took a drag on his cigarette. 'Then someone calls out *come in spinner*. And the spinner tosses the pennies. Gotta be at least ten feet in the air otherwise, it's a *no-throw.* The ringer makes sure it's played dinkum. If the pennies fall both heads up you lose and if they're both tails up, you win.'

'What happens if they land with one head and one tail?' Jimmy asked.

'Nah, that's no good. The spinner keeps tossing til he gets a pair. D'you wanna go and join the game?'

Jimmy looked at his father, who frowned.

'No, thank you.'

'How about you, mate?'

Another man chipped in. 'Here, watch out for him, likely he's got a two-headed penny.'

Tom smiled. 'Thank you, but I will decline.'

The cook shouted, 'C'mon, you buggers, where's my spinner?'

Within minutes, only a handful of people remained in the galley.

'Funny lot, these Australians, I can hardly understand a word they say,' said Jimmy.

'What takes you both to Le Havre?' Tom asked.

'We've signed up for work with the Imperial Graves Commission,' Jimmy answered solemnly.

'I'm going there too,' said Tom.

'It's bloody demanding work,' said the man seated next to

Da. 'Picked up a chest infection, so they had me out of there. Thought it was that bloody Spanish flu to start with,' he coughed into a handkerchief. 'You're a bit of a young'un for that sort of work,' he pointed to Jimmy.

'Both my brothers were lost. Da says it's the right thing to do.'

As his father walked away, Jimmy whispered, 'Don't think bad of him. Da hasn't spoken since my ma died, of a broken heart, they say. Words make him choke. I hear him sobbing in the night.' He followed his father.

'Fuck,' said the man retrieving a flask from his pocket; he gulped a mouthful. 'Bert Frost,' he offered Tom his hand.

'Tom Bellamy.'

Bert crammed tobacco into the bowl of his pipe. 'So, what takes you to France?'

'I'm working with the War Graves Commission ... and to try to understand.'

Bert looked surprised. 'Understand? None of it makes any sense, mate.'

Tom inclined his head.

'Strewth,' he said, drawing hard on his pipe. 'My dad, brother and me had a nice little farm in Mildura. Chas was two years older than me. Apple of Mum's eye, that's for sure. He got married while I was playin' the field, if you know what I mean. Then along comes this lot. We was in. Chas and me, off to see the world. First, stop Egypt. I seen all of them pyramids in books but here we was, right in front of them, having our picture taken and ridin' on camels and so on. Got my first dose of the clap.' He laughed.

'I've heard quite a bit about the Australians in Gallipoli. Were you there?'

'Yeah. Bloody silly tricks we got up to. Chas had this idea to put his slouch hat on a stick and raise it up just above the trench wall. Silly bugger. Full of bullet holes it was, but he still wore it. What about you?'

'BEF. I was in the cavalry.'

Bert offered his flask and Tom accepted.

'We landed at Boulogne in August. Advanced along the line of the canal, which ran as straight as a Roman road through to Mons, without any confrontation. We reached our ground and made shallow trenches. First few days, we rode out to meet advance patrols of the enemy, but we quickly overwhelmed them. It all seemed so easy. I remember that I was distracted from thoughts of battle because I was intrigued with the vista. Patches of woodland, a few green spaces but huge slagheaps dominated the scene. Dotted in between, a factory here and a private house there. Then the battle began.'

Bert drained his flask. 'Worst I remember was one of the first charges in Gallipoli. We went over one hill, then rested in the shadow of a second. Some Tommies were already taking cover in a trench there. Then wallop. A shell exploded right in the trench. Bits of those blokes flyin' everywhere. Bastard Turks. They put petrol in the bombs and them that wasn't blown apart, burnt to death. Screams. Never heard nothing like it. Our blokes went to try and drag them out. Snipers picked them off. That's where we lost Chas. Next thing, we're off to France and those bloody trenches.'

Tom inspected Bert's lined face. The grey stubble of his beard partially hid a purple scar that ran the length of his right jaw. 'What was it like at the end? The armistice, I mean.'

'We knew it was coming because word had gone along the line for a while. It was like you didn't want to do any more killing but you didn't want to be the last corpse. Then suddenly, it was over. Our captain shouts out: *The bloody war's over. It's over!* Like a bunch of stunned mullets, we were. We went on for a while, you know, work as usual. Then this wave of exhaustion came over me and I could see all the blokes felt the same. We was sobbing. Grown men.' He cleared his throat. 'The faces of all my mates who'd gone kept appearing in me mind. I couldn't believe I was still standing. The next few days were a bit of a blur. We had to pack stuff up, but we were too scared to walk out of the trenches for fear of getting shot at. The thought of our mates lying out there in the mud eventually drove a bunch of us to go over the top. We did what we could,' he said, shaking his head. 'Then the news of demobilisation started. Rumour was they were sending most to England and some to Egypt and Mesopotamia. Well, I'd had my fill of travelling. So, me and my mates went to the captain and said, "Bugger goin' to England, we need to find our mates." Couple 'a days later, Captain gave us each a pick, shovel, wire cutters, rubber gloves, a stack of canvas and cresol. We found a load of wooden stakes and then stood there lookin' at each other, like a bunch of dumb monkeys, thinking *... so how the hell do we get there?'*

'Where were you wanting to go?'

'Villers Bretonneux. That was where we lost most of our mates.' He fell quiet for a moment. 'Anyway, Dewey and Bob purloined an old ambulance, scrounged around for parts and the next morning we was on our way.'

'I admire your determination.'

'Thanks,' he sneered. 'So, what about you. Where'd you end up?'

Tom took a deep breath. 'Our orders were to stand and fight. There was to be no retreat. We couldn't let the German army break through and reach the coast. By October, we were in La Bassee and that was my last stand. I was injured when a shell burst in front of me, killed my horse and I woke up in a German POW hospital. Arrived home and then woke up in Weston Super Mare.'

Bert looked puzzled. 'I reckon you missed a bit there, mate.' He rummaged in his pocket and pulled out a pipe. 'Here, you might want this where you're going.'

'Thank you but I don't smoke.'

'Take it, mate. I promise you'll need it.' He pressed the pipe into Tom's hand and winked.

~

Tom awoke to the sound of machinery. He quickly rose, pulled on his haversack, and found Jimmy and his da talking to a group of men who were busy dismantling beds.

'We've arrived,' said Jimmy, his cheeks pink with excitement. 'We're going down to the lower deck. They'll tell us when we can disembark. Here, look at that, Da.' Jimmy pointed to a machine lifting cargo off the ship and putting it down on the ramp. 'It looks like the Swansea Ferris Wheel. They're taking beds off the ship.'

'They're going to the French. Poor blighters haven't got much left,' said a sergeant pushing past. 'Those men engaged by the CWGC will find a bus waiting for you at the end of the wharf. Please make sure you have all your belongings and follow me.'

The wharf was teeming with activity. As the bus drove off, Tom turned to take a last look at the ship and, for a moment, thought he saw Bert waving.

3rd August 1919

Dear Sir,

I apologise for taking so long to write, however, since arriving in France I must say, life has been hectic. However, I am revelling in my first day off for five weeks, spending a little time at base camp. A hot bath and a decent bed last night and now a top-class rum in the canteen this evening has done wonders to restore the spirit.

The journey here was quite harrowing. After disembarking at Le Havre, we travelled by bus for the first three hours until the road disappeared, then transferred to horse and cart. The landscape was an appalling scene, littered with barbed wire, shell holes, trenches and, unexploded shells and other devices protruding from the mud.

In our group, we find twenty men from different military units and backgrounds, including veteran soldiers and men who had never seen frontline service. There are also civilians, including a Welsh man and his boy I met on the ship. We were thrown together in this new unit, with no sense of cohesion, until the good Sergeant Howell took over command.

The work is gruesome and heartbreaking to see the way the men are buried. We have found ten or more huddled in the same grave. Many have been dead twelve months or more, so you can imagine the need for a strong constitution. I am developing one. What keeps us going is the knowledge that we are finding lost men not previously identified and that our work may set the minds of families at ease.

It was too much for the young Welsh boy, which is not at all surprising. He has redeemed himself by working in the records office and doing an excellent job in recording details about each body recovered. These records will prove invaluable over time.

The hour is late, and I must return to camp early tomorrow morning but before I finish this letter, I might ask a great favour of you. Would you be so kind as to send me a decent tobacco for my pipe? The stuff they hand out here is quite abominable. Yes, I am now smoking a pipe, kindly given to me by an Australian soldier I met on the journey here. He said I might need it and he was right.

I hope this letter finds you well. Please give my good wishes to Grace and say hello to Percy. I expect the Phillips family are all settled in by now.

Respectfully,

Thomas

29th August 1919

Thomas, my dear boy,

Goodness, what a time your letter took to arrive. I have sent a package of 'Prince Albert, crimp cut' tobacco. I am assured of its superior quality; I hope you approve.

News from home. Grace's baby arrived on the fourteenth of July. Mother and son well. He is a bonny child. I have found Grace to be fine company, and she has settled in well and happily. Also, Percy has been a grand help since my little turn. He has a remarkable skill for fixing my old machinery and saved me quite a few bob, I can tell you. He uncovered Father's old cider press and has *been tinkering with that and spending hours in the old orchard. Mrs Phillips is a dear lady and appears to be having a wonderful time with her little grandson, a great help to Grace. Mr Phillips is a blessing; his administrative skills are to be admired. We have taken to spending a bit of time together each afternoon in the garden. Harold is working well under Percy's guidance. So, you see, Llancillow is functioning well.*

How are things there? I read in the Times about the enormous need for funding and manpower. This is a remarkable challenge you have taken on. I admire you so. We do hope you will make it home for Christmas. Percy tells me he wants to organise a Wassailing in the new year, goodness knows what that means.

Well, my boy, do take care and stay in good health. I shall look forward to hearing from you when you have time.

Sincerely,

Crabbe

~

Tom felt a tinge of something he found difficult to name. *What does the Major mean by a 'little turn'? Grace has a son ... how I regret not being there when she had the baby.* He folded the letter and placed it in his bedside drawer.

January 1920

Percy banged on the kitchen door with his elbow.

'What've you got there?' Grace asked.

'Pippins,' he replied, setting a box on the kitchen table. 'Now, all I need is some good spices. What have you got in the larder?'

'Just a minute. Don't march that mud into my pantry, thank you.'

Percy grinned, kicked his boots off and set them next to the Aga. 'Sorry, dear sister.'

'What are you looking for anyway?'

'Christmas spices,' he said, studying the jars. 'What would they be exactly?'

'Ginger, cloves, cardamom, cinnamon, that sort of thing. If you tell me what you want them for, I might be able to help.'

'The Wassail.'

'What?'

'Where's the Major?'

'He's resting. Now slow down and tell me what this is all about.' Grace looked fierce with her arms folded across her chest.

'In a couple of days, it's the fifth of January. The Twelfth Night of Christmas, the darkest night of the year and traditionally the time to Wassail the orchard.'

The kitchen door opened and in came Sarah.

'Ma wants to do the Wassail, don't you Ma?'

'What dear?'

'That's enough,' said Grace.

'I'm sure the Major will agree. We can get Cyril, his wife, and his lad too. If only Tom was here. we could invite his father and Alice ...'

'What's all this merriment about?' Asked Crabbe, entering from the dining room.

'Oh, I was just about to make you some tea, Major.'

'Yes, please,' Crabbe replied. 'So? Will you share the news?'

Grace filled the kettle and placed it on the hob. 'Percy's got some project in mind.'

'Wassailing the orchard, Major. It's nearly Twelfth Night.'

'Ah.' Crabbe rubbed his hands together. 'What a splendid idea. I believe I have Father's old Wassailing bowl somewhere. Back of the larder,' he said, walking into the pantry.

Grace shot Percy a not terribly happy look.

'Here it is,' Crabbe said, revealing a large, two-handled, polished wooden bowl covered with hessian. The Phillips family are here, but who else shall we invite?'

'I was just saying, how about Cyril and his family. It doesn't look like Tom will be here but what about inviting his family?'

'Yes, I'll get on the phone to the Bellamy's. We'll invite them to stay the night, plenty of room.'

'Marvellous. Now, all we need is the cider punch,' Percy said, turning to Grace.

'I see. Alright, I'll consult my Mrs Beaton's … but tea first.'

~

On Thursday afternoon, driving the Crossley, Percy collected Edward, Alice, Mrs Chadwick and their overnight bags. They arrived at Llancillow's gate, followed by Cyril, Mrs Tapsley and Harold, in their new Ford Model T.

'Looks like the Council roadbuilding job is paying off well, Cyril.'

'Indeed, it is.' Cyril grinned, revealing a mouthful of gaps and yellow stumps.

They all hurried in through the kitchen door.

'Goodness, hello everyone, please go through to the dining room. Major Crabbe is waiting to greet you.' Grace swiftly dispatched the crowd, apart from Mrs Chadwick, who insisted on staying to help.

'Oh, that's so kind of you. Have you met my mother?'

'Hello, I'm Sarah, lovely to meet you.'

'Likewise, I'm Maisie, and who is this little poppet?'

'This is Matthew, my grandson,' said Sarah.

'Maisie, would you help me carry in the tea?'

Laughter and happy chatter filled the dining room.

Alice sat next to Grace. 'So, tell me, Grace, how are you? Are you happy here?'

'I am, Alice. I can't tell you how good the Major has been to me. I am content and at peace.'

'That's so good to hear. I know Tom was concerned about you before he left. He'll be so relieved to know you are happy. I do miss him.'

'Yes, we all miss Tom. Let's hope he comes home soon.'

~

By five o'clock, darkness had fallen. They all rugged up against the chill, but still and rainless night and led by Crabbe and Percy, began their procession to the apple cider orchard. Each man carried a lighted torch of Herefordshire Thorn, constructed from a stem of hawthorn, the upper branches tied together at their very tips to form the framework of a sphere, then stuffed with straw and decorated with ribbons. The glow of the flames reflected in the wide eyes of little Matthew, clutched closely to Grace's breast.

Earlier that day, Percy had set twelve small piles of dry timber in a ring around the Wassail tree. The group entered the orchard and reverently gathered in a circle around it.

'The song,' proclaimed Percy and they all joined in singing the words they had rehearsed earlier:

Old apple tree we wassail thee
And hoping thou will bear
For the Lord doth know where we shall be
Til apples come another year
For to bear well and to bloom well
So merry let us be
Let every man take off his hat
And shout to the old apple tree

Percy removed the lid from the pitcher of warm cider punch and filled the Wassailing cup held by Crabbe. Grace handed Percy a piece of toast which he dipped into the punch and pushed into a crevice in the bark of the tree.

'Wassail!' the group called.

Next, Crabbe poured the cup of punch onto the roots of the tree.

'Wassail!' again the group shouted.

'Light the fires!' cried Percy. Everyone cheered as the cup was refilled and passed around.

As they walked back to the house, Crabbe leaned on Percy's shoulder. 'My boy, you have done us proud,' he said. 'I have only one sadness and that is that Thomas was not here to share this celebration.' The two men continued in silence.

CHAPTER TWENTY-FIVE

The autumn of 1919 had been unusually mild; however, the continuous rain made the digging extremely arduous in heavy clay soil. Tom watched the steam rising from his colleagues' clothing, strung out on a makeshift line inside the hut. He lit his pipe to combat the thick, sour smell that filled the room. He was alone apart from four exhausted men, quietly playing cribbage, in the far corner.

'Evening.' Sergeant Howell pulled off his greatcoat and spread it over the back of a chair near the heater. 'I was hoping to find you here,' he said, settling in a chair next to Tom. 'I have some news. A fresh crew are arriving in the next few days, and I have recommended to Commander Pearce that you be appointed as the group leader.'

'When you say 'fresh', do you mean untrained?'

'Yes. Don't worry, they've all been vetted and they're keen to work. You'll soon have them ship-shape.'

'Where are they coming from? England?'

'I believe so, they are all demobbed soldiers. Poor sods, no chance of work for them over there. So much for Lloyd George and his promise of a 'land fit for heroes'.'

'Well, at least they may be better prepared for this God-forsaken place. Assuming they have had frontline service.' Tom knocked the ash from his pipe. 'I would like to stay and talk but I'm afraid I don't think I can keep awake. It's been a long day. I'm off to my bed. Talk tomorrow.'

'Yes, of course. I think I'll do the same.'

~

Early the next morning, Tom was called to see the Commanding Officer.

'Ah, Bellamy, come in.' Pearce held open the door and ushered Tom to sit. 'I believe Sergeant Howell has told you about the new men arriving on Wednesday.'

'Yes, sir, he said he had recommended me for group leader.'

'That's right. You'll have twenty men. Sergeant Howell will assist you in a three-day training programme and then set to work at this location.' Pearce spread a chart on the desk and tapped the ordnance map with his pen. 'This is the spot.'

Tom bent to examine the map. 'But sir, that area has already been searched.'

'Twelve months ago, yes. It will be a good spot for the men to hone their skills. Break them in, so to speak.'

'I understand. when do we start?'

'First thing tomorrow, so I want you there to meet the men by four o'clock today.'

'Sir, about my current team, who will lead that?'

'You know the men better than I, Bellamy. Please select a new leader.'

Tom hurried down the hallway. He found young Jimmy banging away at a typewriter like a two-finger expert at quite some speed. 'Hello, Jimmy, glad I found you. I'm just running out to find the team,' he said, pulling on his protective clothing.

'Oh aye?' replied the boy.

'I'm being sent to another team,' explained Tom. 'Can't say much now, but I must find your Da. I want to tell him he's now unit leader.'

'Oh bless, he'll be tickled pink about that.'

'Must dash.'

He found the men bent to their work. Da looked up as he saw Tom approach and held up his cupped hand. 'German, I think.'

'Can I have a word,' shouted Tom.

These good men, Tom thought, as one by one, the men dropped their implements and climbed out of the pit. *How stoic and yet compassionate they are.* 'Men, it has been a privilege to work with you.'

'Eh up,' scoffed Harry.

'I'm being moved to a new team,' Tom continued. 'Da, I'm nominating you as the unit leader.'

'What, no time for drinks?'

'No, I'm sorry. Orders,'

The men looked from one to another until Harry slapped Da's back. 'Congratulations,' he said. 'Oh, and good luck to you, Tom.'

'I guess the drinks are on you then, Da,' said another.

The men laughed and returned to work.

~

Tom's new team soon learned the ropes after their initial training. A week later, it was time to move to a previously undisturbed site. All through November, the unusual weather pattern remained; mild and wet. The constant rain turned the land into a quagmire. Although the work continued, by the end of the month, Tom's team had diminished to himself and nine diehard workers.

'This is it, lads,' he said as the lorry pulled to a halt and the men disembarked. 'The information we have here was provided by a photograph taken from a British plane in 1917. How dependable that is now, I don't know. It clearly shows eight pits, dug in two parallel lines just around here. This was over a mile behind the German lines at the time the photograph was taken. Some of those pits have been backfilled.' He turned to the men. 'I think it's fair to say we have a big job ahead of us. Let's get started, we'll work in two teams.'

The men pulled the gear out of the lorry.

'The first thing we're going to do is look for clues that indicate a body or bodies might be here. These men were buried in mass graves by the German army, so we won't find the obvious rifles or stakes protruding from the ground bearing helmets or equipment. We'll look for any partial remains, small bones and pieces of metal brought to surface. Check out those rat-holes.'

The two teams set off, working parallel to each other.

'Over here,' one of the men shouted, holding something up for the others to see.

'And here,' called a man from Tom's team.

Each team set to work around the finds. Within the hour one team had found the first of the bodies.

'Come and help,' Tom instructed.

Both teams gathered at the one site and peered into the excavation.

'There must be at least ten in there,' said Tom. 'They seem to be quite whole. Work in pairs, see if you can grab a body each.'

As they pushed through the wet, slimy chalk to take hold of an arm or leg, their hands sank into soft flesh and slime.

'Oh Christ.' One of the men slipped and the arm he had pulled simply disconnected. They struggled to pull out the bodies but the most they could do was pull out one piece at a time. It was sickening work, but they persevered until the first pit was cleared. They placed the bodies on cresol-soaked canvas for careful identification.

'Search the pockets. Check for identification discs and personal effects; watches sometimes have useful inscriptions. Let's see if we can clean up some of the badges and buttons so they can be identified,' Tom instructed.

'I've found some cutlery in these puttees. Looks like a man's initials and number.'

Later that day, Tom addressed the men. 'Good job, men. Let's get these bodies back to HQ. It's been a tough day and we're back for more of the same tomorrow.'

1920

Two months wore on with no real break from the task. Tom was concerned for his team. He noticed a depressed mood, apparent amongst some of the men in his charge. Petty arguments broke out over trivial events. Relief came in January when severe frosts prevented the work from continuing. Four days of time off at the base camp was the temporary solution.

On returning to base, Tom sought out Howell. He found him that night at the canteen. 'Sergeant Howell, could I have a word in private?'

Men crowded at the bar, drinking, becoming rowdy. Tom found a quiet table in the corner. 'I'm glad I found you, I've been wanting to talk to you.'

'How can I help?' Howell asked.

'I'm finding it difficult to control the men in my team. I think it's just the emotional strain which, of course, is the nature of this kind of work. I know they are exhausted; we all are. I've overheard a couple of them talking and the gist of their grievance is that they feel they were forced into this work because they had tried, and failed, to find employment back home. So, essentially they had no option but to come here.'

'I agree with you. The first wave of volunteers were people committed to the programme. Take Da and his lad. They believe that every man they find in some way honours the two boys they lost.' He watched the behaviour of the men at the bar, a skirmish had broken out. 'It's tricky. We are desperately short of men, but I agree, this is not work for that kind. I'll have a word to the captain in the morning.'

Tom and Howell caught up the next day.

'Your team is not alone. I spoke to the captain this morning and he tells me that there is an investigation underway. The daily sick-parades have increased in number dramatically. There are numerous reports of men suffering from nervous breakdowns and other stress related illnesses.'

'I can't say I'm surprised. What do you think will happen?'

'Already, they have started to return some of the least suitable men back to England. There's also going to be some sort of filtering system, so men can't apply for a position here if their only motivation is employment. It's early days, we'll be even shorter of manpower but at least we'll have a workforce we can rely on. Captain Pearce wants us to set up a training programme for a new batch of men expected to arrive in March. Meanwhile, medical units are to be set up to interview the current team members and determine whether they are mentally sound for this work.'

'And if they find men who are not sound?'

'They'll be going home.'

~

By July, Tom felt the situation had changed dramatically. New teams were working well. The level of efficiency had improved. The concept by some workers that their reputation depended on finding the highest possible number of bodies in the shortest possible time, with little attention to the important work of identification, was now a thing of the past.

~

In late October, Tom was summoned to the captain's office.

'Ah, Bellamy, come in, take a seat. I'll come straight to the point,' said Pearce, shuffling through a collection of papers. He looked Tom in the eye. 'I've recommended you for a rather special task.' Pearce packed his pipe with tobacco before continuing. 'You're a good man, Bellamy, right for the job.' He found the paper he'd been looking for and waved it in the air. 'It's hush, hush at the moment. Political strategies and all that guff. In short, the directive is to find an unknown soldier. Gawd knows there are enough of those poor blighters around. Problem is,' he paused to light his pipe. 'They want no repercussions. No chance of the identity showing up.'

'I see, sir.'

'A collection of suitable subjects will be exhumed from various battlefields and brought to the chapel at Saint-Pol-sur-Ternoise, near Arras. This is where you come in, Bellamy. You and the other two men appointed to this task, Hough and Williams, will conduct thorough investigations to ensure the complete anonymity of the soldiers. Six will be selected, placed in unmarked coffins, then one will be selected to be returned to England and laid amongst kings.' Pearce blew hard into his handkerchief. 'You'll also be joined by Staff Sergeant Howell.'

'Might I ask, how will the one be selected, sir?'

'Ah, you'll hear more about that when you arrive in Saint-Pol. Any other questions?'

'I don't believe so.'

'Right, good man. You better get packed. Transport will arrive this afternoon to take you to Saint-Pol.'

Tom packed up his belongings and walked to HQ to await the transport.

'Hello Tom, I've been looking for you.' Jimmy; said. 'There's a letter for you.'

Tom turned the letter over and recognised Grace's handwriting. He tucked it in his tunic pocket. 'Thank you, Jimmy.'

'You goin' somewhere?'

'Yes, I'm being posted.'

'Oh. Well, take care then.'

'You too, Jimmy. You've done really well.' Tom felt his words were empty.

~

The journey to Saint-Pol had been lengthy and uncomfortable. Along the way, Tom watched the familiar scenery slip past the lorry. He was almost immune to the destruction of this land laid waste by war. He pulled his pipe and tobacco out of his pocket. 'I hope you don't mind if I smoke,' said Tom to the driver. The driver shrugged. Although he had attempted conversation to pass the time, there was none to be had, the driver merely grunted in response to Tom's banter, so he gave up trying. He remembered the letter from Grace and began to read:

> 'Dear Tom,
>
> It is with great sadness that I must inform you of Major Crabbe's death on the twentieth of September.
>
> You will remember that he had a series of small seizures earlier this year. Unfortunately, this last one was extremely severe, and he was taken very quickly.
>
> I was fortunate to have been with him when he passed. In his last breath, he spoke of his fondness for you. He called you the son he had never had.
>
> The Major's solicitor has written to enquire when you might return for the reading of the will. I have explained that you are in France at present undertaking important work. However, he says that the will indicates you are the sole beneficiary and that is why you are required to attend. He will not proceed without you.
>
> Please don't worry, my parents, Percy and I will stay here taking care of things as best we can.
>
> I shall look forward to your safe return.
>
> My sincere condolences,
>
> Fond wishes,
>
> Grace Phillips'

Tom was now glad of the silence and his surly companion's lack of conversation. He could be alone with thoughts and memories of his dear friend and mentor.

~

It was almost dark when they arrived at GHQ, a construction of metal sheets attached to the remnants of a stone wall from a municipal building. The driver waited for Tom to retrieve his pack before, without a word or a wave, he drove off.

'Good evening, Tom,' Staff Sergeant Howell called in his Welsh baritone. 'We've been expecting you. Please come in, the other gentlemen are already here.' He cleared his throat. 'Welcome, gentlemen. I've been ordered to brief you on this project, which I believe you have already been told is top secret. I'm sure you are all tired and hungry, so let's adjourn to the mess, we can talk over some hot food. Bring your packs with you and we'll drop them off at your lodgings along the way.'

The men followed Howell down a labyrinth of corridors.

'Bit of a rabbit warren, eh?' Williams declared.

'Just to the right, there is your accommodation.' He pushed open a door and stood aside so the men could pass.

Three iron beds, each with a metal bedside table, were set against the stone wall. A paraffin heater glowed with a blue light in one corner, emitting a musty perfume. A small table and a couple of chairs were set against another wall.

'Home, from home,' Williams quipped.

In the mess, the men were served hot stew and a mug of tea.

'Thank you, Toddy. These three men will head a special project. Messrs Bellamy, Hough and Williams. Please,' said Howell, indicating the men should eat. 'Toddy used to cook at the Grosvenor in London, so you're in good hands.'

The men tucked into the fragrant stew and dumplings.

'Let's start with introductions.' Howell nodded at the man opposite.

'Derek Hough. I saw service here in northern France. June '16 to September '18.'

'Stan Williams. April 1915, invalided out November 1917,' he tapped his artificial leg.

'Bellamy, Tom. BEF, captured October '14. Spent the rest of the war in a German POW camp.'

Each man appraised the other.

Howell continued. 'I'm Staff Sergeant Howell. I lost too many young men in this war. Some of them we've been digging up in bits and pieces for this last year.' He searched the faces of the men. They revealed a common sadness. 'I believe you have been told some details about the project,' said Howell, as he spread a map across the table.

The men finished their stew and pushed the bowls out of the way.

'The exhumation work has continued with no special instructions for any of the units. As far as they're concerned, it's business as usual. Tomorrow, you will each be driven to one of these selected areas, sites of some of the bloodiest battles. Tom, you'll be taken to Ypres. Derek, Arras. Stan, the Somme. In each of these locations, the remains of three unidentified British bodies have been exhumed and set aside. Your task is to each select two of the most suitable candidates and transport them here to Saint-Pol. You know what is expected?'

'No risk of identification,' said Hough. The other three nodded in agreement.

'Any questions so far? Right, I should advise that this whole area of north-eastern France is a quagmire right now. It's been tipping with rain for weeks. Not only that, but this is all naturally boggy ground. More than one thousand miles of canals stretched through this area, they were obliterated during the fighting.' He ran his finger over the map. 'The wettest of them all is here, around Ypres.' Howell caught Tom's eye before continuing. 'The northeast is in a shambles because of the constant fighting during the five-year occupation by German forces. The area in and around Ypres was particularly devastated. Any questions?'

'I have a question,' said Tom. 'How long have we got to complete this operation?'

'Five days,' replied Howell. 'You must get back here with the bodies by the seventh of November.'

'Five days?' Hough gasped.

'Pheww,' Williams whistled. 'We'll do it,' he said.

'There will be a lot of work to do when you return. I'm not at liberty to discuss that at present.'

'How do we get to our destination?' asked Tom.

'You'll each be accompanied by a military man who will drive you there and back in a field ambulance. You'll be accommodated in the nearest GHQ to the site and transported each day. Tom, I'll be travelling with you. Derek and Stan, you will meet your drivers in the morning. Breakfast will be at six-hundred hours. Please be packed and ready to leave shortly after that. Now, if there are no more questions, I suggest you get some rest. Goodnight, gentlemen.'

~

The familiar scenes of waste and destruction materialised in the grey morning light. An empty, barren landscape as though the war had left behind bleak ghost towns and villages.

Sergeant Howell glanced at Tom. 'Alright, there?' he asked.

'Yes, fine,' replied Tom as the Ford ambulance bounced along the pock-marked remnant of a road.

'We're coming up to St Quentin; we'll be able to get a hot

drink and some food there. And we'll need to refuel.'

Tom felt compelled to read the letter again. He reached in his tunic and unfolded the paper. Tears stung his eyes as he pondered on the past and regretted the loss. He stared at the delicate script, the fine, even letters of Grace's pen. Howell interrupted his thoughts.

'From here on, at places, this waste is twenty miles broad.' Howell muttered something undistinguishable under his breath.

They arrived at St Quentin GHQ in time for a hot lunch and a chance to stretch their legs. They ate in silence until Howell said, 'We've still got a long journey in front of us. I'll go and check the vehicle has been refuelled. See you out there in fifteen minutes?'

Back on the road, they came across groups of men carrying heavy equipment.

'Chinese,' said Howell. 'Under British officers, they're clearing up the fields, collecting rusty iron and barbed wire, old shells and rails.' He slowed the ambulance to let men cross the road. 'Using dynamite to blow up the German redoubts for steel girders.'

'Dynamite? That's not going to help the retrieval of bodies, is it?'

Howell shook his head in agreement just as he spotted a column of black smoke. He slowed the vehicle. Three Chinese men ran into the road ahead of the ambulance, waving their arms for the vehicle to stop. Just off the road was a cart laden with wire and metal poles; a donkey munched carelessly on weeds.

Tom and Howell climbed out of the vehicle.

'Aidez. Aidez,' one of the men called.

'D'you speak French, Tom?'

'A bit. Better than I speak Chinese.'

The workers ran towards the smoke, pleading with Tom and Howell to follow. When they arrived at the scene, they found two dead bodies in a small crater and a woman sobbing. She held a boy in her arms.

Howell knelt to examine the boy. He felt for a pulse but there was none. He shook his head.

Amidst the shouts and wailing, Tom said, 'Messieurs, le fils est mort, je suis desole.'

'C'mon Tom, there's nothing we can do here. We need to get moving.'

They drove through terrain scarred with shell holes and smashed redoubts and weeds growing thigh high amidst the tumbled earth. Occasionally they saw peasants trying to plant in the boggy soil.

'It's just a bloody quagmire,' whispered Tom. 'How will these people ever recover?' He spread his hands in consternation.

'Getting food in is the main problem. The farmers are trying to salvage what they can of their machinery and equipment but it's going to take a long time to clear the land of the abandoned military equipment. You wouldn't catch me ploughing those fields with all those unexploded shells and collapsing tunnels, not for quids.'

Both men fell silent, deep in their own thoughts, as the miles rolled by.

Near to midday, Howell pulled the vehicle up.

'Need a piss,' he said.

'Me. too.'

They lit up their pipes and leaned against the warm engine.

'How much further to Ypres?' asked Tom.

'Four, five hours. Hungry?' He fetched sandwiches and water bottles from the vehicle.

'Tell me, Sergeant Howell, you're still here. Don't you have a family to go home to? '

'My father was a coal miner; he died when I was just a lad. Ma, bless her, she died in 1915. So that just left my wife. Ah, she was a beauty, a lovely woman. We were married just before the war started.' He paused. 'I wasn't the same man when I came back.' Howell sighed. 'And you? D'you have family?'

'My father, yes. A sister. Mother died last year in bloody awful circumstances. Now I've just found out my dear friend and mentor has died,' Tom said, tapping the letter in his breast pocket.

'Sorry to hear that.' Howell patted Tom on the shoulder. 'We better get moving.'

It was dark by the time they arrived at police headquarters in the Minnepleine district of Ypres. People, pushing and pulling carts, filled the street, illuminated with gas lights that reflected on evanescent structures.

'This city was razed,' said Howell. 'All this is temporary stuff, to house and shelter the people. They have already started to rebuild in brick; you've got to admire their spirit.'

Tom followed Howell into the timber and iron building that housed the police, the local government office and, down a network of corridors, Ypres GHQ.

'Ah, Staff Sergeant Howell.' The officer put down his pen, removed his spectacles and rubbed his eyes. 'You made good time.'

'Yes, sir,' replied Howell. 'This is Mr Bellamy, Captain

Forbes.'

'Excuse me for not getting up,' said Forbes, extending his hand to Tom.

Outside the thin walls of Forbes' office, a raucous commotion erupted. Flemish voices reached a crescendo and then receded to a low grumble.

'Just another squabble,' explained Forbes. 'Nearly six thousand people have flooded back into Ypres. Most are not locals, enticed by the prospect of a temporary accommodation, funded by government. Trouble is the past residents of Ypres, those brave enough to return, are also trying to retrieve what's left of their dwellings, so there's insufficient shelter, insufficient food but no lack of hot tempers. Anyway,' he said, shuffling some papers on his desk, 'Getting to the point, we've found several likely candidates for you, and I expect you'd like to get on with the job first thing.'

'Yes, sir,' replied Howell.

'Righto, get yourselves down to the mess and find something to eat. One of the lads there will show you your bunks for the night.'

'Thank you, sir. After you,' said Howell, opening the flimsy door for Tom. 'This way.' Howell led Tom down the corridors. 'Captain Forbes lost both his legs in sixteen,' he whispered over his shoulder.

~

Early next morning, Tom found Howell in the front office, studying a mud map on the police constable's desk. 'Thank you, Constable; that should help.' He rolled up the map and winked at Tom. 'The whole place is a rabbit warren. The old maps bear little resemblance to what's left. They're still trying to discover dirt tracks and lanes that were destroyed. Why they bother to relay cobbles, I can't guess,' he said, pointing some old men working on the side of the road.'

'How d'you replace two thousand years of history?' Tom answered.

They drove in silence the rest of the way, past endless temporary huts until they left the town limits and returned to the familiar beleaguered landscape.

Howell pointed to a collection of huts in the distance. 'That's it, Bard Cottage Cemetery,' he said, turning off the road and following a track towards the huts.

'Sounds very civilised,' Tom replied mockingly.

'I'm not surprised they found our men there. Boezinge is the name of the area. It was used as a cemetery from June 1915 right through to October 1918. Men buried here were from West Riding Division and 38th Welsh Division.' Howell squinted. 'They've recently brought in remains from the surrounding area, including thirty-two graves from Marengo Farm Cemetery. There's over sixteen-hundred men buried here, and God only knows how many more lie beneath.'

A man in overalls waved the vehicle to stop. He walked round to the driver's side. 'Hello, Ivor, boy. What's taken you so long to get 'ere, then?' He laughed, exposing a mouthful of broken teeth.

'Dai, how are you, man?' Howell laughed and pointed to Tom. 'I brought Mr Tom Bellamy with me. Meet Dai Davies.'

Tom leaned forward to acknowledge the greeting.

'Dai, we're on limited time. Can you show us what you have?'

'Follow me.'

'You have a lot of men working here. How many squads?' Tom asked.

'Yes, we've got a lot of locals working here. Officially, it was a Zone Rouge, considered too dangerous to allow people to return at the end of 1918. Risk of stepping on a shell, see, so many of the buggers failed to explode. The local people been trying to make a fresh start, rebuild their homes, businesses, farms, churches. Not to mention public buildings, roads, bridges, railways, and canals. Some bastard's got to clean up; that's why there's so many of 'em here, they get a couple of bob a week to remove the abandoned weapons and ammunition. They fill in craters, tunnels, and, sometimes, they help us do the exhumations. They find coins every now and again. We let them keep those. None of the personal stuff though, fountain pens, rings, bracelets, rosary beads,' he spoke as if he was mentally ticking off a list. 'Found this yesterday,' he fiddled in his breast pocket. 'A lock of hair in a leather heart,' he paused. 'All objects are carefully examined and conserved to see what they might yield towards an individual's identity.'

Dai sounded matter of fact, but Tom knew it was self-preservation that caused the men to speak like this.

'Here we are.' Dai led them through a ramshackle door. He nodded towards three wrapped bundles on stretchers. It was cold and gloomy inside the tin shed. 'I'll get you some more light.'

Silently and reverently, the two men changed into blue dungarees. Dai returned with lamps and a young worker followed him carrying a tray with mugs of tea. They waited until the young man left.

'What can you tell us?' asked Howell.

Dai cleared his throat, lit the two lamps, and spread out a chart on the bench. 'First two were found here.' He tapped the grid with his finger. 'This was an area where we found bodies three and four deep. We found this fellow, his skeleton intact, in a crouching position,' he pointed to the first bundle. 'There were only scraps of clothing, enough to convince us he was a British soldier. He was wearing boots made by Unity Co-op Society Ltd. 1913. He'd been lying in the bottom of a crater. Nothing much left around him except these.' Dai showed them a small box placed on the stretcher.

'Well, the date on the boots is significant. This was probably a 1914 soldier. We'll examine the box shortly. Please continue,' said Tom.

'Next, this fellow, we finally found most of him after a careful search was made. My men removed the body from the grave, then they placed his skull at the top of the grave and made a geometric pattern of his bones; he's still missing a finger from his left hand. He had a silk handkerchief clenched in his right fist. Nothing else to identify him apart from a scrap of what looks like tartan, in the box there.'

Tom and Howell exchanged glances.

'Next man?'

'Number three. The sticky nature of the clay in these parts means that we can't sieve earth to find objects or small fragments of bone. Finger probing is the only effective way. We've turned up a lot of spoons that way. That's what we found around this fellow. Eight of them, each with a different service number scratched on the back.' Dai reached for the third box and showed it to Tom and Howell. 'See? There's a bit of a cap badge there too and some buttons,' he said, pushing the objects around with his finger. 'Scraps of khaki, his skeleton is complete but no boots, not even a strap. Guess the Germans took those.'

'Thank you, Dai, we'll take it from here,' said Howell.

'Dirt,' exclaimed Tom.

'What?'

'We need two barrels of dirt from the vicinity where you found these bodies, please.'

'What the 'ell for? Don't you think we've already been through it with a fine-tooth comb? We search with our bloody fingers for buttons, buckles and boots, not to mention bones.' Dai spat the words.

Howell stepped between the men. 'C'mon now, Dai, Tom's not having a go. We need the dirt to take back with us. I'm sorry we can't tell you more but it's important.'

'Right.' Dai stomped off.

'Let's get on,' said Tom. 'Number three, these spoons,' he examined them under the light. 'Look, this one has RB 3 I think that's a 5.'

'Rifle Brigade, this has LF, can't make out the number, though. I would say that's the Lancashire Fusiliers,' added Howell.

'Why so many spoons? Was he collecting them d'you think?' Tom picked up another. 'For each of these service numbers, a possible owner could be pointed out, but with uncertainty concerning which regiment he belonged to, his date and place of death, or theatre of war, his identity couldn't be guaranteed.' He examined the fragment of a metal cap badge before handing it to Howell. 'Does this mean anything to you?'

Howell shook his head. 'The buttons are just general issue. Let's look at number two.'

Tom took the fragile piece of tartan. 'It's clearly a tartan weave,' he said, taking a small brush and bottle of liquid out of his bag. He reached into his tunic pocket and pulled out a small piece of Pear's soap. 'Work's a treat,' he said as he cautiously rubbed the tartan and held it up to the light. 'I'd say that was blue and green.'

Howell squinted. 'I agree, that'll be Black Watch colours. And this?' he said, pointing to the silk handkerchief.

Tom carefully spread the delicate cloth on the table and dabbed it with the wet brush. 'It's frayed at the corners but there seems to be some stitching here, look.' He continued to work on the cloth. 'Red stitching, little hearts, I think.'

'Nothing else in the box?'

'Just rusty metal scraps, nothing identifiable.'

'This last fellow then.' Tom examined the boots. 'Considering they've been submerged in wet clay, they're in good condition. Look, the soles and heels show slight wear.'

'He'd be BEF then. Might have been one of yours.'

'Well, he wasn't cavalry otherwise, he'd have been wearing riding boots.' Tom turned the boots to read the maker's name. Unity Co-op Society Ltd. 1913, that's not a name I'm familiar with.'

'Hah,' scoffed Howell. 'Forgive me, but I don't imagine you would have shopped there. The Co-ops have been around for over fifty years, catering for us poor beggars. They are all over the place. Up north, down south, even Cardiff has the Co-op.'

'So that doesn't help us pinpoint the place of issue then.'

'Even though number two has little to identify him, the scrap of tartan leads to the Black Watch. Any number of wives or sweethearts would have pressed a hanky into the hand of their man before he left. Silk suggests that it may have been a wealthy woman. Does it matter that one finger is missing?'

'What about number one?' asked Howell, examining the boots again.

'I'm sure that he was a BEF soldier, although it's odd that he was wearing Co-op boots. That suggests to me that he was a volunteer, perhaps a Territorial, he stepped up to the call and prepared himself.'

'That brings us to number three, the man with the spoons.'

'Hmm,' Tom mused. 'Is there a chance that one of these spoons could be his? Impossible to determine, it creates a very slim opportunity though.'

'Well, we can only take two of them – what do you think?'

'I say number one.'

'I agree.'

'And the Scot.'

'Agreed. I'll fetch Dai.'

'We need that soil.'

Howell returned with Dai.

'I understand that you want the soil, but you'll have to give the men time. They're out there now, in the pissing rain. They've orders to bring it back here as soon as possible.'

'Can you find us a bed for the night, Dai? We'll need the soil before we leave. There's not much daylight left, so best done in the morning.'

'Yes, I'll find you both a bed, but you'll have to put up and shut up.'

'Of course,' said Howell. 'It will give us a chance to catch up. I have a good bottle of whisky in my pack.'

'Aha. All's forgiven then. C'mon, let's get to the mess. Bring your stuff.'

~

The following morning, nursing a sore head, Tom caught up with Dai and Howell in the mess.

'Here, get some of that into you,' said Dai, winking at Howell, he pushed a plate of sausages across the table to Tom.

Grease congealed on the plate. 'No, thank you. Just some hot tea and toast for me.'

Dai laughed.

Howell checked his watch. 'The barrels have been loaded. Let's get back to headquarters as fast as we can. Thank you, Dai, old friend.'

~

Heavy rain made the drive arduous as Howell strained to focus on the potholed road. The weather cleared in the early afternoon as they reached police headquarters in the Minnepleine.

'Let's take a break here and find some food,' said Howell.

'Good idea, I could use something to replace the lining in my stomach. I'm not used to hard liquor.'

Howell slapped Tom's shoulder. 'Follow me.'

~

Satisfied with a hot meal in the police canteen, they continued their journey to St Pol.

'You were in the first battle of Mons, Tom. Did you get anywhere near Ypres in fourteen?'

'No, we retreated west towards Aras from Mons. Why do you ask?'

Howell shrugged. 'I just wondered if you got to see Ypres before it was smashed to pieces. It was a remarkably lovely city. I was there in October 'fourteen, Second Battalion Welsh Regiment. Right in the centre of town was this towering, ornate building. They called it the Cloth Hall. There wasn't much left of it by the time we were gone. It's this bloody flat land,' he said. 'There was just a bump of a hill to the south where the Germans had massive guns installed. They bombarded the town until it was flattened. We lost a lot of good Welshmen here.'

Tom surveyed the shattered landscape and tried to imagine what it was like. *Shops, houses, schools, municipal buildings, churches ... what must it have been like for the inhabitants?*

They continued the journey, both deep in their own thoughts.

On arrival at St Pol, the team reunited. The strain of the last three days etched in their features. Grim faced, Howell's words broke the silence that had engulfed the crew. Through tightened jaw, he ground out the words, 'Right, lads. Let's get them inside.'

Reverently, the four men carried the coffins into the small chapel. They lowered them onto trestle tables and covered them with Union Jacks.

'What now?' Tom asked.

Howell answered, 'The hut will be locked and guarded until midnight when Top Brass arrive. Somehow, they will decide. C'mon lads, I'm knackered. Let's get some grub and then I need a good, long kip.'

~

At midnight, a general entered the chapel. He walked slowly, pausing at each flag-shrouded coffin twice, before placing his hand on one of them. He had made his choice. This soldier would forever be acknowledged as 'The Unknown Warrior'.

CHAPTER TWENTY-SIX

'Tom, they're transferring our man to Dover on HMS Verdun, due to leave today from Boulogne. I want you to go with him,' said Howell.

'Me? Why aren't you going?'

'I still have a lot of work to do here. I haven't been demobbed yet. You're a civilian now. Anyway, you've done your bit, man. Get on home while you've got the chance. Hey, make sure those six barrels of soil are watched over as well,' Howell laughed.

The two men shook hands. 'I won't forget you, Sergeant. You're a good man.'

'Stop yacking and get on with it.' Howell turned and walked away.

~

In Boulogne, Tom joined the mile-long cortege as it passed through the streets of the town to the strains of a military band playing Chopin's Funeral March. Children and townspeople lined the streets and watched in silence, with bowed heads. He recalled his first arrival in Boulogne in August 1914. How different that was; crowds cheering and pretty girls blowing kisses.

He watched the coffin and six barrels of soil from the battlefields, taken on board. Three huge wreaths, each carried by two men, were placed beside the coffin, and four guards assumed their stations.

After a flurry of activity, HMS Verdun slipped anchor and headed into the Channel.

The cold, brisk wind cut into Tom's thin frame. He pulled the collar of his greatcoat up around his ears as he watched the Port of Boulogne disappear in sheets of rain.

'Below decks for me,' said an older man. 'Out of this bloody wind.'

Tom followed him to the shelter of the lower deck, where men sat huddled in small groups, speaking in soft voices.

'The name's Treloar,' said the man.

'Bellamy,' replied Tom, offering his hand.

'What brought you to this momentous day, Bellamy?'

'I've been working with the War Graves Commission.'

'Brave man. Not a job for the faint hearted, I imagine. I lost my son in this war. At least we had him home when he died.' Treloar reached into his coat pocket and brought out a card. 'Treloar and Wells, Undertakers,' he said. 'It was a privilege to bring the coffin for this man who represents so many lost.' Treloar handed Tom the card. 'Did you see it? The coffin.'

'No.'

'Magnificent it is. Constructed of fine oak timbers from the trees of Hampton Court Palace, no less. Did you know the King himself selected a medieval sword from his own private collection, which was fixed to the coffin lid?'

~

At three o'clock in the afternoon, Tom returned to the deck as the Port of Dover came into view. He stood to attention when a nineteen-gun salute fired from the quay. Not a soul on board could fail to be gripped by emotion as the ship docked and a band played Land of Hope and Glory.

~

As she climbed into the car, Grace waved to her mother. This was the first time she had left her child, but the anxiety of separation was only hers. She watched little Matthew giggling and waving, secure in his grandmother's arms. She took a deep breath, smoothed her skirt, and settled into her seat.

'Here we go, love,' said Percy, manoeuvring the vehicle through the gates. They both waved at Matthew as he closed the gate behind them.

Grace removed the card from her purse and read it again. It had come as quite a surprise. Lady Morton had not been kind in the past and made it clear she wanted nothing to do with Grace. For whatever reason, Her Ladyship sent the invitation, Grace now felt only gratitude for this opportunity.

Percy made light conversation along the way, but she felt the full weight of the day and answered in monosyllabic words.

'Here we are. We made it in good time, the train is just coming in. Have you got everything you need?'

'Yes, thank you, don't get out, love. I can manage.' She kissed him on the cheek, glad to board the train and hopeful of a carriage to herself.

'Can I come in?' asked a woman. She sat opposite Grace, fidgeting and tugging at her hat, which sat low over her brow. Her skirts rustled as she was jolted by the sudden movement of the train, she grabbed the arm of the seat to steady herself. 'Silly me,' said the woman. 'Not used to such fancy transport. Goodness, this moves along at a pace, doesn't it?' she added nervously.

'Are you travelling far?' Grace asked.

'I'm going to see my Stan. He's coming home today.'

'Oh?'

'He's coming up by train. Not this one. Well, I don't think so anyway.' She laughed nervously. 'I would have liked to have gone to Dover. That's where they first come in, but I couldn't afford two train trips, see. It would have been a sight there though, I'll bet.'

Grace turned her gaze to the window. Drizzle collected on the dirty glass, leaving brown trails across the muted vista. *Like tears,* she thought. She wondered if she would weep again as she occasionally did at unexpected moments, although always privately and less each time. She knew in her heart the memory of Freddie's kind face that had only ever looked with love upon her would not disappear along the procession of years to come, although the sting of bereavement had already diminished.

The *clickety-clack* rhythm slowed as the train approached the next station. With a hiss and a screech, it slowed to a stop.

'Blasted weather,' spat a robust woman as she pulled open the carriage door. She placed her basket on the seat and shook off her mac in the corridor before sitting next to Grace. 'Ghastly.'

'Indeed,' Grace replied and edged along the seat to give the new passenger more room.

'Thank you, dear. Anyone for a biscuit?' she said, plucking a tin from her basket.

Grace declined.

'I'd love one. Thank you ever so much. I've not had anything to eat or drink since I caught the cart to the station this morning. My name's Deidre.'

'Nice to meet you, Deidre. I'm Mrs Bourke, but you may call me Martha,' she exclaimed, wiping crumbs from her ample bosom.

'There are still a lot of people on the platform,' remarked Grace.

'Yes, they'll be adding more carriages now. Can you hear that clanking sound? That'll be the couplings.' Martha wiggled her head in a *know-it-all* way. 'So, Deidre, where are you off to?'

'I'm going to see my Stan,' she replied.

'Your husband?'

'No, hahaha,' she cackled. 'Stan's my boy.'

'I think Deidre is going to London for the *ceremony*,' added Grace.

'That's right. My husband said I was crackers, but what does he know, eh?'

'Ah,' sighed Martha, straightening her back and cocking an eyebrow. 'I believe it is my dear William they are bringing home.'

Deidre was dumbstruck for a moment. 'I know it's my Stan. He was such a brave boy. Though I begged him not to go, he went all smiles and with a *cheerio*.' A smudge of tears spread slowly across her lined face.

Martha twitched. 'I am sure it is my William. Of course, they would only bring back an officer. Not a common soldier. Not for such an honour as this. William was a captain. He was a hero. Everyone said so. I have received information from reliable sources confirming that the place he was found, items he was carrying all corroborate it is my William.'

'Can't be right,' said Deidre, wiping her tears and blowing her nose into a frayed handkerchief. 'My husband says nobody knows who's in the coffin. I know cos I'm his mother. Doesn't a mother always know?'

'And what about a wife? William and I were childhood

sweethearts. We had a bond like no other. There is no doubt in my mind that William has come home.'

The carriage filled with new passengers. Deidre blew her nose hard; Martha tilted her head towards the luggage rack. New tentative conversations began amongst the carriage occupants, all women, dressed in unadorned mourning black, an outward display of their inner feelings. Whispers gathered like prayer in the carriage ... *'He was a good husband. That makes it harder to bear.' 'I begged him not to go but he said it was his duty.' 'There are no children as we'd only been married six weeks.'*

Grace listened to the outpouring of grief. In so many ways, she wanted to claim Freddie as the unknown soldier, returned. Her heart ached to place Matthew Frederick in his arms and say the words, 'Here is our son.' She gazed with compassion at the women and felt compelled to say, 'Yes, it will be your man. It will be your husband, Martha, and your son, Deidre, it will be my Freddie and not just them, but the sons, fathers, brothers, husbands of every woman. We will know in our hearts that he is our very own beloved they are laying to rest today. Safe, in the arms of us all.'

The train gathered speed, bearing the women closer to their destination. Their restlessness and longing echoing in the mournful whistle and billowing steam.

~

At Victoria Station, Tom watched as, under the scrutiny of Treloar, the coffin was taken off the train by eight Coldstream Guards and placed on a gun carriage drawn by six black horses. Despite the chill, Tom felt sweat in his armpits, his throat was dry with emotion and a sudden rush of exhaustion waved over him.

Tom took his place amongst former servicemen, standing

four abreast in the entourage, behind the heads of the Armed Forces. 'I shouldn't be here.'

'What?' the man standing next to him whispered.

'This place rightfully belongs to Sergeant Howell.'

'March on!' The order echoed along the platform. In the pale winter sunlight, the parade moved off, watched by an enormous crowd as the coffin was borne through the streets. There was no sound except for people sobbing and the clop of horses' hooves.

~

Grace took her place in the congregation of one thousand women who had lost husbands or sons during the war. The scattered whispers and occasional scrape of furniture on the ancient, tiled floor of Westminster were the only sounds that interrupted her thoughts. In this moment, she felt like the outside world ceased to exist. *I'll never forget you, Freddie. Your son is healthy and strong. I am now at peace in this communion with you.*

~

As the chimes of Big Ben sounded eleven o'clock, the coffin was carried through the north transept door of Westminster Abbey while the choir sang 'O Valiant Hearts'.

Tom, in the troop of four hundred former service men, remained inside the transit as uniformed pall bearers carried the coffin to the west end of the Nave past a guard of honour of one hundred holders of the Victoria Cross.

And so it ends, thought Tom. *After all these years of loss and grief. As if we can understand, let alone mourn so much loss. Will this ceremony be enough to quell the longing for lost brothers, husbands, fathers, and sons?* At that moment, he thought of Grace. Of all she had given and all she had lost.

With a rustle, the congregation stood to sing Rudyard Kipling's solemn recessional hymn 'God of our fathers'. The chorus resounded with passion, singing as if their hearts would burst. The massive organ throbbed the melody which echoed around the ancient walls and reverberated through the feet of the congregation.

Grace felt light, uplifted, as she sang with fervour, while tears ran freely down her face until the music stopped and solemnly, King George V began the recessional walk followed by Mary, his Queen, and a succession of dignitaries, and politicians.

Tom's stomach churned as trumpeters sounded Reveille. His heart hammered in his chest. He squeezed close his eyelids as the vision rose of horses, wide-eyed, nostrils flared, foaming mouths, the sound of them snorting. The kick and jerk of muscle beneath him as his mount propelled him forward. He felt the drag of the leather reigns; his knees clamped tightly to the girth. With one arm outstretched, sword in hand, he hurtled towards the dark line. Bullets wined past, men and horses screamed as they fell. Finally, a blinding flash of fire and burst of shell and then the pain and darkness.

~

Grace joined the line of mourners filing past the grave, now covered with an embroidered silk funeral pall, four guardsmen stood reverently at each corner. An usher signalled the mourners to keep moving towards the north transept. All was quiet now except for the tramp of feet. Beyond the transept door, shafts of pale sunlight lit up the exit and reached up to the cavernous ceilings. She stepped out of the line as she neared the door. 'Tom? Is that you?'

He sat with his head bowed, slumped, exhausted. On hearing Grace's voice, he looked up. His face wet with tears.

'Grace?'

'Will you come with me?' Grace asked, holding out her hand to him.

Together, they walked beneath the Great North Door into the cold, still air.

'Tom, you look pale. Have you eaten?' asked Grace.

He shook his head.

'Shall we find somewhere? I'm cold, hungry and feel like I've run a marathon.' She looked around, not sure which direction to take. 'Let's go this way.'

'Wait just a minute, Grace.' Tom stopped to look at the huge throng of people gathered outside the Cathedral. 'So many.'

'Yes, it beggars belief, doesn't it? Look, they are queueing to file past the grave. Goodness knows how long that will take; there must be thousands of people waiting there. Let's go, I fear I will faint if I stay here much longer.'

They walked down Great Smith Street until they found a tearoom, with a short queue outside. Ten minutes later, they were in the warm and seated at a table.

Tom looked into Grace's eyes. *Those lovely eyes,* he thought. *The first thing I remembered when I woke up in hospital.* He wanted to talk, to tell her about everything that happened in France. To ask her about Llancillow, about Percy, about her son but his throat felt constricted and painful with emotion.

A waitress brought them sandwiches and a pot of tea. They ate and drank, absorbed in their own thoughts, the silence between them awkward.

Four women sat at the next table. They held hands and each took a turn to speak:

'I'll never forget you, Father. Never.'

'Charlie, today you have been laid to rest, but you were already safe in my heart.'

'Johnny, I begged you not to go and now they've brought you back.'

'My dear Frank. I forgive you. I'll take little Annabelle to see you soon. She says he remembers your smell.'

The four women hugged each other before leaving the café.

'Oh goodness.' A sudden, unexpected tear rolled down Grace's cheek. She dabbed it with her handkerchief. 'I'm sorry,' she said.

Tom yearned to comfort her but felt inadequate. He said, 'D'you mind?' and pulled out his pipe and the silver match case from his jacket pocket.

'I didn't know you smoked a pipe, Tom.'

'It started as a necessity but now I rather like it.' He smiled. 'Grace, it's wonderful to see you. I didn't expect you to be at the service.'

'I didn't expect to be there,' she replied. 'Lady Morton sent me her invitation to attend. It was so unexpected.'

'That was kind of her. I didn't expect to be there either. Another man made a similar generous gesture.' He lit his pipe.

'What will you do now, Tom? Do you plan to return to France, or will you assume your inheritance at Llancillow?'

'What?'

'Did you receive my last letter? I wrote to you about the Major and the reading of his will.'

'Yes, I did, thank you. It's just that it never occurred to me that the Major would do such a thing. Include me in his will, I mean.'

'He was a dear man and so fond of you. He told me that he loved you like a son.'

Tom was speechless. He blinked back tears. *It's all been such a rush; I haven't had time to grieve.*

Grace searched for the right words to say but offered the mundane. 'Percy and Cyril have been managing quite well but I'm sure they will be pleased to see you return. I feel you will be happy with Percy's work on the orchard. He's so proud of the cider apples. Cyril, on the other hand, repeatedly tells me that his bones ache and he's getting too old for bouncing around on a tractor. Harold is turning out well; he's keen to learn and is wonderful with the cattle.'

Tom smiled. 'Dear Percy and poor old Cyril.'

'Father has taken pride in the administration of the farm. He does miss the Major; they became close companions. Each evening, before supper, they would meet for a discussion on the day's events and enjoy a little tipple, as Pa called it.'

He finished his tea. 'To be honest, I have been so immersed in work that I hardly gave a thought to Llancillow. I'm awfully grateful to your father and Percy for keeping the place going. And feel profoundly indebted to you for looking after the Major. I must say, I deeply regret not being there when he died. I wish I could have seen him again. Thank you for writing to me to let me know. And what will you do, Grace? Now that this is all behind us.'

Grace flinched unsure what Tom was implying. 'I'll be alright. We'll all need a bit of time to sort ourselves out. I expect you'll want to make the place your own.'

Tom recognised the anguish in her face. A thousand unspoken words seemed to hang in the air between them at that moment. 'What a damn fool I am. Dear Grace, that's not what I meant,' Tom said, perplexed and trapped in awkwardness. He wanted to look into her eyes and say all the things that stuck in his throat. She smiled at him tenderly, yet with an expression of curiosity and concern. *For God's sake, man,* he chastened himself. *Get a grip. Stop being ambivalent ... speak the truth.* 'These past years, Grace, I had no idea who I was. I felt incomplete, driven to find meaning and what I found was pain and sorrow, all painted into one miserable grey canvas.' His heart beat loud, he felt sure she would hear it.

'Tom,' she said, softly. 'Where there is life, there is hope. Take heart. I believe that today, we are all released from our despair.' A quick blush leapt to her cheeks. 'Life is not meant to be travelled backwards. Tomorrow is yours to embrace.'

He closed his eyes, the everyday sounds that encircled them seemed to dim. Her words tumbled through his mind. He held them close, absorbing them, they brought warmth and peace. He opened his eyes and looked at Grace, her fingers lowering the teacup to the saucer. He watched as her chin tilted and she looked up at him, her lips parted. He felt his heart flutter. He spread his hands on the table and moved them slowly closer to Grace's until their fingertips touched. At that moment, a realisation came upon them that their hopes might be resolved.

Just as there is never one defining moment or beginning in time, there is a feeling only lovers might share ... and that is the awareness that they are poised at the creation of a new and joyful life.

Tom said, 'It's time. Let's go home.'

The End

EPILOGUE

22nd June 1922

Tom held his jacket in the crook of his arm as he walked along the now familiar, well-worn path flanked by hedgerows.

Through gaps, he gazed out to a colourful patchwork of fields nestled amidst rolling hills, where sheep tending their lambs were dotted over the landscape like specks of cotton wool.

The air was filled with the hum of bees and a cacophony of birdsong. He breathed in the sweet air, fresh and expectant.

Tom reached the end of the path; here the hedgerows fell away and before him was a wide lawn and low stone wall. He pushed open a gate and walked across a swathe of buttercups and creamy cow-parsley towards an ancient oak door.

'Anyone here?' he called, but there was no response.

He entered and stood beside the stone alter beneath a glittering stained glass window. The ornate image displayed a young woman kneeling, her hand held out. Her eyes looked to the heavens with a hopeful expression. Behind her, a fountain flowed, and flowers filled the background. Tom marvelled at the intricacy of the design, how the sunlight brought it to life and sent colourful shards of light to dance across the dull flagstone floor.

He heard muted voices coming from the vestry and shortly afterwards, the ancient bells of Saint Godfrey's Church began a joyous peel, echoing across the green fields, sending a message of joy and summoning the faithful. His heart began to beat faster, he breathed deeply to calm his nerves.

Voices, familiar and loved, shared conversations and

greetings with warmth and laughter.

Reverend Witherspoon ushered people into the church.

Tom slipped on his jacket and turned to watch as Percy escorted his mother, Sarah, to a seat in the front pew. She lifted Matthew onto her lap and pulled out a storybook from her handbag.

Percy joined Tom near the alter. They spoke quietly for a few minutes before turning to watch as family and friends were ushered in. Alice and her father, Edward, took their seats in the adjacent front pew, acknowledging Sarah with a smile. Doctor and Mrs Farrington sat in the row behind. Cyril, his wife and son arrived with twin sisters, Ethel and Winney Fanshaw, in company with Gloria Thomas, owner of the village bakery. Soon the little church filled.

Reverend Witherspoon, followed by Mrs Turner, the organist, ceremoniously made their entry. He spoke words of encouragement to Tom, requesting he turn to face the alter, and checked that Percy had remembered to bring the ring.

The congregation hushed as the melodious tones of Handel's 'Air' from Water Music, sounded.

Matthew Phillips stood tall, his chest pumped, his face red, eyes sparkling with tears. He squeezed his daughter's hand as they entered the church and began the slow walk down the aisle.

Grace's eyes fixed on Tom's back. Her face radiant, skin a blush of peach, her chestnut hair knotted in a French pleat; she wore a simple two piece of ivory-coloured linen. A spray of rosemary on her chest, and a posy of forget-me-nots and pink rosebuds in her hand.

Tom turned his head as she approached. Their eyes held each other; the pledge of love already confirmed for all to see.

About the Author

Carol is a member of the Katharine Susannah Prichard (KSP) Writers' Centre in Greenmount, Western Australia, and a long-time member of the Thursday Night writing group. In 2021, Carol was awarded a two-week Fellowship at KSP.

She has been a participant in 'Write-a-book-in-a-day' 2007-2021 and a regular contributor to the Thursday Night Group Anthologies.

Carol was a marriage and funeral celebrant for forty-three years. In that time, she worked closely with her clients, telling their stories to enhance and develop personally rewarding and deeply meaningful ceremonies.

She is passionate about this story, *Remembrance of Love and War*, which reflects the life of her grandfather. Many years of research, including travelling to Britain and France, have culminated in this work.

Carol's second work is of a very different genre. She is collating an anthology of short stories she has written in the field of Australian Gothic. Written over ten years, the stories are based on her personal and work experiences whilst travelling through the Kimberley, Northern Territory and along the Eyre Peninsular.

Carol lives in Woodbridge, Western Australia. She is married to Jim. She has three adored children, Kate, Joanna and Nathanael and four grandchildren ... and not forgetting Gracie, their adorable pooch.

www.ingramcontent.com/pod-product-compliance
Lightning Source LLC
Chambersburg PA
CBHW030250010526
44107CB00053B/1655